Overstreet's Comic Book Price Guides...

THE
OVERSTREET
TOY RING
PRICE GUIDE

THE
OVERSTREET
TOY RING
PRICE GUIDE

SECOND
EDITION

ROBERT M. OVERSTREET

SPECIAL ADVISORS

Bill Campbell, Kevin Cleary, Steve Geppi, Ted Hake, Robert Hall, Mike Herz,
Bob Hritz, Roger Hutchinson, R. C. Lettner Harry Matetsky, Ron Menchine,
Kevin Pipes, Mike Renegar, Bruce Rosen, John Snyder,
Howard C. Weinberger, Robert Yeremian

IMPORTANT NOTICE: All of the information in this book (including valuations) has been compiled from the most reliable sources, and every effort has been made to document, confirm, and double-check all data. Nevertheless, in a work of such immense scope, the possibility of error always exists. The publisher and the author shall not be held responsible for losses which may occur in the purchase, sale, or other transaction of property because of information contained herein. Readers who believe they have discovered errors are invited to send their corrective data via letter. All verified corrections will be incorporated into subsequent editions.

THE OVERSTREET TOY RING PRICE GUIDE

(2nd Edition) is an original publication by Gemstone Publishing, Inc.

Distributed to the book trade by
Collector Books
P.O. Box 3009
5801 Kentucky Dam Road
Paducah, KY 42001
PH: (502) 898-6211

Printed in the United States Of America.

First Printing: August 1996

10 9 8 7 6 5 4 3 2 1

ACKNOWLEDGEMENTS

The creation of this book was made possible by the early inspiration of "Little" Jimmy Dempsey who introduced me to the ring market years ago. But the inspiration to actually get the job done came from the constant encouragement and advice of John Snyder, Bruce Rosen, Steve Geppi, Ed Pragler, Don Maris, Harry Matetsky, Mike Herz and Bob Hritz. These enthusiastic hobbyists gave freely of their time and knowledge to make this book the most comprehensive and informative work on toy rings published.

This edition includes hundreds of new photographs, corrections and new data thanks to R.C. Lettner who spent countless hours indexing, photographing and proofing. Books of this type would not be possible without the selfless hard work of fans like Mr. Lettner. He deserves a real big "Thank You" from us all.

Another fan deserves my heart felt thanks. Ron Menchin, who was the official voice of "The Senators" has supplied hundreds of sports rings for photographing. In his own right, Ron has become an expert on sports memorabilia and has become our official advisor for the sports sections in this edition. We will all benefit from Ron's input. Thanks is also due for his excellent entertaining article in this book.

Special thanks is also due Howard C. Weinberger for his articles and his continued support and advice, especially on the Flicker rings; and Howard's photographer, Jeff Kermath, who spent hours photographing rings included in this edition; to Bruce Rosen who supplied hundreds of rings for photographing as well as the associated data; to Dave Eskenazi who supplied rings for photographing; to Ed Pragler for sending rings for photographing; to Mr. Edmund Macksoud of Uncas for tracking down ancient history on the Superman rings; to Henry Moncure for text revisions and corrections to rings listed; to John Barry of Planet Studios for supplying photographs and to Bob Barrett for sending photographs; to Robert Yeremian for his help in pricing; to Ted Hake for his senior advice and continued support; to A. Kaviraj for his brilliant premium ring gag art.

Thanks is also due Tony Overstreet, Mike Renegar, Benn Ray, Joe Rybandt, Carol Overstreet, Cathy Disbrow and Jeffery Dillon of Gemstone for their help in getting this book to press; and especially to Arnold T. Blumberg for laying out this edition.

The following people supplied needed information and photos for this edition: Dave Anderson, Ron Breidenbach, Paul Burke, Bill Campbell, Paul Deion, Robert Hall, Bill Hughes, Steve Ison, Jennifer Menken, Rex Miller, Danny Fuchs, Kevin Pipes, Scott Rona, Joseph Sain, Art Thomas, Evelyn Wilson, who all have my sincere thanks.

TABLE OF CONTENTS

INTRODUCTION

For decades, ring collectors have searched far and wide for the next addition to their collection. Ads in comic books, monster magazines, toy and antique publications occasionally contain ring offerings of interest. Older rings are always turning up at antique stores, antique shows, auctions, comic book conventions, comic book stores, flea markets and toy conventions. Getting to know who the key ring collectors are will increase your chances of obtaining a rare ring whenever one comes up for sale. In the past, the rarest rings were usually passed on from collector to collector or collector/dealer. Over the years the collector would develop a waiting list of buyers for his rarest rings. He only had to privately contact these prospects when it was time to sell.

There are many shows that can produce finds of collectible rings. One of the largest takes place in Atlantic City in March and again in October. Another important show for rings and premiums is the Dallas Big-D Collectible Show held in July & Nov. Check the ads in this edition for dealers and collectors that buy and sale rings.

Many rings are offered each year to attract new collectors into this market. For instance DC produced the Superman magnet and Green Lantern Squirt rings. Matchbox developed a beautiful set of 68 rings called the "Ring Raiders," and Mattel produced a popular series called "Polly Pockets" with its own styled ring box. Marvel has released its X-Men series and Image, its Spawn rings. Special rings were released along with The Shadow and Phantom movies.

Cereal boxes should always be checked for ring offers. Lucky Charms offered the Lucky Horseshoe ring in 1985 and Kelloggs Sugar Corn Pops offered a beautiful set of 28 football insignia rings in the 1980s. Disney continues to release gold and silver children's rings each year available at the Disney stores and other outlets. Warner Brothers also sells newly designed rings in their catalogue and at their stores.

Ring prices are always changing as the market continues to grow. The wise investor should keep up with the latest sales and discoveries, using this book only as a guide. We hope this reference work will provide up-to-date information for the collector in this new and exciting hobby.

A word of warning: Because of the popularity of collecting rings, many new fantasy and unlicensed rings are appearing in the market. A few reproductions of licensed rings are also being produced (see the section on Fantasy rings and Reproductions). Remember, reproductions have appeared in many collectible markets and there have always been experts available who could tell the difference.

A special thanks to all who helped in the compilation of this edition of those wonderful little toys–the rings!

GRADING

The more valuable the ring the more important accurate grading becomes. A ring in MINT condition is worth more than in GOOD condition and the value difference could be considerable. Rings should be graded with a keen eye for detail and close attention should be given to luster, surface wear and defects, color chipping and fading, damage, plastic altered by heat, plating wear, missing parts, replaced parts and restoration before a grade is assigned. The following grades should be used to more accurately describe the condition of your rings.

MINT (MT): Same condition as issued; complete with full luster and no sign of wear. Rarely occurs in 1930s to 1940s rings. In very rare cases, rings have occurred with unbent prongs on otherwise fitted rings and are worth a premium. Rings in this condition could bring considerably more than the Near Mint (NM) listing.

NEAR MINT (NM): Nearly perfect with the slightest evidence of wear and 90% luster to the naked eye. Generally the highest grade reached by most of the metal rings.

VERY FINE (VF): Wear beginning to show on high points, but 70% of the surface shows luster. Very minor color flaking may be evident but the overall appearance is still very desirable.

FINE (FN): Still enough luster to be desirable. General wear beginning to show. Less than 70% and more than 50% luster evident. Slightly above average condition.

VERY GOOD (VG): Most of the luster is gone, general wear, tarnishing and fading is the general rule. Prongs can be bent but are still complete. On plated rings, base metal can be seen over much of the ring. Paper (where applicable) could be stained but is still legible and complete. Most rings that have been cleaned will fall into this grade.

GOOD (GD): Below average condition. Still complete but prongs can be chipped or bent, color or plating will be gone. Surface abrasion and wear is obvious but all parts must be present.

FAIR (FR): Excessive wear obvious. A minor part may be missing.

POOR (PR): Incomplete and not suited for investment purposes.

GRADE AND ITS RELATION TO VALUE

CONDITION IS THE KEY TO VALUE - Condition plays a large role in determining value for most rings. As one might imagine, the more expensive the ring, the more important condition and accurate grading become. The value of a ring in Mint condition can be as much as 10 times that of the same ring in just Good condition. For a ring to bring the highest value, it must be complete, original, unrestored and in top condition.

MARKET REPORT
by Bob Overstreet

The first edition of this book was published in the Fall of 1994 and was received with much enthusiasm. Since that time, the number of collectors have grown enormously. Unfortunately, the supply of rare and high interest rings have remained scarce. Due to this, the ring marketplace continued to change as dealers and collectors competed for the small number of rare rings that surfaced.

The most exciting event of the past two years to ring collectors was the 1995

> Frank Buck Black Leopard sells for record price of $6075 in fine

Sotheby's auction that placed a high grade collection of rare rings up for bid. Thanks are due to Jerry Weist of Sotheby's, who, realizing the market for collectible rings convinced this prestigeous auction house to hold an auction. With the publicity and high visibility of this collection, everyone looked forward with great anticipation to this auction. Anxious buyers congregated in the auction room, while collectors and dealers at home scrambled for the available phone lines.

> Radio Orphan Annie Altascope brings a high price of $12,650!

As expected, the bidding was fast and heated with several rings bringing record prices! This was quite an achievement for the very first auction of this type. The **Frank Buck Black Leopard World's Fair** in fine

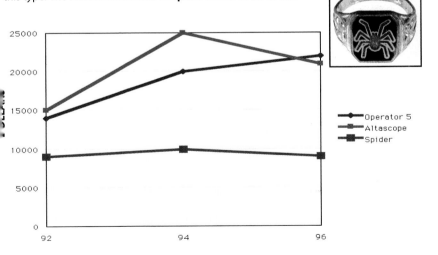

FOUR YEAR GROWTH OF OPERATOR 5, ROA ALTASCOPE, & SPIDER RINGS

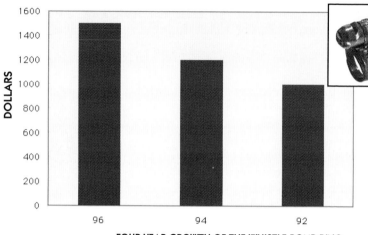

FOUR YEAR GROWTH OF THE WHISTLE BOMB RING

New Discovery Egyptian Sphinx Ring!

condition brought $6,075, almost triple the Guide's list price! Another rare ring that sold for a top price was the rare **Don Winslow Membership** in NM which brought an unbelievable $3,738! Other record sales were: **Captain Marvel** fn-$3,163; **Green Hornet Secret Compartment** vf-$3,450; **Shadow Carey Salt** nm-$1,380; **Howdy Doody Jack in the Box** vg-$3,163.

But the one ring in the collection that got everyone's attention was the very rare **Radio Orphan Annie Altascope** in fine condition that sold for a staggering price of $12,650!!

Buck Rogers Birthstone sells for $800!

Superman Prize ring brings $100,000!!

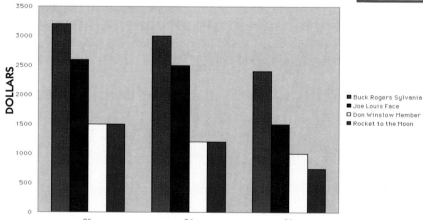

Legend:
- ■ Buck Rogers Sylvania
- ■ Joe Louis Face
- □ Don Winslow Member
- ■ Rocket to the Moon

FOUR YEAR GROWTH OF BUCK ROGERS SYLVANIA, JOE LOUIS FACE, DON WINSLOW MEMBER, & ROCKET TO THE MOON RINGS

The rare R.O.A. Initial gets $5000!

Other important rings that were sold at about Guide list such as the **Melvin Purvis Secret Scarab** vf-$1,035, **Snap, Crackle & Pop** set vg-$920, a group of **Lone Ranger** rings brought $1,200, four **Captain Midnight** rings fetched $1,700, three **Captain Video** rings sold for $1,300, and a **Shadow Blue Coal** ring brought $575.

Melvin Purvis Secret Scarab fetches $1400!

Most of the rings in this collection were assembled over a long period of time and the collector was very fussy about grade. Consequently, many of the rings were in very high grade. Some large lots were purchased by dealers who immediately filled want lists and sent them to excited buyers. There were a few unlisted rings in this collection such as the **China Good Luck** and the **Egyptian Sphinx** rings, which are included in this edition.

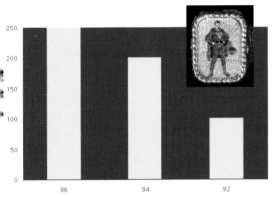

FOUR YEAR GROWTH OF THE SUPERMAN FLICKER RING

A rare variant of the **Tom Mix Straight Shooters** ring turned up from the Robbins archives. Only 5 were found, and all sold quickly to collectors.

The toy ring marketplace has enjoyed brisk sales over the past year. All types of rings from the 1800s to the limited editions of the 1990s sold very well. Many record prices were paid and very few examples of the scarcer rings surfaced for sale.

Atom Bomb ring most requested!

The Atlantic City Extravaganza show in March has always been a great place to hunt rings. Many collectors attend shows of this type in searce of rare and unusual rings. At this event, several scarce rings sold including a mint **Dizzy Dean**, a new unlisted **Writers Guild** ring, a **Tom Mix Deputy** wrapper, a **Hopalong Cassidy Steer Head**, and many others.

A **Superman Action Comics** ring surfaced this year setting off a controversy in the marketplace. This ring is similar to the legendary **Superman Membership Prize** ring but the image of Superman, as well as the base, are different. The base of this ring was made by Uncas, a company still in business today. The company was contacted to see if they manufactured this newly discovered ring. Uncas informed us in writing that they had no record, nor did anyone remember ever doing a Superman ring. In fact, they never had an account with DC Comics to produce any Superman items. There is no evidence at all from this company to substantiate the existance

Valric of the Vikings ring sells for $7500!

of this ring. While the ad for the ring used "Action Comics" instead of "Member" in advertising this ring, the real focus w on Superman Comics and the Superman radio show. To participate in the program, you had to become a member firs This is why "member" was put on the "official" ring, not "Action Comics."

Lone Ranger Marine Corp sells for $1000!

However, as one noted collector stated, "since records are sketchy and often lost, someone could have done this ring as a proto-type." Until more information surfaces, we may never know for sure when this ring was made–1940s, 1960s or 1980s?

Superman Gum Ring brings $27,500!!

Golden Age (1890s-1940s): One of the most requested rings from this period is the **Lone Ranger Atomic Bomb** cereal premium. This ring is beautifully designed with its gold base, silver bomb and red tail fin Over 6 million were produced from the late 1940s to the early 1950s

Tennessee Jed goes for $600

Almost everyone had this ring and have fond memories of taking the red tail fin off the back and looking into its atomic chamber to see the atoms smashing in the dark. Another requested ring, the **Superman Prize** ring in vf, sold for $100,000! Another **Prize** ring in vg sold for $28,550! A **Superman Gum** ring brought $27,500 and another $20,000; a **Superman Candy** ring in low grade got $20,000. **Valric o the Vikings** in vf sold for $7,500; a high grade **R.O.A. Initial** brings $5,000. Some other sales are: **Baseball Hall of Fame** vf-$250; **Buck Rogers Birthstone** vf-$800; **Buck Rogers Ring of Saturn** vf-$850; **Buster Brown Club** $80; **Captain Hawks Sky Patrol** vf-$300; **Captain Hawks**

Monster Cereal Fruiit Brute sets record at $300!

Secret Scarab nm-$1800; **Captain Marvel** vf-$1750; **Dick Tracy Hat** vf-$300; **Dick Tracy Secret Compartment** fn-$400; **Gabby Hayes Cannon** vf-$250; **Green Hornet Instructions**-$250; **Hopalong Cassidy Bar 20** vf-$250; **Howdy Doody Jack-In-The-Box** vf-$5,000; **Huskies** vf-$600; **Jack Armstrong Baseball** vf-$850; **USA/KKK**-$650; **Lone Ranger Six Shooter** fn-$150; **Lone Ranger Military** vf-$1,000; **Melvin Purvis Secret Scarab** vf-$1,400; a group of **Post Tin** rings (37) sold for $860; **Radio Orphan Annie Initial** vf-$5,000; **Roy Rogers Microscope** vf-$150; **Shadow Blue Coal** nm-$750; **Shadow Carey Salt** nm-$1,500; **Sky King Navajo Treasure** vf-$165; **Sky King TV** w/photos vf-$250; **Sky**

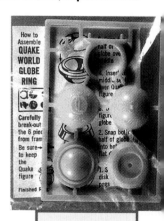

The very rare Quake World Globe sells for $1500!

14

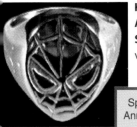

King Teleblinker vf-$150; **Spider** vg-$3,000; **Straight Arrow Cave** vf-$275; **Superman Candy** vg-$20,000; **Superman F-87 Plane** vf-$256; **Superman Gum** vg-$27,500; **Tennessee Jed** vf-$600; **Tom Mix Look Around** vf-$175; **Tom Mix Magnet** vf-$100; **Tom Mix Target** vf-$305; **Valric The Viking** vf-$7,500.

Spider-Man 50th Anniversary brings $3000!

Silver Age (1950s-1970s): Cousin Eerie-$60; **Flintstones**-$25; **Green Hornet Flicker 11 pack)**-$275; **Icee Bear**-$75; **Ironman**-$50; **Judy Jetson**-$30; **Keebler Elf**-$75; **Marvel Fant. Four**-$75; **Monkees-Davey**-$75; **Monster Flicker**-$100; **Monster Fruit Brute**-$300;**Olympic Eagle**-$40; **Quake World Globe** (in pkg.)-$1,500; **Beatles-Ringo**-$20; **Rocky**-$25; **Schlitz Beer**-$20; **Scooby Doo**-$35; set of 17 cardboard **NHL**-$170;

Shadow Movie Gold sells for $400!

Smokey the Bear-$20; **Star Trek** plastic-$75; **Marvel Super Hero** 3 packages-$225; **Spiderman Vitamin**-$110; **Superman** 1976 Nestle-$50; **Superman Flicker**-$200; **Zorro picture**-$50.

Bronze/Modern (1980s-1990s): Comic companys, Toy companys,

Shadow Bust Gold goes for $395!

Warner Brothers, Disney, Goosebumps and others produced interesting collectible rings in the past few years. All the Stabur strip character rings have enjoyed increased demand. A few recorded sales are: **Archie Silver**-$375; **Batman-Diamond Gold**-$1,500; **Batman Riddler**-$33; **Casper (Spook)**-$50; **Dagwood Silver**-$425;

Spawn Gold sells for $1025!

Disney Skull Gold & Silver-$20 ea.; **Hagar The Horrible Gold**-$600; **Silver**-$200; **Mask Figural & Key Chain**-$50; **Mask Movie**-$25; **Mortal Combat Gold**-$400; **Silver**-$50; **Phantom Silver**-$275; **Predator**-$100; **Ren & Stimpy**-$10; **Shadow Bust Gold**-$395; **Shadow Movie Gold**-$400; **Silver**-$100; **Spawn Gold**-$1025; **Spiderman 50th Anniversary**-$3,000; **Superman Bronze**-$75; **Superman of America Gold**-$750; **Silver** -$395; **X-Men Diamond Gold**-$1500; **Silver**-$150; **Xavier Institute Gold**-$525.

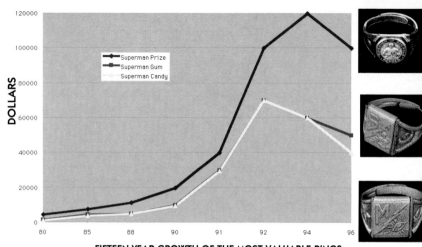

FIFTEEN YEAR GROWTH OF THE MOST VALUABLE RINGS

Chart legend:
- Superman Prize
- Superman Gum
- Superman Candy

Y-axis: DOLLARS (0, 20000, 40000, 60000, 80000, 100000, 120000)
X-axis: 80, 85, 88, 90, 91, 92, 94, 96

THE MOST VALUABLE RINGS
(THE SUPERMAN RINGS)

Since the Superman rings were first offered as a premium back in the 1940s, th mystique of these elusive objects has endured over half a century. Today they are th most sought after and revered rings in the market. As much as 15 years ago the mark was still small and these rings were very rare with only a few examples every bein offered for sale. When a sale did occur, the price paid was always a record. All the know examples were locked into old time collections for years. By the early 1990s there wer many collectors waiting for the chance to buy these rings, and they were continuous making cash offers to the owners. When the price became right, a few rings were final sold which in itself fueled the market even more. Prices paid began to sharply increas to unheard of levels, irregardless of grade to $10,000, $15,000, $20,000, $25,000, $30,00 and more. Soon most of the known rings were now owned by new players. The ol timers that sold had reaped a handsome profit!

As news of sales went out over the grape vine along with numerous buying ac appearing coast to coast, a few more rings surfaced. Just in the past 4 years, for exampl the population of the Candy ring increased by 50% (most low grade), while only 2 lo grade examples of the Prize ring surfaced. There were no gum rings found. In 1991 an 1992 these rings were hot, selling for high prices upward to $125,000. Low grade ring sold for high prices and high grade sold for high prices. But soon, as the waiting list c buyers deminished, and more than one example was available for sale, grade becam more and more important.

Today low grade examples of these rings will not bring the prices they did just 3 or years ago. As the chart for the record prices during each period indicates, the market i currently adjusting its perception of the value of these unique rings, especially in grade.

If a line is drawn from 1980 to the present for each ring, a more realistic growt pattern is realized, taking out the anomaly of the sharp spikes of 1991 and 1992. Th future of these rings in the marketplace will depend on how many new players com into the field coupled with the number of new finds.

We should keep in mind that the vast majority of owners of these rings paid a ver high price in relation to the spike of 1991 and 1992. Most will keep them for a long tim while others will probably wait for the next price cycle to sell. Remember, a sligh change in demand for these rare rings could start the next price spiral.

100 MOST VALUABLE TOY RINGS

VALUE	RANK	RING TYPE
$100,000	1	Superman Of America (prize)(comic books)
$50,000	2	Superman Secret Compartment (gum)
$40,000	3	Superman Secret Compartment (candy)
$22,000	4	Operator Five
$21,000	5	Radio Orphan Annie Altascope
$14,000	6	Superman Tim
$9,500	7	Sky King Kaleidoscope
$9,000	8	Spider
$8,500	9	Cisco Kid Secret Compartment
$7,500	10	Valric of the Vikings
$6,000	11	Frank Buck Black Leopard (W. Fair)
$6,000	12	Tom Mix Deputy
$5,500	13	Howdy Doody Jack in the Box
$5,500	14	Radio Orphan Annie Initial
$5,000	15	Lone Ranger Gold Ore
$4,500	16	Radio Orphan Annie Magnifying
$4,000	17	Lone Ranger (ice cream)
$3,750	18	Knights of Columbus
$3,200	19	Buck Rogers Sylvania Bulb
$3,000	20	Buck Rogers Repeller Ray
$3,000	21	Frank Buck Black Leopard (bronze)
$3,000	22	Green Hornet (plastic)
$3,000	23	Spiderman (gold)
$3,000	24	Tonto (ice cream)
$2,600	25	Joe Louis Face
$2,500	26	Captain Marvel
$2,500	27	Tom Mix Spinner
$2,200	28	Quisp Figural
$2,000	29	Frank Buck Black Leopard (silver)
$2,000	30	Lone Ranger Photo (test)
$1,600	31	Captain Midnight Mystic Sun God
$1,600	32	Clarabelle Face/Hat
$1,500	33	Batman Bat Signal (gold)
$1,500	34	Captain Video Flying Saucer (complete)
$1,500	35	Don Winslow Member
$1,500	36	Joe Louis Figural
$1,500	37	Rocket To The Moon (complete)
$1,500	38	Whistle Bomb
$1,200	39	Captain Hawks/Melvin Purvis Scarab
$1,200	40	Captain Midnight Signet (1957)
$1,200	41	Dick Tracy Monogram
$1,200	42	Jack Armstrong Dragon's Eye
$1,200	43	Major Mars Rocket (complete)
$1,200	44	Radio Orphan Annie Triple Mystery
$1,200	45	Shadow Carey Salt
$1,050	46	Spawn (gold)
$1,000	47	Archie (gold)
$1,000	48	Captain Video Pendant
$1,000	49	Green Hornet Secret Compartment

VALUE	RANK	RING TYPE
$1,000	50	Lone Ranger Secret Compartment-Navy
$950	51	Sky King Aztec Emerald Calendar
$925	52	Ted Williams Baseball
$900	53	Sky King Mystery Picture
$850	54	Buck Rogers Ring of Saturn
$850	55	Lone Ranger Secret Compartment-Army
$850	56	Lone Ranger Secret Compartment-Marines
$850	57	Roy Rogers Hat
$850	58	Space Patrol Cosmic Glow
$800	59	Barnabas Collins (Dark Shadows)
$800	60	Lone Ranger Secret Compartment-Airforce
$800	61	Shadow (gold)
$750	62	Bullet Pen
$750	63	Golden Nugget Cave
$750	64	Rin Tin Tin (complete)
$750	65	Rootie Kazootie Lucky Spot
$750	66	Superman of America (gold)
$750	67	Vincent Price
$750	68	X-Men (gold)
$650	69	Batman Prototype
$650	70	Cisco Kid Hat
$650	71	Hagar The Horrible (gold)
$650	72	Jack Armstrong Baseball Centennial
$650	73	Joe Penner Face Puzzle
$650	74	Quake Figural (Captain)
$650	75	Snap, Crackle & Pop (Pop)
$650	76	Tim
$650	77	U. S. Marshal
$625	78	Captain Video Secret Seal (copper top)
$600	79	Huskies Club
$600	80	Quake Leaping Lava
$600	81	Quake Volcano Whistle
$600	82	Quisp Meteorite
$600	83	Quisp Space Disk
$600	84	Quisp Space Gun
$600	85	Shadow Blue Coal
$550	86	Gene Autry Eagle
$550	87	Howie Wing Weather
$550	88	Range Rider
$550	89	Shirley Temple
$550	90	Snap, Crackle & Pop (Snap)
$525	91	Captain Midnight Whirlwind Whistle
$525	92	Captain Video Secret Seal (gold)
$525	93	Roy Rogers Saddle
$500	94	Buster Brown
$500	95	Captain Midnight Flight Commander
$500	96	Captain Midnight Initial Printing
$500	97	Clarabelle Horn
$500	98	Clyde Beatty Lions Head
$500	99	Mickey Mouse Figure 1931-1934
$475	100	Captain Midnight Marine Corps

HISTORY

From the beginning of time man has been fascinated and intrigued with the mystique of rings. Before the discipline of science, during the middle ages and beyond, in a world of sorcerers, wizards and witches, some believed that rings exist that possess special powers over man.

Boris Karloff used a ring to bring down his victims in the famous 1933 movie "The Mummy." Carl Barks picked up on the idea and wrote his first complete story "The Mummy's Ring" (Four Color #29, 1943) which was a smash hit to comic book collectors. A red ring played a major role in the recent 1994 film "The Shadow." In baseball collecting, the Pennant and World Series rings are highly prized and are on collectors' want lists. Price guides exist on antique rings of a generic nature and are quite popular. It only seems reasonable that our industry should have a guide on comic related rings, both premiums and store bought.

Beginning in the 1930s the premium ring was an early device given away to children to trace consumer response to various products. The producers were quick to use words like "mysterious, mystic, scarab, lucky, cosmic, ancient, dragon, Egyptian, Aztec, secret, magical," etc. reinforcing this ancient belief that rings truly do possess magical and secret properties.

Cereal companies, sponsors of radio and television shows, beverage companies, food producers, movie studios, comic book companies, toy producers, sports promoters, etc. gave away many different types of premiums including rings to survey what type of products their customers were buying. At the same time, the first comic books and Big Little Books began to appear.

The earliest premium ring is the **Lone Wolf Tribal**, made of sterling silver, which was offered in 1932 by Wrigley Gum (the sponsor of a popular radio show) to test listener response. Soon after this historic first, the famous comic strip character Little Orphan Annie got her own nationally broadcast radio show. Now known as "Radio" Orphan Annie, dozens of premiums began appearing on the market, including some of the rarest rings ever offered anywhere. The ROA Altascope (only 7 known) was the last ring offered before the radio show was canceled and is the rarest of the ROA rings. The ROA magnifying and initial rings are the next most difficult ROA rings to

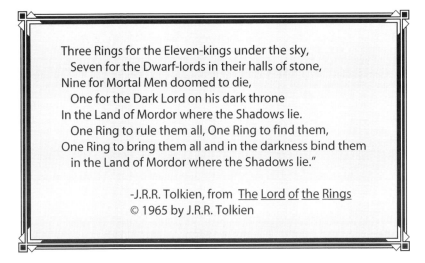

Three Rings for the Eleven-kings under the sky,
   Seven for the Dwarf-lords in their halls of stone,
Nine for Mortal Men doomed to die,
   One for the Dark Lord on his dark throne
In the Land of Mordor where the Shadows lie.
   One Ring to rule them all, One Ring to find them,
One Ring to bring them all and in the darkness bind them
   in the Land of Mordor where the Shadows lie."

     -J.R.R. Tolkien, from The Lord of the Rings
     © 1965 by J.R.R. Tolkien

find. Other popular characters' rings from the 1930s included Buck Rogers, Tom Mix, Frank Buck and Melvin Purvis. The Tom Mix Deputy ring from 1935 was very difficult to acquire and today is one of the 10 rarest rings.

Box tops, candy or gum wrappers, coupons, etc. were required in most cases to receive the premium. The radio advertisers believed that the amount of response each product received was an indicator of its acceptance level. The responses could even be used as regional indicators by offering certain premiums exclusively to certain geographic areas. Some rings were only offered in a small area while others, like the Kix Atom Bomb, exploded all over the country.

The earliest rings were made of metal and usually exhibited excellent quality in design and material (some were even gold plated) and are highly prized by collectors. Most of the early metal rings were made by the **Robbins Company**. In recent years there was a very exciting "archive find" of rings and ring parts from this company which included complete rings as well as a few one-of-a-kind prototypes and different ring bases only.

During the 1940s the sponsors of popular radio shows such as *The Shadow*, *The Lone Ranger*, *Sky King*, *Green Hornet* and *Superman* offered premium rings to listeners. The Lone Ranger Atom Bomb, also given away through Kix cereal in 1946, was the most successful premium ever with over 1 million produced. Today this ring is still revered as one of the most beautiful and desirable because of its breathtaking design and eye-catching gold, silver and red colors.

> *The earliest children's toy ring is the **1893 Columbian Exposition** made of sterling silver.*

The most valuable of these rings is the **Superman of America membership ring** which was shipped to 1600 winners of the Action Comics contest in early 1940. Only 12 complete examples of this ring are known to exist, with all but one in less than near mint condition.

Plastic first appeared in 1907 (bakelite) and was followed by Catalin and Plaskon which were in common use during the 1920s for radio tube bases, appliance knobs, dial windows and other poured molded items. The phenol plastics were in use by the 1930s and polystyrene showed up in 1938. Tupperware first appeared in 1942. Rings using plastic made their appearance in the late 1930s (see The Majestic Radio ring and 1939 World's Fair rings) and by the 1950s the number of rings made of this cheaper material rivalled the metal ones and soon surpassed them.

Television (a new concept of combining radio with movies) was invented in the 1920s and saw limited broadcast use as early as 1933, and by 1938 was being commercially broadcast in several of the nation's largest metropolitan areas. Among those who saw its potential in the 1940s was William "Hopalong Cassidy" Boyd who specifically retained control of the TV rights to the cowboy movies he made in the 1930s. His vision reached fruition by the late 1940s when he became a regular TV star.

After World War II, TV broadcasting exploded resulting in a huge expansion of the audience for premium offers. Soon, many premiums were being offerred through popular television shows. No one could have predicted the impact this new entertainment medium would have in such a short period of time. By 1950 the first television comic book, **Howdy Doody**, was published. The **Howdy Doody Jack in the Box ring** is the rarest plastic item from this era. Just as in radio, the premiums were used to test viewer response.

Western comic books jammed the stands in 1948 and science fiction comics began to appear in 1950. The most popular characters from the movies were marketed to the public in comic books, on radio and eventually on television. Gene Autry, Roy Rogers, Gabby Hayes, Hopalong Cassidy, Space Patrol, Captain Video and others had their rings too.

During the 1960s dozens of plastic rings of television show celebrities abounded. Addams Family, Dark Shadows, Beatles, Davy Crockett, Munsters, Tarzan, Batman are just a few. Cereal personalities such as Quisp and Quake also had their series of rings. In fact, the Quisp figural ring is the most valuable after 1959.

The 1970s saw rings from *Star Wars* (film), *Star Trek* (TV), McDonalds (hamburger chain), Huckleberry Hound (TV), Captain Crunch (cereal), etc.

Companies continued promoting their characters during the 1980s with G.I. Joe, Gumby, Marvel Comics character rings, Lucky Charms (cereal) and others. One of the most ambitious ring programs ever initiated was the 1990s Ring Raiders with an amazing 68 rings in the set!

Today, the comic book companies are producing high quality rings directly for the collectors market. Spawn by McFarlane, X-O, X-Men, Spider-Man, Superman, Green Lantern, Teenage Mutant Turtles, G.I. Joe and Diamond Comic Distributors' promotional rings such as Batman, The Shadow, and X-Men.

USING THIS BOOK

This reference work is the most complete, accurate, and comprehensive listing and photographic index of collectible rings ever attempted. All listings are arranged alphabetically by the name of the character, event, type, style, company or subject. The listings are placed on each page <u>vertically</u> and should be referenced from top to bottom. It is our goal to eventually show an illustration for <u>every</u> listing.

Some of the scarcer and more interesting rings may have additional illustrations to show more detail. Boxed notations are also used to explain in greater detail the functions of particular rings. Before purchasing a ring, check the illustration and description in this book to be sure all the parts are included. Complete ring sets are listed <u>as</u> <u>sets</u> when known with a complete photographic reference where possible. The rings of a set are linked with arrows pointing down (usually located in the lower left corner of each illustration). The price is linked to the set above with an arrow pointing up. Rings missing from sets will be included whenever possible in future editions.

Additional information includes dates as well as a description (if needed) and price range. Pay close attention to detail when comparing your ring with the illustrated example to make sure identification is accurate. Many rings appear similar and lack identifying markings making this reference the only way of correctly identifying certain rings. Take this book with you on all your ring buying trips.

If you have a ring that should be included in future editions, please send a detailed description with a photograph to the author.

Collecting rings is a fascinating challenge and many can be purchased at very moderate prices. Unlike some collectibles, rings are very easy to display because of their small size. If handled properly rings maintain their look and beauty with very little effort.

Price guides exist for antique rings of a generic nature and are quite popular. With the ground swell of interest in the collectibility of premium rings, it is only fitting that our hobby have a price guide and the "legitimacy" which it confers. The future of ring collecting looks bright as new collectors enter the market every day, and it's easy to see that the era of serious ring collecting is here!

STARTING A COLLECTION

Today the comic book companies are producing collectible rings based on our favorite logos and comic characters. These are available through most comic book stores or can be ordered via mail order catalogs (e.g. Warner Brothers, Disney, etc.). Most of these offerings are limited editions and sell out quickly, so be prepared to pay a premium price if you purchase them from dealers or collectors after production is discontinued. Of course the older rings are difficult to find. They can be bought from reliable dealers and at comic and collectible shows throughout the country.

Before starting your collection, consider studying the photographs in this guide to broaden your knowledge of the rings you may want to collect. Pay special attention to the details and visual subtleties of each ring. This is important because there are a few cases where older rings have been duplicated in recent times and are similar in design. The new rings are never exactly identical to the originals and usually look "brand new" in appearance.

Frequently collectors discover rings unknown to the market and not listed in this guide at toy shows, antique shows, premium shows, and comic book conventions. When these new discoveries are documented, they will be added to future editions of this book.

Many of the premium rings came with a mailing envelope or box and papers (referred to by collectors as instructions). Ring paper is usually scarce and is a very valuable and an interesting addition to any ring collection. Other rings appeared in groups attached to cards. When searching for rings at shows, don't forget to look for the larger card sets. They can sometimes be easy to overlook.

Rings were offered in cereal box promotions, newspaper comic sections and comic book ads. These advertising pages make a ring collection display more colorful and interesting.

Most rings are still inexpensive and affordable to collectors. The market is young and new discoveries are always possible to the energetic searcher. Many of the rare rings lack identifying markings, making it possible to discover rare rings in unlikely places (flea market bargain bins and the like).

With ring collecting becoming popular, collectors are looking for an affordable way to showcase their growing premium ring collection. One of the latest display ideas is the new "Toy Ring Display Case." These cases are made of a "revolutionary" crystal clear, soft (yet very strong), lightweight plastic. These cases allow you to both display and protect your growing collection. The best part is, they're only $10.00! Even better is if you order 4 or more cases, that low price drops to an even lower $7.95! An individual case allows you to display 35 rings, each in their own padded compartment. To order, contact **The Collector's Display Case Company**, Route 2 Box 73 Fremont, NE 68025-9635. Or give them a call at 402.721.4765.

THE TOP RINGS

The following rings pictured represent the most valuable known. Many are extremely rare, some with less than 25 known examples.

Superman Prize
1940s, $100,000

Radio Orphan Annie Altascope
1940s, $21,000

Cisco Kid Secret Compartment
1950s, $8500

Superman Secret Compartment (gum)
1940s, $50,000

Superman Tim
1949, $14,000

Valric of the Vikings
1940s, $7500

Superman Secret Compartment (candy)
1940, $40,000

Sky King Kaleidoscope
1940s, $9500

Frank Buck Black Leopard, N.Y. Worlds Fair
1939, $6000

Operator 5
1934, $22,000

Spider
1930s, $9000

Tom Mix Deputy
1935, $6000

Howdy Doody Jack In The Box
1950s, $5500

Knights Of Columbus
1940s, $3750

Spiderman (gold)
1993, $3000

Radio Orphan Annie Initial
1940s, $5500

Buck Rogers Sylvania Bulb
1953, $3200

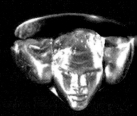

Joe Louis
1940s, $2600

Lone Ranger Gold Ore
1940s, $5000

Buck Rogers Repeller Ray
1930, $3000

Captain Marvel
1940s, $2500

Radio Orphan Annie Magnifying
1940s, $4500

Frank Buck Black Leopard, bronze
1938, $3000

Tom Mix Spinner
1930s, $600

24

COLOR RING SECTION BEGINS: The following pages contain photos of many rare and interesting rings from advertising characters, baseball, cereal, comic book, cowboy, football, movie, newspaper strip, political, radio, toy, TV, & World's Fair.

Alice In Wonderland
1933 (movie) $175

Baseball Domed Logo, Cubs
1954, $60

Baseball, Spokane Hawks
1938, $150

Barbie
1980s, $15

Baseball Domed Logo, Milwaukee
1954, $60

Basketball Flicker
1960s, $20

Baseball
1969, $60

Baseball A's
1990, $30

Baseball Flicker Group
1960s, $40

Baseball Atlanta
1993, $75

Baseball Baltimore
1970s, $10

Baseball Hall of Fame
1939, $200

Baseball Mets
1960s, $20

Baseball Cardinals
1982, $75

Baseball Houston Error

Baseball Milwaukee

Baseball Chicago
1993, $20

Baseball Mets
1970s, $15

Baseball New York
1993, $60

Baseball
1969-72, $35

Baseball Play Ball Card
1969-72, $40

Baseball Padres
1970s, $15

Baseball St. Louis
1993, $75

Baseball Pirates
1960, $60

Baseball Yankees
1940s, $250

Baseball Pirates
1971, $15

Basketball Seattle
1979, $40

Batman Ring Watch
1989, $20

Batman Box
1966, $40

Batman

Batman Figure
1990s, $4

Batman Vending Machine Flicker
1966, $35

Batman Flicker
1960s, $25

Batman Rubber
1966, $4

Batman Nestles
1980s, $50

Battlestar Galactica
1978, $40

Bazooka Joe Mailer/ring
1940s, $400

Beatles
1964, $15

Captain Crunch Whistle
1970s, $60

Belt Buckle
1950s, $60

Capt. Hawks Air Hawks
1930s, $150

Big Boy
1970s, $2

Cabbage Patch Kids
1983, $20

Cameo
1950s, $10

Capt. Hawks Sky Patrol
1930s, $300

Boogey Monkey
1960s, $10

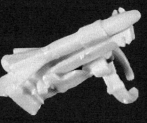

Captain Crunch Rocket
1970s, $150

Captain Midnight Flight Commander
1941, $500

Capt. Midnight Initial Printing
1948, $500

China Luck
1940s, $150

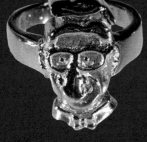

Chilly Willy Face
1970s, $10

Crackerjack
1950s, $20 each

Carl Barks Gold
(prototype)(1 of 3) 1995, $200

Davy Crockett Flicker
1950s, $400

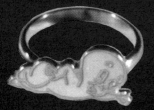

Civilian Conservation Corps.
1930s, $40

Casper Silver
1970, $20

Cat Woman
1991, $10

Cowboys & Indians Paper
1960s, $15

Dennis The Menace
1960s, $40

Donald Duck Figure
1935, $150

Egyptian Sphinx
1940s, $150

Dizzy Dean
1936, $250

E.T. on Card
1982, $25

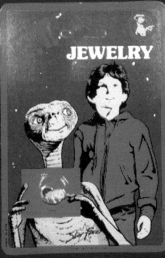

E.T. on Card
1982, $28

Doll
1980s, $2

Disney Sugar Jets
1950s

RINGS OF THE FUTURE

Every year new rings are being produced. From the fun Looney Tunes rings, featuring some of today's best animation, to the chilling holographic Goosebumps rings, rings are becoming more and more popular as entertainment collectibles. With the release of Warner Bros.'s Batman Forever, several new Batman rings exploded into the ring market, showing licensing companies that the manufacturing of collectible rings is a unique and successful marketing idea.

The masters of marketing, Disney, also released some great rings. From Mickey and Minnie to Pocahontas and Aladdin, Disney marketed collectible rings by themselves, or in Pocahontas's case, with some of their movie toy lines. This allowed collectors an opportunity to collect unique rings in a variety of different forms, thus bringing more excitement to the hobby. Because of these successes, Disney plans to offer many more premium rings in the future.

Many other companies have also started to create new premium rings for advertising, promotion and fun. The future will reveal many older rings that collectors were not aware of, that much we are sure of, but it will also provide new and exciting modern rings. Collectors, while studying the past, must also look to the future for dynamic, undiscovered premium rings.

RINGS IN THIS GUIDE

This book contains over 4,000 illustrations, which are individually described, dated and priced.

The following guidelines for ring listings in this reference work will apply. Rings are listed alphabetically by character, company, sets or type. Rings based on comic characters, celebrities, sports figures, movies, TV shows, fictional characters, etc. are included. All rings are made of metal, precious metal, plastic, paper, cardboard, etc. Most rings were offered as premiums by the sponsors of radio shows, TV shows, movies, cereals, candys, gums, etc. and are included. Other listed rings were sold to the public through ads in comic books, stores, mail offerings, catalogues, etc.

Another category of rings included are the new collectible rings being produced by distributors, comic book companies and others with the collector in mind.

All "paper" associated with each ring will be listed, illustrated and priced when available. Items associated with the advertising and promotion of certain rings may be included which could consist of ring cards, actual ads, headers for gumball machines or display promotional signs.

Not included in this work are many of the generic gumball machine rings and general toy rings produced past and present. Basically, the criteria for inclusion of a ring is based primarily on collector demand and interest and historical importance. Please notify the author if you have rings not listed that should be included in future editions.

REPRODUCTIONS

A reproduction ring, or "repro" as its' called in the hobby, is a ring that has been created to resemble a previously manufactured ring. However, in all cases a professional dealer or collector can tell the difference. In some cases the fakes are well done and can fool the beginning collector.

There are several ways to distinguish repros from originals. Here are some helpful hints in determining the real treasures from the fakes.

Note the markings. Many reproductions do not have the same exact markings as the originals or they may have been cast (created) differently. An example of this would the G-man Club ring. In the reproduction version of this ring, a cast line (or the line that is formed when they put two pieces together) runs horizontally through the top of the ring. In the original, there was no cast line present. In other examples, the rings' designs on the base are different, paint looks to "new" or the images on the top may not look crisp and defined. Collectors that are serious about ring collecting should familiarize themselves with the many different ring designs and styles in this book so that they may be confident in their future purchases.

Materials A variety of materials were used in the creation of premium rings. From base brass to a host of other different alloys, these rings were created in all sorts of metals. Because of that, it is hard to determine the original materials that were used to create the ring unless you have access to an original ring. Once you have seen an original, it's usually easy to tell the difference. If you're not sure, take a look at the metal itself. Does the metal have sharp edges around the ring base? Are any scratches brighter than the surrounding metal? In many cases, questions like these may give you the answers you need.

Too Good to be True Although collectors often "find" great bargains at garage sales and flea markets, many repros have found a place in these markets as well. The best example of fraud would be the placement of the cheap repro's of the Spider Ring at these garage sales. With less than 20 known original Spider toy rings in existence, and valued over $10,000, fakes of these rings began to appear at flea markets. Prices ranged anywhere from $5 to $2,500. Unfortunately, these simply crafted repro rings (sold as originals) fooled many beginning collectors. Flea markets and garage sales are still excellent sources for new finds, however, collectors should exercise caution with dealing with large purchases at cheap prices.

Fantasy Pieces A Fantasy ring is basically a ring that has not been "licensed" for creation, and was made without permission from the owners of the property. Examples would be the Lighting bolt (Shazam) ring and the brass "hornet "(Green Hornet) ring. These rings are not reproductions, because they did not exist previously. Most fantasy rings in this book are priced at $1. The reason for this is because as long as the rings are produced in quantity, the value will not be able to increase in a secondary market. However, in some cases where rings are discontinued or produced in a limited edition, the price could increase in the future. Most of these pieces could retail for more than one dollar, but it is not this books purpose to encourage unlicensed products.

Beatles

World's Fair

Coca Cola

Giant

Mickey Mouse

ABOUT RING PRICES

The prices in this guide are in U.S. currency and reflect the market just prior to publication. These reported prices are based on (but not limited to) convention sales, dealers lists, stores, auctions and private sales. The author invites sales lists, sales reports or any other information pertaining to ring information or sales.

PRICES IN THIS BOOK ARE FOR ITEMS IN
GOOD AND NEAR MINT CONDITION

The values listed are for complete examples and represent **Good** and **Near Mint** condition where only two prices are shown. All rings valued at $500.00 or more will show the Good, Fine, and Near Mint values. The more valuable and scarcer rings may have additional grades priced to reflect a wider spread in the value.

Other rings that generally turn up incomplete will be priced in this way with additional prices for the missing parts. Examples are: Rocket to the Moon ring came with 3 rockets. Prices are listed for the ring and also for the rockets. The Captain Video Flying Saucer ring has prices for the base as well as the saucers which are usually missing. The Radio Orphan Annie triple mystery ring usually occurs with the top missing, so prices for the top and base are given.

When rings appear on cards or in sets, both the individual price and the set price may be given.

The values in this book are **retail prices**, not dealers' wholesale prices. Dealers will pay a percentage of the listed prices when buying inventory and this percentage will vary from dealer to dealer. Some dealers are only interested in buying rings in strict near mint or mint condition, while others will buy in all grades.

KING OF THE COMIC BOOK PREMIUMS!

In the Summer of 1994, the very rare Supermen Of America prize ring ("Superman prize ring" in collector's short hand) sold for $22,500 in good (GD) condition. This is a new record for a ring in that grade.

But even more significant is the fact that this is the HIGHEST PRICE EVER PAID for any comic memorabilia in good (GD) condition. No comic book, premium, toy, or original art has sold for $22,500 in good (GD) condition.

With only twelve discovered specimens, the Superman prize ring is on the way to achieving the status of legendary….

Many people ask about the origin and rarity of the prize ring. The following is a detailed explanation of the story behind what many feel is the King of the Comic Book Premiums: the 1940 Superman Prize Ring!

Origin Of The Ring

The Supermen of America club was originally announced in the first issue of *Superman* during the summer of 1939.

To clearly see the relationship of this ring to comic book history, note that just six months before the end of this contest, *Superman* #1 was sent out to eagerly-waiting comic book readers.

Then, as a follow-up to promoting club membership, a contest was held with over 2,000 "dandy free prizes" to be awarded to the winners. The contest consisted of asking Superman Club members to write (in 100 words or less), "What I would do if I had the powers of Superman." On January 28, 1940, this first major superhero-related contest ended.

One of the major prizes was a rather striking silver-finished, gold-topped ring with red accent paint carefully applied around the letter circle on top. The promoters of the contest claimed they would award 1,600 of the rings to the authors of the best 1,600 letters. No one really knows if 1,600 rings were actually given away.

Some historians have questioned this number, speculating that the contest coordinators didn't really have that many rings to give away at all. As was often the case during the '30s and '40s, many comic book related contests exaggerated the number of possible winners. Although this approach used dubious ethics, it is possible that the larger number of prizes offered increased the "size" of the contest and the "hope" of those entering. Whatever the truth to this unanswered question of collectibles history, the reality is that few specimens survive today!

How Rare Is The Ring?

In 1992, some 50-plus years later, a high grade example of the famous ring sold for an astounding $125,000. The record prices paid for this ring each time one comes up for sale had prompted many collectors to ask, "How rare is the ring?"

Today, only 12 specimens of the ring have surfaced and all of them are presently in the hands of collectors. Nine of the rings grade good (GD) to fine (FN), while the remaining three are very fine (VF) or better.

To add to the issue of scarcity, from 1974 until 1992 there has never been a single one of these rings available. Then in 1992, as the price began to escalate, five rings sold in rapid succession, with each sale establishing a new price record. Two new toy rings were discovered in 1995.

Discovery Of Ring #10

Diamond International Comic Distrubutor President and CEO Steve Geppi had been running ads offering to buy the ring for more than three years. In 1992, Steve received a call from a retired elderly lady… regrettably on the verge of losing her home because of overdue bills.

She told Steve she was sure she had the ring he was looking for… and that it was one of her most treasured possessions. It seems her father had won the ring in the contest way back in 1940 and then gave it to her as a gift.

She wore the ring around her neck for two years after it was given to her, but she decided to put it away for safe keeping when she noticed it had started to show wear. She kept the ring in her jewelry box for more than 50 years! The ring is in average condition.

Thinking the ring might be worth only a few thousand dollars at most, she was pleasantly surprised when Steve offered her $40,000 for it. When Steve made the offer, she happily accepted and promptly paid off her mortgage with money to spare.

More Rings In The Future?

It's likely, as collectors continue to search junk shops, flea markets, and antique shows across the country, a few more examples of the rarity might surface. And with more opportunities for documented sales, only the Shadow knows what higher prices lurk in this ring's future.

But even if the number of rings in the market double, the Superman prize ring will continue to be one of the most historically significant and highly sought-after items in the world of collectibles.

THE SPIDER RING

In October of 1933 a new action hero debuted on newsstands across America. His name was The Spider and he waged a relentless war against the overlords of crime. The Spider wore a black hat and cape and a trademark ring featuring a crimson spider.

THE SPIDER-MASTER of MEN! became a pulp magazine sensation.

Clubs were the trend of the day and **THE SPIDER Magazine** wasted little time forming "The Spider League for Crime Prevention." Members were called SPIDERS and a column called "The Web" was featured in each issue of **THE SPIDER Magazine**. SPIDERS were to help Uncle Sam's G-Men ferret out criminals and alert constituted authorities.

SPIDERS could order a Spider ring for twenty-five cents in coin or stamps. The ring was just like the one The Spider wore when he left the mark of The Spider on the jaw of a despicable gangster.

Less than 20 of the original rings have been documented, and a high grade ring can bring up to $10,000.

OPERATOR 5 RING

In April of 1934 a new kind of hero appeared on the newsstands to instill patriotism in an America that was reeling from the Great Depression.

His name was Jimmy Christopher and his code number was Operator 5. Jimmy Christopher was a special agent with the United States Secret Service and his mission was to uncover subversive elements bent on the ultimate destruction of the United States.

His secret symbol was a skull with a number five centered in it's forehead, signifying membership in all elite covert strike force.

OPERATOR 5 Magazine was an instant hit and a club for kids called "The Secret Sentinels of America" was formed. When you joined the Secret Sentinels, you could purchase the famous ring with the Operator 5 secret symbol on it for twenty-five cents in currency or stamps.

Today this premium ring in high grade condition sells for over $20,000, and there are only six documented owners of the original.

New Record For The Ultra Rare Magnifying Rings

Early in 1941, Kellogg's announced to the children of California, "Boys & Girls, be the first to get your new **Viking Magnifying** ring." The ring had a picture of Prince Valric, a young Viking hero, on the top. It also had a new gimmick, a small magnifying glass attached to the top which could magnify the picture of Prince Valric five times. This magnifying glass was so powerful kids could use it to burn a hole in paper using the sun's rays or destroy whole colonies of ants.

This advertisement also had a continuing story about Valric's escape form the dangerous wicked Grimm. Of course once Valric had his daily fare of nourishing rye grain, he made his escape! To make this story fit into the product sell, the ring was offered by obtaining a coupon from, of all things, All Rye Flakes, plus you had to ante up 10¢ as well.

Today this ring is one of the rarest of all to find. It ranks 10th among all the rings listed in the **Overstreet Premium Ring Guide** with a population of only 6 known. A nice example of this ring just sold for a whopping $7,500, setting a new record!

The makers of Quaker Rice Sparkies liked the look of the ring and decided to offer one for the radio *Orphan Annie* show late in 1941. Using the same technique with the magnifying glass and changing the face on the top to Orphan Annie, the premium was announced on the radio show as a tie-in with the new Secret Guard Club. However, the Club was a bust and few rings were made.

The United States was now in a war and Little Orphan Annie was not convincing as a leader of the Secret Guard or a potential superhero. Very shortly thereafter, she went off the air giving way to Superman and Captain Marvel to save the day on radio and in the comic strips. The age of Little Orphan Annie was over. All items that were offered, along with membership to the Secret Guard, are very scarce and are rarely seen, even in many top collections of comic memorabilia. This ring ranks 15th in the **Overstreet Guide** with less than 20 known examples in collections.

COLLECTING OR INVESTING?

Thoughts on the hobby
by Howard C. Weinberger

It is now obvious to the experienced ring collector that the publication of the first **Overstreet Ring Price Guide** has dramatically affected the collectible ring market.

The positives are the validation of ring collecting as a credible and fun hobby that has attracted many new and enthusiastic people, as well as the recognition of premium rings as an important part of the American culture. The negatives are the fact that it is getting harder to find many of the older rings. Whether this is temporary or not, we do not yet know. For many years it has been the habit of some dealers to price all rings at the top price regardless of the actual grade. Unfortunately, this practice continues today. They either do not understand the principle of grading or are simply abusing the hobby's guidelines as explained by the **Overstreet Price Guide**, auction houses and others.

As with any collectible, it is always advisable to collect what you love rather than what is hot! Collectibles markets can be unpredictable. What is hot today can certainly be cold tomorrow. If you collect what you love, you will not be concerned day to day what your collection is worth. However, market speculation will always be there, and if you are lucky and a bit sensible, it can certainly be profitable as well.

Here are some thoughts on the collectible ring market and how it can go forward for both the collector and speculator.

Most of the Golden Age premium rings prior to the 1950s and 1960s are known. It is unusual to discover a Golden Age premium ring not yet known. Certainly these older rings are deemed the blue chips of the hobby. Their numbers are extremely limited, especially in top grade condition. Also, most of these rings are singles or stand-alones (one single ring in a promotion versus an entire set or series).

Tennessee Jed look-around

The values of these rings continue to evolve as the market decides what is most desirable and scarce. *Desirability* and *scarcity* are two very important considerations. It is fair to say that **Billy West** or **Tennessee Jed** premium rings, for example, are not plentiful. However, most people today would not know who these characters were. So, even though these specimens may be scarce, a lot of people may not care to collect them, even though they have earned a place in the Golden Age of rings. A more recognizable figure, especially one still known to young people today, is probably going to be more desirable and will fetch a higher price in most situations. Billy West was known to one maybe two generations before fading from the scene, whereas Superman and Batman are still alive today, almost 60 years after their creation. So five year old kids today will still fondly remember these characters 30 years from now, as we did, which will certainly continue to make the older premiums of these known heroes even more valuable.

New discovery from the Golden Age! Egyptian Sphinx ring!

One of the best things about most of the older rings, besides their obvious beautifully detailed design & high quality, is there functionability. They did something! Whistles, sirens, secret compartments, decoders, glow-in-darks, look-arounds, flickers, etc. Many contemporary rings, on the other hand, are made of inexpensive materials and just display a simple logo or a picture.

Once we get into the 1950s and later, other considerations enter the market. "Sets" of rings began to emerge as product marketers found new bait to make kids come back again and again. Whether in a gumball machine or a cereal box, you had to continue to buy in order to get another ring to complete a full set. This is a particular part of the hobby that is starting to get attention. For example, the first **Overstreet Ring Price Guide** illustrates the set of twelve **Green Hornet** flicker rings at $20 each. This is where it gets complicated. A casual ring collector that just wants an example of a **Green Hornet** ring in their collection certainly does not want the ring of the couple kissing.

Green Hornet kissing ring not as desirable as the Green Hornet mask ring

They would want the Green Hornet logo ring or the ring showing his face. But does that also mean that the ring of the couple kissing has become scarcer because no one wanted it and it consequently was thrown away more often? And how about the fact that Bruce Lee was Kato in the *Green Hornet* TV series. There are Bruce Lee collectors out there that care nothing about rings or the Green Hornet. They only want the **Kato** flicker rings from the set for their Bruce Lee collection. This creates the crossover market. You will run into this a lot. There are collectors of Buster Brown, Howdy Doody, Lone Ranger, Quisp and many more. See what I mean? There is a lot to consider. This will also make it more difficult to complete full sets going forward. It is inevitable that certain single rings within sets will demand higher prices than others.

Green Hornet Bruce Lee Kato ring wanted by Bruce Lee collectors as well as Green Hornet collectors creating a crossover market.

Complete sets, in my opinion, will eventually become the most desirable commodity of the contemporary rings (1950s to present). Think about it. Flicker rings and more recent rings are certainly more available than the Golden Age stand-alones. You can usually find a single **Batman**, **Looney Tune** or **Laugh-in** ring for example at a show or a dealers shop. But it is rare to see someone offer a complete set. Furthermore, it has been my experience to see the same few rings of a particular set over and over again, while other rings in a set are never seen. Example: You will usually see one of the individual characters of the **Monkees** (Davy, Micky, Peter or Mike), but try to find the **Monkeemobile**, or the **Speedy Gonzales** from **Looney Tunes**, or the **Judy Carne "Sock it to me"** from the **Laugh-in** set.

Howdy Doody, another crossover market ring wanted by general ring collectors as well as Howdy Doody collectors.

GOOD LUCK! It makes sense to believe that this is where the Boomer Era rings (1950s, 1960s & early 1970s) will become rare and scarce relative to the Golden Age stand-alones that are rare and scarce as individual rings. In sports card collecting it is common to get the complete set cheaper than buying all the cards individually, but the opposite is true for complete ring sets. A complete set will become more valuable than the single rings. As collectors attempt to complete sets, it will be interesting to see which rings are really the rarest. HAPPY HUNTING to everyone.

Dr. Doolittle

Monkees

Felix the Cat

Superman

Universal Monsters

TOUGHEST FLICKER SETS

1. Superman	?
2. Universal Monsters	6
3. Doctor Dolittle	12
4. Baseball Teams	56
5. Space	6
6. Rocky & Bullwinkle	6
7. Frankenberry/Count Chocula	6
8. Dances (Twist, Frug, Jerk, etc.)	5
9. Monkees	12
10. Tom & Jerry	4
11. Wizard of Oz	12
12. Mork from Ork	4
13. Man From U.N.C.L.E. (b&w)	2
14. Tarzan	6
15. Space (small)	?

TOUGHEST INDIVIDUAL FLICKER RINGS

1. Davy Crockett
2. Howdy Doody TV
3. Rootie Kazootie (Thick Lens)
4. Ben Hur
5. Mister Softee
6. Huck Finn
7. Buster Brown (Red/White color)
8. Punt Pass & Kick
9. Robert E. Lee
10. Howdy Doody (Thick Lens)

Davy Crockett

Rootie Kazootie

Mister Softee

Howdy
(Thick Lens)

Count Chocula

Arby's

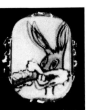
Looney Tunes

McDonalds

TOP FLICKER ACTION

Some of the best flicker action is found on:

1. Felix the Cat (set of 3)

2. McDonald's (set of 4)

3. Tarzan (set of 6)

4. Looney Tunes (set of 16)

5. Frankenberry and Count Chocula rings

6. Arby's Looney Tunes (set of 10)

TOP 25 SPORTS RINGS

1) Joe Louis Face	1940s	$ 2,600
2) Joe Louis Figural	1940s	$ 1,500
3) Ted Williams	1940s	$ 925
4) Jack Armstrong Baseball Centennial	1939	$ 650
5) Huskies Club	1936	$ 600
6) Joe DiMaggio Club	1940s	$ 400
7) Baseball, Game Ring	1949	$ 300
8) Football, Bowman Gum	1948	$ 300
9) Baseball, Dodgers	1940s	$ 250
10) Baseball, Yankees	1940s	$ 250
11) Baseball, Giants	1940s	$ 250
12) Dizzy Dean	1936	$ 250
13) Dizzy Dean Winners	1936	$ 250
14) Andy Pafko	1949	$ 235
15) Baseball, Babe Ruth Club	1934	$ 200
16) Baseball Hall Of Fame (gold)	1939	$ 200
17) Baseball Hall Of Fame (silver)	1939	$ 200
18) Baseball, Atl. Crackers	1954	$ 160
19) Baseball, Bowman Gum	1949	$ 150
20) Baseball, Spokane Hawks	1938	$ 150
21) Baseball, All-Star	1995	$ 125
22) Football, Wash. Redskins	1991	$ 125
23) Basketball, Bowman Gum	1949	$ 110
24) Baseball, Bakelite	1920s	$ 100
25) Baseball, N. Y. E.	1937	$ 100

COLLECTING SPORTS RINGS
by Ron Menchine

In traveling throughout the United States during the late 1960's and early 70's as the Voice of the Washington Senators, I was constantly on the lookout for baseball memorabilia. Although I did not see a great many baseball rings, I would always buy them whenever I did. They were nearly always reasonably priced and great conversation pieces when I'd actually wear them.

At a Sports Collector's Convention in Detroit in 1969, I acquired a ring that came out 30 years earlier celebrating the Baseball Centennial (1839-1939). It was quite attractive and a real bargain at $25. I didn't know any more about it other than it was really a neat item. As far as the ring's origin, I had no idea who put it out and under what circumstances. That information and a lot more came a quarter of a century later when I had the pleasure of meeting John K. Snyder and Robert Overstreet two years ago while working on a story for **White's Guide to Collecting Figures** magazine.

But until that time, I was still picking up novelty baseball rings whenever I'd see them, which was not very often.

I found my Andy Pafko Scorekeeper Baseball ring at an Antique Shop in Hagerstown, Maryland in the 1980s for only $20. I later learned that the ring was put out by Muffets, a Chicago company in 1949. Pafko was the "hitting and fielding star of the Chicago Cubs" as the promotional advertising for Muffets pointed out. The ring cost 15 cents plus the blue box top from a package of Muffets and the offer expired September 15, 1949. A fine all-around player who batted .285 over 17 seasons, Pafko

The Andy Pafko Scorekeeper ring and paper.

was undoubtedly selected by Muffets on the strength of his 1948 season with the Cubs when he batted 312, drove in 101 runs leading the Cubs. In addition, he led all National League Third Basemen in Assists with 314 and double plays with 29. Muffets put him in very select company when he became only the second Player Muffets honored with a ring, the immortal Babe Ruth being the other in 1934. Originally 15 cents plus the Muffets box top, the Pafko ring today brings in excess of $200.

I found my first plastic baseball ring at a Pennsylvania flea market in the 1970's. It was red and had the name and logo of the Detroit Tigers in the middle. Although I did not know it at the time, I later discovered it was available in Kellogg's cereal in 1960, the last season Major League baseball had 16 teams. I also learned the rings came in red, white and blue emphasizing baseball is as American as our flag.

1978 Los Angeles Dodgers

While attending a Baltimore Orioles game at Memorial Stadium in 1984, I was lucky enough to be there when, as a special promotion, fans were given facsimile World Championship rings commemorating the Orioles 1983 World Series victory. Ballpark Giveaways such as this have contributed to the tremendous interest in novelty sports rings that exist today.

For years Major League Baseball clubs held special days to lure additional fans to the ballpark. Although the St. Louis Browns haven't had a team since 1953, they proved to be great innovators

1976 Cincinnati Reds

in the area of Ballpark Giveaways. On May 1, 1945 they celebrated the flag raising of their first and only American League Pennant by giving all fans in attendance a special pennant shaped for the game against Cleveland. Bat Day, the first popular giveaway event of modern times also had its origin in St. Louis. Rudy Schaefer, long time assistant to Bill Veeck at both Cleveland and St. Louis learned early in 1952 that a mid-west bat company was going out of business. Schaefer sold Veeck on the idea of purchasing the stock of

1982 St. Louis Cardinals

bats at a bargain price and giving them away at a future Browns game. In a game that normally would have attracted a Corporal's Guard, thousands of fans turned out for the event. It wasn't long before every Major League team featured Bat Day. Other Special Events followed but were primarily limited to other baseball equipment such as balls, caps, gloves and uniform parts. Naturally, most of these promotions were geared for youngsters, but it wasn't long before adult giveaways were included as a bonus for attending special events. It worked like magic as thousands of additional fans trooped to the ballpark. Because of the immense popularity of these giveaways corporate sponsors began clamoring to underwrite the cost of these promotions. In the early days of ballpark giveaways the ballclubs themselves picked up the tab. Now the sponsors gladly pay for the promotions because the free publicity they receive more than compensates them for any costs involved. Starting in the mid 70s, a plethora of giveaways such as rings, cups, mugs, clocks and watches, baseball cards, beach towels, sun visors and umbrellas were an added incentive to attend a game.

1986 New York Mets sponsored by Tropicana.

1988 Baltimore Orioles

Facsimile championship rings like the '83 Orioles ring I received at the ballpark the following season were ideal and extremely popular giveaways. I ultimately learned there were many others. The first I am aware of commemorated the Cincinnati Reds 1976 championship and was a Riverfront Stadium giveaway the following season. Another was a Los Angeles Dodgers 1978 National League Championship ring. The earliest dated facsimile championship ring is a 1960 Pittsburgh Pirates World Championship ring but this was a promotion for the Giant Eagle food chain in the 1990s. This ring has become particularly sought after because it not only commemorates one of the most exciting World Series in history (when the Pirates beat the Yankees in the seventh game on Bill Mazeroski dramatic 9th inning home run), but it was the also the first World Series for Pirates Hall of Famer, the late Roberto Clemente. Other known facsimile championship rings are: 1982 World Champions St. Louis Cardinals, 1983 Baltimore Orioles, 1986 New York Mets sponsored by Tropicana, 1988 LA Dodgers, 1990 Oakland A's American League Champions sponsored by Giant Eagle. There are undoubtedly others that have been produced and I welcome hearing from anyone who has additional information or any for sale.

1954 Chicago Cubs

Baseball Hall of Fame

Ron Menchine was the official voice of the Washington Senators, author of several books on baseball, and is a collector of pre-1960 baseball memorabilia.

Pittsburgh Pirate Plastic

1995 Baseball All-Stars

PREMIUM RINGS WE'D LOVE TO SEE!

ART & CONCEPT BY A. KAVIRAJ

BILL 'N ANNE CAMPBELL

1221 Littlebrook Lane

Birmingham, AL 35235

BUYING - SELLING - TRADING

Radio and Box Top Premiums (Rings, Badges, Decoders, Manuals)

Character Watches, Boxes, Inserts, Bands, Parts, Hands, Dials

Western Hero Items including Cap Guns and Holsters

Comics, Big Little Books, Pop-Ups

Capt. Marvel, Capt. Midnight, Capt. Video, Buck Rogers, Tom Corbett Space Cadet, Doc Savage, Shadow, Tom Mix, Lone Ranger, Superman, Batman, Little Orphan Annie, Mickey Mouse, Donald Duck, Popeye, Howdy Doody, Hopalong Cassidy, Roy Rogers, G-Man, Gene Autry, Jack Armstrong, Davy Crockett, Paladin, Rin Tin Tin, Sgt. Preston, Zorro, Green Hornet, Sky King, Straight Arrow, Buster Brown, Flash Gordon

For personal collection: Capt. Marvel items wanted. Also especially need Whistle Bomb Ring, Big Bad Wolf and Donald Duck 1934 Wrist Watches with leather bands.

DIRECTORY OF SHOPS
(PAID ADVERTISING -STORE LISTING)

You can have your store listed here for very reasonable rates. Send for details and deadline for the next Guide.The following list of stores have paid to be included in this list. We cannot assume any responsibility in your dealings with these shops. This list is provided for your information only. When planning your trip, it would be advisable to make appointments in advance.

Items stocked by these shops are listed just after the telephone number and are coded as follows:

(a) Premium Rings (old)
(b) Premium Rings (new)
(c) Toys from '30s - '50s
(d) Toys from '60s - present
(e) Star Wars Merchandise
(f) Superhero Collectibles
(g) Disney Memorabilia
(h) Decoders & Other Premiums

(i) Movie Posters & Memorabilia
(j) Original Art
(k) Comics & Related Material
(l) Star Trek Items
(m) Trading & Collectible Cards
(n) Cowboy Memorabilia
(o) Other

FLORIDA

Whiz Bang! Collectibles
948 E. Semoran Blvd.
Casselberry, FL 32707
PH: (407) 260-8869 (a-o)

Tropic Comics East
5439 N. Federal Hwy.
Ft. Lauderdale, FL 33308
PH: (954) 351-0001
(c-f, i-m,o)

Tropic Comics South Inc.
742 N. E. 167th. St.
N. Miami Beach, FL 33162
PH: (305) 940-8700
(c-f,i-m,o)

Tropic Comics Inc.
313 S. State RD 7
Plantation, FL 33317
PH: (954) 587-8878
(c-f,i-m,o)

MISSOURI

Decades Of Toyys
3315 Woodson
Brecken Ridge Hills, MO
63114-4718
PH: (314) 427-8693
(a-h,l,m,o)

NEW HAMPSHIRE

Ron Toth
72 Charles St.
Rochester, NH 03867-3413
PH: (603) 335-2062
(a-d,f-h,n,o)

OHIO

Toys Toys Toys
110 Main St.
Bellville, OH 44813
PH: (419) 886-4782
(d-f,i,l,n)

TEXAS

**Third Planet Sci-Fi
Superstore**
2718 Southwest Freeway
Houston, TX 77098
PH: (713) 528-1067
(b,d,e-g,i-m,o)

CLASSIFIED ADVERTISING

Toy Ring Display Case: Display, Organize, and Protect up to
70 rings! $10.00 ea. plus S&H, 4 or more ONLY $7.95 plus
S&H Visa/MC Accepted. Shelf or wall mount, lock together
when stacked. L.S.A.S.E. Dept. TR1 Collectors Display Case
Co. RT2 Box 73 Fremont NE 68025-9635
(402-721-4765)

SUPER RARE LOA ALTASCOPE RING VF/NM LESS THAN 10
KNOWN. WILL CONSIDER ALL REASONABLE CASH/TRADE
OFFERS. LSASE PLUS $1.00 BRINGS LIST OF PREMIUMS
ETC. FOR SALE. JOE FAIR RD-2 10 CRESTWOOD DR.
NEW CASTLE, PA 16101 (412) 6542413 (4-7 PM BEST)

I sell toy rings. Call Bobby Segal (814) 355-2542. Or send Want List: P.O. Box 39 Julian, PA 16844

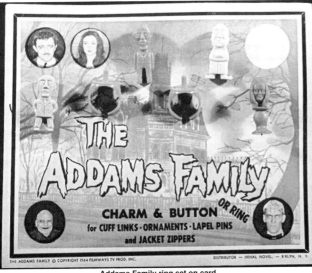

Agent 007
1960s (paper)(black/green)
$8-$22

Addams Family ring set on card
1964 (T.V.)(plastic)(set of 4 on card)(rings & bases produced in different colors)
(red, blue, brown, black, amber, pink known)
With Card $160
Individual Rings $2-$4 ea. for all colors

Agent 007 (1)

Uncle Fester

Lurch

African Tribal
(see Savage Tribal Ring)

Agent 007 (2)

Agent 007 Face (paper),
1960s
$8-$22

Agent 007 (3)

Gomez

Morticia

Agent 007 Face
1995 (round)(metal)
(color)(fantasy)
$1

Agent 007 (4)

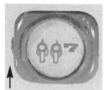

Agent 007 (5)
1960 (paper insert)(set of
5)(blue, green
& red bases)
$10-$22 each

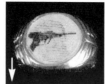

Agent 007 Flicker(4)
007 gun to picture of Sean
Connery face.

Agent 007 Flicker (6a)

Agent 007 Flicker (8b)
Figure in karate outfit with
hands together to same
man defending himself
against a child.

Agent 007 Flicker (1)
"James Bond" to picture of
Sean Connery face.

Agent 007 Flicker (5)
"O.S.S." to picture of Sean
Connery face.

Agent 007 Flicker (6b)
Man in white suit with arms
behind his back to same
man armed with a sword.

Agent 007 Flicker (9a)

Agent 007 Flicker (2)
"007" to picture of Sean
Connery face.

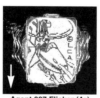

Agent 007 Flicker (6)
"633" to picture of agent.

Agent 007 Flicker
1960s (small round)(6 diff.)
$10-$26 ea.

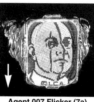

Agent 007 Flicker (7a)

Agent 007 Flicker (9b)
Odd-job face to his hat hitting a man in the head.

Agent 007 Flicker
1960s (12 diff., original
base)(in color, plastic)
$15-$30 ea.

Agent 007 Flicker (4a)

Agent 007 Flicker (7b)
Face (half white, half flesh
with a scar) to same man
being punched "POW".

Agent 007 Flicker (1)
Cartoon James Bond in
white sport jacket to a
diver underwater in yel-
low bathing suit behind a
shark

Agent 007 Flicker (3)
"117" to picture of gun.

Agent 007 Flicker (4b)
Picture of two helicopters (1
yellow, 1 white) to close-up
of yellow copter.

Agent 007 Flicker (8a)

Agent 007 Flicker (2)
A missile standing on
launch pad inside of a
volcano to missile taking
off out of volcano opening

Agent 007 Flicker (3)
Dark skinned man with
blue hat strapped onto
head to same man with
veil over face holding a
weapon.

Agent 007 Flicker (4)
Picture of two helicopters (1
yellow, 1 white) to close-up
of yellow copter.

Agent 007 Flicker (5)
"007" gun picture to close-
up of James Bond holding
his gun.

Agent 007 Flicker (6)
Man in white suit with arms
behind his back to same
man armed with a sword.

Agent 007 Flicker (7)
Face (half white, half flesh
with a scar) to same man
being punched "POW."

Agent 007 Flicker (8)
Figure in karate outfit with
hands together to same
man defending himself
against a child.

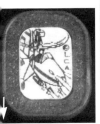

Agent 007 Flicker (9)
Odd-job face to his hat hitting a man in the head.

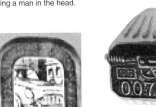

Agent 007 Flicker (10)
Yellow Aston Martin (sports
car) to ejector seat with figure shooting out of sunroof.

Agent 007 Flicker (11)
White yacht cruising to
same yacht moved futher
along.

Agent 007 Flicker (12)
Spaceship in space with
cone opening and figure
coming out to close-up of
figure walking in space.

Agent 007 Flicker
1960s (12 diff., blue base)
$10-$22 ea.

Agent 007 Gun
1967 (plastic)(from 007 kit)
$10-$24

Agent 009 Identi-Kit
1960s (card set with 007 ring)
Complete $55

Agent 007 Gun,
1960s (metal)
$5-$10

Agent 007 seal
1960s (metal, heavy)
$25-$55

Air Force (see U.S. Air Force)

Alexander
(see Post tin)

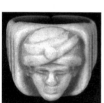

Aladdin Type Cameo
1990s (plastic, green color)
(gumball)
$2-$4

Aladdin
1995 (metal/plastic)
(round, color)
$2-$4

Aladdin - Genie
1995 (metal/plastic)
(color)
$2-$4

Aladdin - Jasmine
1995 (metal/plastic)(2 diff.
color variants, pink and
white)
$2-$4 each

Aladdin - Jasmine
1995 (metal/plastic)(rectangle)(3 diff. color variants)
$2-$4 each

Aladdin - Jasmine
1990s (plastic)(Crest,
color)
$5-$10

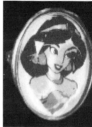

Aladdin - Jasmine
1990s (metal)(oval)
$2-$5

Aladdin's Lamp
1950s (plastic)
(gumball, yellow base)
$15-$40

Aladdin's Lamp
(casino giveaway?)(plastic)
(red/black)
$10-$30

Aladdin's Lamp
1970s (plastic,
gumball)(Canada)
$5-$10

Alice in Wonderland
1933 (metal)(enameled)
released at time of movie)
$50-$175

American Airlines
(see Junior Stewardess)

Andy Gibb
(see Movie Star photo)

Allyson, June
(see Movie Star photo)

Alvin
1960s (plastic)
$20-$40

**Andy Pafko Scorekeeper
Baseball Ring**
1949 (metal)(Muffets)
$75-$235

HERE'S YOUR NEW
Andy Pafko
SCOREKEEPER
BASEBALL RING

IT RECORDS:
* ★ OUTS
* ★ STRIKES
* ★ BALLS

Personally Autographed by
ANDY PAFKO
Hitting and Fielding Star of the Chicago Cubs

NOW—you can keep an accurate check on every pitch and every play in the ball game—whether you're playing yourself or watching it out at the park or on television.

Just think, your new Andy Pafko Scorekeeper Baseball Ring will never let you get caught napping. If you're an infielder you'll know for sure when to start that double-play and when to play the batter. As an outfielder, you'll always be sure to peg to the right base. Correct, split-second

thinking like that will win many a ball game for you.

You'll want your whole team to have those wonderful, useful new Rings as part of their regular equipment. The attached order blank makes it easy. First, round up the gang! Show them your ring. Then for each additional Andy Pafko Scorekeeper Baseball Ring you want, send just 15c in coin and 1 Muffets box top to: MUFFETS Baseball Ring, Dept. 4, Chicago 77, Illinois.
M-5.42

ORDER BLANK

Muffets Baseball Ring, Dept. 4, Chicago 77, Illinois

Please send me _____ Andy Pafko Scorekeeper Baseball Ring(s). For each Ring I enclose 15c (in coin) and the blue box top from a package of Muffets.

Name _____

Street or R.F.D. _____

City _____ Zone _____ State _____

Supply Limited! Offer Closes September 15, 1949
Offer Good Only in the United States

Andy Pafko paper
1949 (scarce)
$75-100

Andy Panda
1970s (plastic)(Canada)
$1-$2

Animaniacs (see Looney Tunes)

Annie (see Radio Orphan Annie)

Apollo Flicker (4)

Apollo Flicker (5)

Amazing Marvel Super Heroes
1966 (set on card)
Complete $50-$100
Ring Only $10-$20 ea.

Apollo Flicker (3)

Apollo Flicker (6)

Apollo Flicker (2)
"First Man on the Moon"
July 20, 1969 to picture of
rocket launching from earth.

Apollo Flicker (5)
"Michael Collins" to face
with space suit on (no
helmet).

Apollo Flicker (11)
(shows both images)

Apollo Flicker (7)

Apollo Flicker (3)
"Neil A. Armstrong" to
face with space suit on
(no helmet).

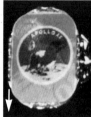

Apollo Flicker (6)
Apollo II logo to picture of
Eagle and Columbia
docking.

Apollo Flicker (8)

Apollo Flicker (12)

↑ **Apollo Flicker** (12 diff.)
1960s (Blue base)(scarce
set)(1st man on moon
7/20/69)
$5-$20 ea.

Apollo Flicker (4)
"Edwin E. Aldrin Jr." to
face with space suit on (no
helmet).

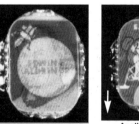

Apollo Flicker (7)
"Columbia" picture to
"Eagle" picture.

Apollo Flicker (9)

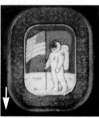

Apollo Flicker (10)

Apollo Flicker (1)
Apollo II logo to "Apollo 11"
cartoon figure of all three
figures together.

Apollo Flicker (8)
"The Eagle has landed" t
picture of Eagle landed.

Apollo Flicker (9)
"That's one small step for man, one giant leap for mankind" to Armstrong stepping off ladder.

Apollo Flicker (10)
"We came in peace for all mankind" to Armstrong on moon in suit standing by flag.

Apollo Flicker (11)
Apollo 12" angled picture of rocket with moon in background to astronaut stepping on the moon.

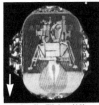

Apollo Flicker (12)
"Apollo 12" picture of ship on moon to ship taking off of the moon.

Apollo Flicker
1960s, (12 diff.)
(silver base)
(scarce set)
$10-$35 ea.

Apollo Flicker
1960s Armstrong, Aldrin & Collins photograph faces to picture of Eagle sitting on moon with earth in background
$15-$30

Aquaman Dome
1970s (metal)(small, color)(see Robin)
$10-$20

Arby's Logo
1970s (plastic)(brown and white)
$2-$4

Arby's Bugs Bunny Flicker

Arby's Porky Pig Flicker

Arby's Daffy Duck Flicker
(obverse & reverse)

Arby's Yosemite Sam Flicker

Arby's Flickers
1987 (set of 4)
$15-$50 ea.

Astronaut Rings
1960s (on card)(Mercury 7)
(1st U.S. Astronauts, set of 7)
On Card $200
Ring Only $10-$20 ea.

Archie
1993, Staber
Silver (50 made) - $325
Gold (5 made) - $1000

Astronaut
1960s (aluminum)
$10-$20

Army (see Sky Birds, Smith
Bros. & U.S. Army)

Arthur Godfrey Photo
(see Real Photos)

Arthur Murray Spinner
1976 (Murray Go Round)
(Also see Tom Mix
Spinner)(metal)
$100-$210

Baba Looey Flicker
1960s
$50-$100
(no photo available)

Baba Looey (see Quick
Draw McGraw)

Atlanta Crackers
(see Baseball --)

Babe Ruth (see Baseball)

Back To The Future
(see Hill Valley High)

Atlas Club
1941 (Sterling)
$90-$175

Bam!
1976 (paper over
plastic)(DC)
$1-$2

Bambi
1960s (aluminum)
$20-$40

Barbie Heart
1980s (metal, color)
$5-$10

Barbie on Card
1962 (no illo.)(1st Barbie
ring?)
$30-$60

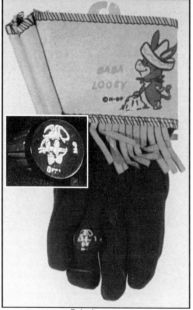

Baba Looey
1960s (Ring on glove)(Dixie)
Complete w/glove $75
Ring Only $20-$40

Barbie Recess Ring
1980s (metal)
On Card $15
Ring Only $2-$6

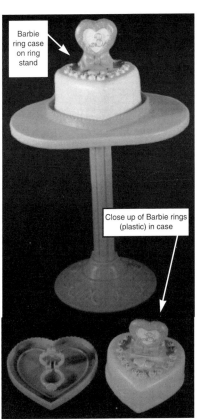

Barbie ring case on ring stand

Close up of Barbie rings (plastic) in case

Barbie Wedding
1992 (packaged with doll, 2 rings, and table)
Complete $30
Rings w/table $20

Barnabas Collins
1969 (Dark Shadows)(gum wrapper paper needed to order ring)(in color)(scarce)
$75-$125

Barney
1993 (enameled)(TV dinosaur)
$2-$5

Barry Goldwater Flicker
1960s (plastic, blue base)
Barry to "I'm for Barry"
$5-$15

Barney
1990s (plastic/paper)(TV dinosaur)
.50-$1

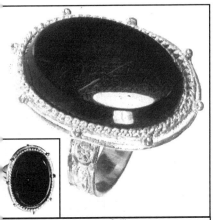

Barnabas Collins
1969 (Dark Shadows, T.V.)(Gum)(2 versions)
GD $400, FN 600, NM $800

63

Baseball: The rings in this section consist of All Star, Championship and World Series facsimiles, vending machine and original rings usually sold at the ball parks, through the mail, or offered as cereal premiums. Each year, original, high quality rings are produced in a very limited quantity for players and staff of various teams at most major championship and bowl game events. Due to the scarcity and popularity of these rings, various sponsors began producing facsimiles of the originals to be given away at a later date at the park of the championship team.

The originals as well as salesman's samples of these rings command top dollar of usually $1000 or more.

The very first facsimile ring is believed to be the 1976 Cincinnati Reds World Championship ring issued as a ball park giveaway in 1977. The Pittsburg Pirates offered a facsimile ring (dated 1960) of the 1960 World Champion-ship which was sponsored by Giant Eagle stores. This ring was given away at the Pittsburg ball park in the 1990s.

Other high quality rings were produced and sold at the ball parks and are not championship facsimiles. Nearly all ball park facsimile championship giveaways were sponsored by an advertiser who frequently put their logo on the side of the ring.

Baseball Aluminum Cereal Box (front view)

Baseball Aluminum
(shows ring in cellophane wrapper as it was placed in cereal box)

Baseball (see Andy Pafko, Bazooka Joe, Dizzy Dean, Jack Armstrong, Joe Dimaggio, Kellogg's Picture & Ted Williams)

Baseball All Star
1995 (metal)(prototype)(see-through top)
$60-$125

Baseball Aluminum
Begin listing

American League

| BALTIMORE ORIOLES | BOSTON RED SOX | CHICAGO WHITE SOX | CLEVELAND INDIANS |

| DETROIT TIGERS | KANSAS CITY ATHLETICS | NEW YORK YANKEES | WASHINGTON NATIONALS |

Illo from cereal box

Baseball Aluminum (Cereal Box)
1957 (back view)(contains ad for complete set of aluminum rings)(rings were inserted in cereal box)
Cereal box Complete $75-$150

American League Rings

Baltimore Orioles

Detroit Tigers

Boston Red Sox

Kansas City A's (Athletics)

Chicago White Sox (two views shown)

New York Yankees

Cleveland Indians

Washington Nationals

National League

BROOKLYN DODGERS   CHICAGO CUBS   CINCINNATI REDLEGS   MILWAUKEE BRAVES

NEW YORK GIANTS   PHILADELPHIA PHILLIES   PITTSBURGH PIRATES   ST. LOUIS CARDINALS

Illo from cereal box

National League Rings

Chicago Cubs

Cincinatti Red Legs

Baseball Aluminum
1957 (aluminum)(16 in set)(Kellogg's Shredded Wheat cereal premium)(one ring came in each cereal box)
$10-$25 ea.

Baseball, Astros
1970s (orange/aluminum)
$10-$20

Baseball Bakelite
1920s (part of set?)(black bakelite plastic)(the first baseball toy ring)(player unidentified)
$50-$100

Baseball, Atlanta Crackers
1954 (metal)(gloves over crossed bats on side)
$75-$160

Baseball, Baltimore Orioles
1988 (Equitable Series) (Limited edition giant ring given away to v.i.p.'s & players only at various equitable series sites)(bases vary by location)
$45-$85

Baseball, Babe Ruth Club
1934 (gold color metal, Muffets)(glove between crossed bats on side)(also see baseball, Atlanta Crackers, Dodgers, Giants & Yankees)
$75-$200

Baseball, Baltimore Orioles
1970 (World Champions) (adjustable in box)
In Box $75
Ring Only $20-$60

Baseball, Baltimore Orioles
1970s (metal)(color)
$5-$10

Baseball, Baltimore Orioles World Series
1984 (metal)(ballpark give-away)(facsimile)
$20-$50

Baseball Cardinals
1982 (National League World Champions)(metal)(gold color)(ballpark give-away)
$40-$75

Baseball, Celestrium Florida Marlins
1993 (1st year)(Balfour)(metal)(celestrium top)
$30-$75

Baseball, Celestrium Milwaukee Brewers
1993 (Balfour)(National League)
$30-$75

Baseball Celestrium Rings
Made for Major League baseball, NBA, NFL and NHL by Balfour Jewelry Co., Mass. They all originally sold for $95.00 + $4.00 P&H.

Baseball, Celestrium Atlanta Braves
1993 (metal)(Balfour)(celestrium top)
$30-$75

Baseball, Celestrium St. Louis Cardinals
1993 (Balfour)
$30-$75

Baseball, Celestrium Chicago White Sox
1993 (metal)(Balfour)(celestrium top)
$30-$75

Baseball, Celestrium Texas Rangers
1993 (American League)(metal)(Balfour)(celestrium top)
$15-$30

Baseball, Celestrium Colorado Rockies
1993 (metal)(Balfour)(celestrium top)
$30-$75

Baseball, Celestrium Toronto Blue Jays
1993 (metal)(Balfour)(celestrium top)
$30-$75

Baseball, Big League Package/Paper
1994 (front & back shown)
Complete $2-$5

Baseball, Big League
1994 (metal)(blue over gold)
$10-$20 ea.

Baseball Bowman Gum
1949 (Pirates shown)(One for each team)(also see Football, Bowman)
$75-$150

Baseball Centennial
(See Jack Armstrong)

Baseball Cereal
1960 (red, white, blue plastic variants)(baseball set of 16)(Kellogg's Shredded Wheat cereal box premium)
In Package $55
Ring Only $20-$50 ea.

Baseball, Chicago White Sox
1960s (red/aluminum)
$10-$20

Baseball, Cincinatti Reds
1977 (metal)(1976 World Championship facsimile)(1st known facsimile ring)
$20-$60

Baseball, Detroit Tigers
1970s (metal)
$10-$20

Baseball, Dodgers
1940s (metal)(scarce)
(gold color)(Brooklyn)(glove over crossed bats on side)(also see baseball, Atlanta Crackers, Babe Ruth and Yankees)
$100-$250

Baseball, Dodgers
1978 (National League Champions)(silver color)(ballpark giveaway)
$20-$60

Baseball Domed Logo, A's

Baseball Domed Logo, Cardinals

Baseball Domed Logo, Cincinatti Red Legs

Baseball Domed Logo, Cubs

Baseball Domed Logo, Detroit Tigers

Baseball Domed Logo, Indians

Baseball Domed Logo, Milwaukee Braves

Baseball Domed Logo, Orioles

Baseball Domed Logo, Washington Nationals

Baseball Domed Logo, White Sox

Baseball Domed Logo
1954 (gold color metal)
(possible set of 16)
$30-$60 ea.

Baseball Flicker
1960s (modern base)
$1

Baseball Flicker Candy
1960s (orange base)
Cartoon baseball player swinging a bat with tree in background.
$1-$2 ea.

Baseball Flicker Candy Athletics, pitcher

Baseball Flicker Candy
Braves, infielder

Baseball Flicker Candy
Dodgers, hitter

Baseball Flicker Candy
Orioles, catcher

Baseball Flicker Candy
Red Sox, pitcher

Baseball Flicker Candy
Cardinals, catcher

Baseball Flicker Candy
Dodgers, pitcher

Baseball Flicker Candy
Pirates, catcher

Baseball Flicker Candy
Reds, infielder

Baseball Flicker Candy
Cubs, pitcher

Baseball Flicker Candy
Giants, catcher

Baseball Flicker Candy
Pirates, infielder

Baseball Flicker Candy
Reds, pitcher

Baseball Flicker Candy
Cardinals, catcher

Baseball Flicker Candy
Giants, infielder

Baseball Flicker Candy
Orioles, hitter

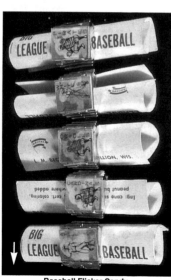

Baseball Flicker Candy
1960s (group showing paper inserted through rings)

Baseball Flicker Candy
Senators, hitter

Baseball Flicker Candy
Tigers, pitcher

Baseball Flicker
White Sox, pitcher

Baseball Flicker Candy
Yankees, pitcher

Baseball Flicker Candy
Tigers, hitter

Baseball Flicker Candy
White Sox, hitter

Baseball Game paper
page 1 & 2 (scarce)- Both pages
$80-$100

Baseball Flicker Candy Box
1960s
Box only $100

Baseball Flicker Candy
1960s (set of 56)(14 teams w/4 of each team)(A pitcher,
catcher, hitter & infielder flicker for each team)(L.M. Becker
& Co.; came w/candy rolled in paper w/ring attached)(gold
base)
Ring Only $15-$40 each
Wrapper $1

Baseball, generic
1969 (metal)(heavy, gold,
color)(Major League logo)
$30-$60

Baseball Game Ring
1949 (pin ball)
(Kellogg's)
$100-$300

Baseball, generic
1950s (sterling)
$10-$20

Baseball, generic
1970s (metal)
$1

Baseball Hall of Fame
1939 (metal)(silver color base)(National baseball museum, Cooperstown, N.Y.)
$75-$200

Baseball, Heavy Chicago White Sox
1994 (metal)(sold at Disney World)(in color)
$10-$20

Baseball, Heavy New York
1993 (heavy metal)(color) (Citibank ballpark giveaway)
$20-$60

Baseball, Giants
1940s (gold color metal, (glove over crossed bats on side)(also see baseball, Atlanta Crackers, Babe Ruth, Dodgers & Yankees)
$100-$250

Baseball Hall of Fame
1939 (metal)(gold over blue)(National baseball museum, Cooperstown, N.Y.)
$75-$200

Baseball, Heavy Chicago Cubs
1993 (heavy metal)(color)
$10-$20

Baseball, Heavy New York
1994 (metal)(sold at Disney World)(in color)
$10-$20

Baseball, Heavy Houston Rockets (see Basketball-)

Baseball, Heavy Oakland A's
1994 (metal)(sold at Disney World)(in color)
$10-$20

Baseball Hall Of Fame
1950s? (Cooperstown, NY) (metal, red/silver)
$10-$20

Baseball, Heavy A-s (Oakland)
1990 (heavy metal)(color) (American League champions)(sponsored by Gatorade)(facsimile)
$15-$30

Baseball, Heavy N.Y. Mets
1993 (heavy metal) (no color variant)
$10-$20

Baseball Hall Of Fame
1970s (Cooperstown, NY)(copper)
$5-$10

Baseball, Heavy Atlanta
1993 (heavy metal)(color) (shows NBA mistake on side)
$30-$75

Baseball, Heavy Pirates
1990 (heavy metal)(color) (Eastern Division champions)(Giant Eagle food stores, ballpark giveaway)
$20-$60

**Baseball, Heavy
St. Louis Cardinals**
1993 (heavy metal)(color)
$30-$75

Baseball, L.A. Dodgers
1990 (heavy brass & enam-
el)(Kelloggs Shredded
Wheat cereal premium)
$15-$30

**Baseball Logo
N.Y Mets**
1970s (plastic)
$2-$4

**Baseball, Metal Logo
Cincinatti Reds**
1970s (metal)(color)
$5-$15

**Baseball, Heavy
Toronto Blue Jays**
1993 (NFL on side in error)
(metal)
$30-$75

**Baseball Logo
Astros**
1960s-70s (plastic)
$2-$4

**Baseball Logo
Yankees**
1970s (plastic)
$2-$4

**Baseball, Metal Logo
Dodgers**
1970s (Black/yellow)
$5-$15

**Baseball Knot Hole
League of America**
1938-1939 (metal)(silver
color)
$75-$150

**Baseball Logo
Boston Red Sox**
1960s-70s (plastic)
$2-$4

Baseball, Mark Fidrych
1976-77 (metal, plastic
dome)(black & white top)
$40-$80

↓

↑ **Baseball, Metal Logo
Giants**
1970s (metal)(2 varia-
tions)(color)
$5-$15

**Baseball, L.A. Dodgers
World Champions**
1988 (brass & enamel)
$20-$40

**Baseball Logo
Dodgers**
1970s (plastic)
(white over blue)
$2-$4

**Baseball, Metal Logo
Cardinals**
1970s (metal)(color)
$5-$10

**Baseball, Metal Logo
Mets**
1970s (red/yellow)
$5-$15

Baseball, Metal Logo Padres
1970s metal)(color)
$5-$15

Baseball, N.Y.E.
1937 (sterling)(V.A.H.)
$40-$100

Baseball, Phillies Giant Paper Weight
1993 (National League Champs)(metal)(beat Atlanta 4 games to 2)
$15-$50

Baseball NY Mets
1961-62 (metal)(1st seas was 1962)
$30-$60

Baseball, Metal Logo Pirates
1970s (metal, color)
$5-$15

Baseball N.Y. Mets
1960s (metal)(color, square)
$10-$20

Baseball, Phillies
1993 (National League Champs)(metal)(Subway sandwiches ballpark give-away)(facsimile)
$20-$40

Baseball, Pirates
1960 (World champions) (heavy metal)(Giant Eagle Food Store giveaway) (color)(Outfielder Roberto Clemente's 1st series)
$30-$60

Baseball, Metal Logo Seattle Mariners
1970s (metal)(color)
$5-$15

Baseball, Metal Logo Yankees
1970s (red/yellow)
$5-$15

Baseball, N.J. F.U.
1940s (10 years)(Joix)(metal)
$15-$50

Baseball, New York Mets
1986 (metal)(Tropicana premium)(championship facsimile)(large supply recently surfaced)
$5-10 in package

Baseball, Pirates
1969 (Aluminum)(color)
$10-$20

Baseball, Pirates
1971 (World champions)
(metal)(color)
$5-$15

**Baseball Plastic
Boston**

**Baseball Plastic
Cincinatti**

THE PLASTIC BASEBALL RINGS

The plastic baseball rings come in various colors: Black, light blue, dark blue, green, red and yellow. All city names on the rings are in old lettering. All team nicknames come in silver lettering with the exception of yellow which comes only with the nickname in gold. There are no known city names on the yellow rings. At the same time, the color plastic rings were issued (1969 - 1972), white based rings featuring iridescent colors were also produced at the same time. The iridescent colors used are: Blue, green, purple, bright red and dark red. All feature the team nicknames with the exception of the dark red which comes only with the city names.

**Baseball Plastic
Braves**

**Baseball Plastic
Cleveland**

**Baseball Plastic
California**

**Baseball Plastic
Cubs**

**Baseball Plastic
Angels**

**Baseball Plastic
Athletics**

**Baseball Plastic
Cardinals**

**Baseball Plastic
Detroit**

**Baseball Plastic
Astros**

**Baseball Plastic
Baltimore**

**Baseball Plastic
Chicago**

**Baseball Plastic
Dodgers**

Baseball Plastic
Expos

Baseball Plastic
Mets

Baseball Plastic
Orioles

Baseball Plastic
Pirates

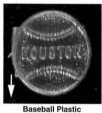

Baseball Plastic
Giants

Baseball Plastic
Minnesota

Baseball Plastic
Padres

Baseball Plastic
Pittsburg

Baseball Plastic
Houston

Baseball Plastic
Montreal

Baseball Plastic
Philadelphia

Baseball Plastic
Red Sox

Baseball Plastic
Indians

Baseball Plastic
New York

Baseball Plastic
Phillies

Baseball Plastic
Reds

Baseball Plastic
Kansas City

Baseball Plastic
Oakland

Baseball Plastic
Pilots

Baseball Plastic
Royals

**Baseball Plastic
San Diego**

**Baseball Plastic
Tigers**

**Baseball Plastic
San Francisco**

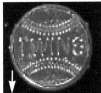

**Baseball Plastic
Twins**

Baseball Plastic
1969-72 (on card)
Complete $18-$35

**Baseball Plastic
Senators**

**Baseball Plastic
White Sox**

**Baseball Plastic
St. Louis**

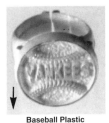

**Baseball Plastic
Yankees**

Baseball Plastic
1969-1972 (plastic)(each
ring came in diff. colors)
$2-$4 ea.

**Baseball Plastic
Texas**

Baseball Play Ball
1969-72 (plastic, diff. colors)
Complete with Card $20-$40
Ring Only $2-$4 ea.

Baseball, Trail Blazesr
1983 (metal)(championship)
$12-$25

Basketball
1949 (Bowman Gum)
(metal base)(gold
finish)(also see Football)
Heavy version $50-$110

Basketball Flicker
1960s (metal)(color,
square)
$10-$20

Baseball, Yankees
1940s (metal)(gold
color)(glove over crossed
bats on side)(also see baseball, Atlanta Crackers, Babe
Ruth, Giants & Dodgers)
$100-$250

Basketball, Seattle Mariners
1979 (All Star Game)(metal)
$20-$40

Basketball Hall of Fai
1980s (Naismith Memo
$5-$10

**Basketball
Celestrium Rings**
Made for Major League
baseball, NBA, NFL and
NHL by Balfour Jewelry Co.,
Mass. They all originally
sold for $95.00 + $4.00
P&H.

Baseball, Spokane Hawks
1938 (metal)
$75-$150

Basketball, Bullets
1978 (NBA World Champs)
(metal)
$20-$40

Basketball, Atlanta
(see Baseball, Heavy
Atlanta)

**Basketball, Heavy
Houston Rockets**
1993 (Error, shown on r
as baseball team)(hea
metal)(color)
$30-$75

Basketball
1949 (Bowman Gum?)
(hollow)(metal base)(also see
Football)(Note: This base is
not as thick as the original)
Later version $20-$40

Basketball, Chicago Bulls
1993 (metal)(3Peat)
$12-$25

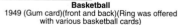

Basketball
1949 (Gum card)(front and back)(Ring was offered
with various basketball cards)

Basketball-Chicago Bulls
1994(metal)(sold at Disney
World)(in color)
$12-$25

Basketball Nets
1970s (metal, color)
$10-$20

Basketball NY Nets
1970s (metal)(World Champions)
$20-$40

Bat
1960s (metal)(silver color)
(fantasy)
$5-$10

Bat & Fink Ring Paper
1960s (vending machine paper)(in color)
$15-$25

Basketball 76ers
1970s (metal)(color)
$10-$20

Bat
1960s (plastic)(vending machine)
without package $5-$10

Batman
1966 (green rubber) (DC) $2-$4

Batman Bat Signal
1992 (Diamond Comics Distr.)
(14k gold w/diamond chips)
(25 made)(DC)
$1500

Bat
1960s (plastic)(in package)
(glows in dark)(Black & white bat versions)
In Sealed Package $20

Batman Bat Signal
1992 (Diamond Comics
Distr.)(silver)
(550 made)(DC)
$250

Batman Clock Flicker
1960s (silver base)
$10-$25

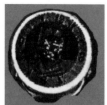

Batman Flicker
1960s (round)
$20-$40

Batman Flicker (3)
"Batman" chest view up
"Bruce Wayne" chest view

Batman Bat Signal
1982 (Party)(plastic)(DC)
$1

Batman Disc
1960s (paper on plastic)
$12-$25

Batman Flicker (1)
"Member Batman Ring
Club" to full figure
"Batman/Robin" side by
side.

Batman Flicker (4)
"Robin" chest view up
"Dick Grayson" chest view

Batman Bat Signal
1990 (metal)(enam-
eled)(DC)
$2-$4

Batman Figure
1990s (metal)
(color, enameled)
$2-$4

Batman Flicker (5)
"Batman" face to full figure swinging on rope

Batman Bat Signal
1990s (plastic)(c.1964)
(Rosecraft on card)(DC)
On Card $20
Ring Only $4-$12

Batman Flicker
1960s (Batman photograph
face (Adam West) to Robin
photograph face (Burt
Ward))(round)
$20-$40

Batman Flicker (2)
"Batman" face to "Robin"
face

Batman Bat Signal
1990s (c.1964) (metal,
cloisonne' w/sparkles)
(Rosecraft on card)(DC)
On Card $20
Ring Only $4-$12

Batman Flicker (6)
"Robin" face to full figure
swinging on rope

Batman Flicker (7)
"Batmobile" to Batman &
Robin swinging on ropes
dropping into the Batmobile

Batma Flicker (1)

Batman Flicker (5)

Batman Flicker (10)
"Joker" face to "POW" fist
punching jokers face.

Batman Flicker (2)

Batman Flicker (6)

Batman Flicker (11)
"Penguin" full figure holding
umbrella to full figure
floating down with open
umbrella

Batman Flicker (8a & b)
"Batcopter" to close up of
Batman & Robin in
Batcopter

Batman Flicker (3)

Batman Flicker (7)

Batman Flicker (12)
"Batman" face to Batwoman

Batman Flicker
1966 (Original silver base)
(set of 12)
$8-$25 ea.
Villians $10-$30 ea.

Batman Flicker (4)

Batman Flicker (8)

Batman Flicker (9)
"Riddler" face to "BAM"
Batman & Riddler fighting

Batman Flicker (9)

Batman Flicker (11)

Batman Flicker (10)

Batman Flicker (12)

Batman Flicker
1966 (blue base)(DC)
(set of 12)
$8-$15 each
Villians $10-$20 ea.

Batman/Robin Action Rings
1966 (flicker for vending machine ring case)(in color)
(showing both sides)
$20-$35

Batman/Robin Action Rings
1966 (4 rings on card)
Set $125

Batman Game
1960s (plastic w/dome)
$10-$20

Batman Gold
1990s (14K gold)(DC)
$30-$60

80

Batman Gold Face
1960s (3D, metal)(DC)
$25-$50

Batman Logo
1980s (Nestle's)(DC)
(rect.)(see Robin)
$25-$50

Batman Logo
1990s (metal,
blue/gold)(DC)
$2-$4

Batman/Ridler
1995 (movie)(sterling)
(Warner's stores)($28)
$28

Batman Logo
980s (Nestle's)(red & blue
variants exist)(DC)
(round)(see Robin)
$25-$50

Batman Logo
1980s (square)(DC)
(Nestle's)
$25-$50

Batman
1970s (plastic bat)
$10-$20

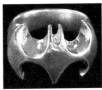

Batman-Sterling
1995 (Warner's catalog)
(sterling)($110)
$110

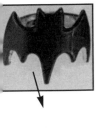

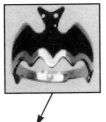

Batman
1970s
(plastic)(black/yellow)
$10-$20

Batman
1966 (in box)(metal)(DC)(3 diff.)
In Box $40
Ring Only $10-$20

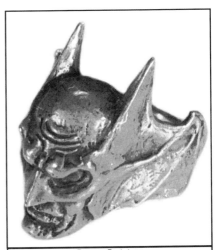

Batman Prototype
1993, (metal)
$650

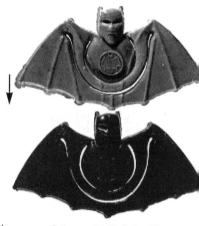

Batman and Robin Collapsible
1960s (rubber)(glows-in-dark)(blue, red & black version)
(4 rings in set,–Batman(2), Robin, & Batmobile)(Canadian)
$10-$60 each

Batman Collapsible
1960s (4 rings on card)(Canadian)
(2 card versions)
Set $250

Batman Ring Watch
1989 (in pkg.)
Complete $20

82

**Battlestar Galactica
(Alien)**

**Battlestar Galactica
(Commander Adama)**

Bazooka Joe Initial
1940s (gold color,
black top)(scarce)
(also used as popsicle
premium)
$150-$400

**Bazooka Joe Lucky
Baseball**
1950 (Gold plated
metal)(size adjustable)(bubble gum wrapper premium)
$30-$75

**Bazooka Joe Lucky Baseball Ring ad
from Action Comics #147, 1950**

**Battlestar Galactica
(Cylon)**

**Battlestar Galactica
(Daggitt)**

**Bazooka Joe Printing
Stamp**
1940s (metal)(gold color)
$60-$150

Beany (2)
1960s (propeller top)(compass base)(plastic)(2 diff.)
Complete $100-$300

Battlestar Galactica
1978 (Universal Studios)
(metal)(photo) (4 in set)(came in box w/ paper)
In Box $20-$40 each
Ring Only $15-$30

Beany (1)

Beatles
1980s (brass & pewter
versions)(also exists
as a repro)
Original $5-$10
Repro $1

83

**Beatles
(George)**

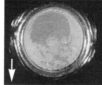

**Beatles Flicker
John**

**Beatles Flicker
(John)**
John to "I'm John" -
"Beatles"

Beatles Flicker (Paul)

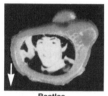

**Beatles
(Paul)**

**Beatles Flicker
Paul**

Beatles Flicker (Paul)
Paul to "I'm Paul" - "Beatles"

Beatles Flicker (Ringo)

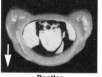

**Beatles
(John)**

**Beatles Flicker
Ringo**

Beatles Flicker
↑ 1960s (set of 4)(gold metal
base)(purple, green, red
& black flicker versions)
$15-$30 each

**Beatles Flicker
(Ringo)**
Ringo to "I'm Ringo" -
"Beatles"

Beatles Flicker
↑ 1960s (Silver base)
(set of 4)
$8-$15 each

Beatles Flicker (John)
Beatles Flicker
↑ 1966 (Blue base)(set of
$5-$10 each

**Beatles
Ringo**

Beatles
↑ 1964 (plastic)
(photo)(set of 4)
(red, blue, yellow, green
colors known)
$8-$15 each

**Beatles Flicker
(George)**
George to "I'm George" -
"Beatles"

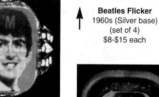

**Beatles Flicker
(George)**

Beatles Ringo
1960s (cereal)(plastic)
$10-$20

**Beatles Flicker
George**

Beetle Bailey
1993 (silver)(Staber)
(20 made)
$250

Belt Buckle
1950s (western)(metal, gold
color)(with 2 jewels in belt)
$30-$60

Betty Boop
1990s (metal enameled)
$10-$20

Big Boy (Bob's)
1970s (plastic)(red and
white)
$1-$2

Belt Buckle
1950s (western)
(metal, silver)
$10-$20

Belt Buckle
1960s (metal)
$2-$4

Betty Grable Photo
(see Real Photos)

Bicentennial Wagon Train
1976 (metal)(painted, color)
$2-$4

Big Boy (Bob's)
1970s (plastic)
$1-$2

Big Foot
(see Buster Brown...)

Big League Baseball
(see Baseball...)

Billy The Kid Saddle
(see Saddle...)

Betty Boop
1990s (9 on card, generic)
Complete Set $5

Big Bad Wolf
1960s (plastic, gumball)
$10-$20

Billy West Club
1940 (metal)(see Tom
Mix Circus &
Cowboy Riding Horse)
$50-$175

Big Boy (Bob's)
1970s (plastic)
$1-$2

Bing Crosby Photo
(see Real Photos)

Black Flame
1930s (Hi Speed
Gas)(metal)(gold color)
$125-$350

Bottle
1950s (plastic)(gumball, advertising)(2 diff.)(also see Captain
Crunch)
$10-$20

Bob Hope Photo
(see Real Photos)

Bowman Gum
(see Baseball-Bowman)

Boxing Flicker
(see Polly Flicker Rings)

Bogey Monkey
1960s (on card)
On Card $10
Ring Only $2-$4

Boxing Flicker
1960s (metal)(Hong Kong
Star)(rectangle, color)(also
see Polly Flicker)
$10-$20

Boy Scout
1940s (silver)(metal)(also
see Cub Scout & Girl
Scout)
$15-$50

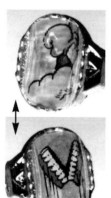

**Boxing Glove to
Flying Teeth Flicker**
1980s (plastic)(color)
$2-$5

Bozo's Circus
1960s (metal)
$20-$80

Bozo Figure
1980s (metal cloisonne')
$10-$25

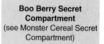

**Boo Berry Secret
Compartment**
(see Monster Cereal Secret
Compartment)

Boot (see Cowboy Boot)

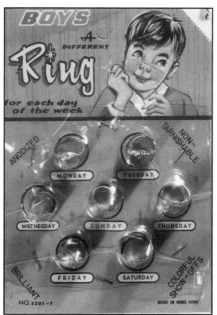

Boys Show-Offs Ring Set
1960s (one for each day of the week)(on card)
$5 set

Brownies
1930s (Several
different stores)
(metal)
$75-$250

Brownies Jumping Elf (2)
1950s (sterling)
$8-$30

Brownies Jumping Elf (1)
1930s (sterling)
$10-$50

Buck Jones Club Ring
1937 (Grape Nuts)(metal)
$75-$160

Bozo (see Clown)

Brooklyn Dodgers
(see Baseball -Dodgers)

Brer Fox Club
1938 (metal)(rare)
$75-$200

Broom Hilda Spinner
1970s (on tree, in package)
In Package $75
Assembled $30-$60

Bronco Rider Flicker
1950s (thick top lens)
$25-$50

*No. 402. Membership
Ring. A beauty! 24-carat
gold finish. Good-luck horseshoe design. Adjusts to fit
any finger. Free for 3
Grape-Nuts Flakes box-
tops.*

**Buck Jones
Club paper**
(scarce)
$75-$100

Buck Rogers Birthstone
1934 (Cocomalt
(birthstones in red, yellow,
green & white known)
$200-$450

Buck Rogers Photo
1940s (metal)
$150-$350

Buck Rogers Repeller Ray
1930s (Cream of Wheat)(green stone)(gold color)
Good - $500
Fine - $1500
Near Mint - $3000

Buck Rogers Ring Of Saturn Paper
1940s (scarce)
$100-$150

you remove the source of energy (by taking the ring away from the light), what happens? The electrons slip back into their old places again. And when they do, energy is created that turns into visible light! When the ring gives off this light, it glows in the dark.

The light is a "cold" light, however. It doesn't send its rays any distance. This means that it can be seen only at close range. It's invisible to people standing only a couple of dozen feet away.

That's about enough of this technical talk, don't you think? But we did want to give you a short explanation of why the Buck Rogers Ring of Saturn has these amazing qualities.

HOW YOU CAN HAVE FUN WITH YOUR RING

Now what you want to know is "how can I have fun with my Buck Rogers ring?" Well, there are plenty of ways.

First of all, you can use it as a secret signal to flash on your pals. You and other Buck Rogers fans can recognize each other *in the dark* with your magic-glow rings. (Just the way Buck used it to tell his friends in the dark. Even on a pitch-black night, your Buck Rogers ring will glow so you and your pals can recognize each other instantly as members of the gang. And remember

—you have to be up close to see the light from the ring. So while you're showing your ring to a friend near you, people 25 feet away won't see a thing. Pretty neat, isn't it?

Here's another way you'll find your magic ring mighty handy. You can use it to "talk" to your friends in the dark *without making a sound.* Just work out a set of signals—a secret code like the ones used in various lodges, fraternities, and underground societies. Then by passing your hand over the ring, so as to cover up its glow and then let it "flash," you can pass on information to a friend looking on without saying a word to him.

For instance, two "flashes" might mean "Danger—let's get out of here." Three flashes could mean, "Go back and round up more of the gang—we need help." It's easy to work out a code in advance to cover whatever emergencies you think you and your pals might run into.

Incidentally, if some one of your friends hasn't gotten his Buck Rogers ring, better suggest to him that he send for it right away so he can be in on the fun, too. (Just tell him to send a dime and a Post's Corn Toasties boxtop to Buck Rogers, Battle Creek, Michigan.)

You'll think of lots of other ways in which this amazing ring really will be valuable. So now go ahead and have fun with your Buck Rogers Ring of Saturn!

8382 Printed in U.S.A.

the MAGIC POWER OF THE RING OF SATURN is yours!

This tells about the magic quality of BUCK ROGERS RING OF SATURN

THE BUCK ROGERS RING OF SATURN

Ever see anything like the Buck Rogers ring before? Bet you haven't. It's really a wonder ring. It has magic qualities that make it glow in the dark with mysterious blue light. You'll have plenty of fun with it!

You heard on the radio how the Ring of Saturn helped Buck Rogers save Dr. Huer from the people on Neptune. That's how valuable it can be! You, too, will find plenty of ways where the ring will be mighty handy. We'll talk about some of them a little later on.

In the meantime, we want to let you in on the secrets of this miraculous Ring of Saturn—tell you what's behind its mysterious properties.

WHY DOES IT GLOW?

You already know how to make it glow. Just wear it awhile in the light. It can be sunlight or light from an electric lamp—it doesn't matter. Then take the magic ring into a dark room, and PRESTO! It glows.

Now *why* does it glow? It hasn't any batteries or wires. The fact is, it doesn't depend on electricity for its light. The light it sheds is really a kind of energy, though, just as electricity is a kind of energy.

Here's what happens. When you let the sun shine on this ring awhile, or let it stand under an electric light, the ring absorbs light energy—it's called *radiant* energy.

ATOMIC SECRETS

Energy takes many forms. You've read about atomic bombs. What gives them their terrific explosive power? It's caused by a sudden release of energy—energy that rushes out when the tiny particles which make up uranium atoms are pushed out of place. These tiny atomic particles are called electrons, protons, and neutrons. When you study chemistry, you'll find that everything in the world is composed of atoms—billions and billions of them.

Now to get back to your Buck Rogers ring—it's made up of atoms, too. Radiant energy (light energy) is powerful enough, in its own way, to push electrons out of their normal positions in the atoms of the ring material. Then when

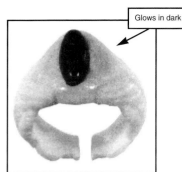

Glows in dark

Buck Rogers
Ring of Saturn
1940s (plastic)(red stone)(Post)
GD $325, FN $580, NM $850

(also see Jack Armstrong Dragon's Eye, Shadow Carey Salt and Shadow Blue Coal)

Buffalo Bill Jr
1950 (metal)(TV)
$30-$60

Bugs Bunny Bullseye
1990 (paper disc)
$5-$10

Bugs Bunny Face
1980 (metal cloisonne')
$8-$15

Bugs Bunny Figure
1980 (metal cloisonne')
$8-$15

Bulb glows in dark

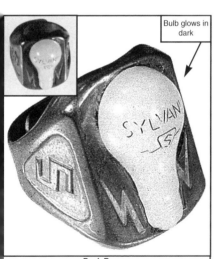

Buck Rogers
Sylvania Bulb
1953 (metal)(glows-in-dark)(Sylvania)(rare)
Good- $800
Fine - $1500
Near Mint- $3200

Buffalo Bill
(see Kellogg's Picture Rings)

Bugs Bunny Dome
1980s (small)(metal)
$10-$20

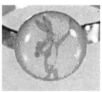

Bugs Bunny Face
1970s (plastic)(blue over white)
$10-$20

Bugs Bunny Face
1980s (metal cloisonne')
$8-$15

Bugs Bunny Face
1992 (pewter)
$10-$20

**Bugs Bunny
Indian Headress**
1993 (Warner,Sterling)
In Box $50
Ring Only $35

The Official Burger King Ring

Burger King
1980s (plastic)
In Box $15-$30
Ring Only $2-$4

Bugs Bunny Ski
1980 (metal cloisonne')
$10-$20

Bullwinkle
1969 (Jay Ward display)(in color, painted)
$35-$70

Buster Brown
1900s (metal, scarce)
GD $250, FN $375, NM $500

**Buster Brown Flicker,
side 2
(Tige)**

↑ **Buster Brown Club
Flicker**
1950s (Buster to Tige)(color)
$30-$60

Bulldog
1960s (metal)(die stamped, color)(Mack truck)
$10-$20

Bullwinkle
1990s (metal, cloisonne')(see Rocky)
$5-$10

Buster Brown Club
1940s (metal)
$25-$75

Bullet Pen
1940s (metal, generic)(very rare)(Robbins archives)(prototype)
$750

**Buster Brown Flicker,
side 1
(Buster)**

**Buster Brown
Big Foot Whistle**
1976 (plastic)(Buster Brown Shoes)
$10-$20

90

Buster Brown
1970s (plastic)(red &
white)
$1-$2

Buzz Corey Space Patrol
1950s (plastic)(photo)(rare)
$150-$300

Buzz Corey (Carol)
1950s (sidekick photo)(rare)
$150-$300

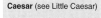

Cabbage Patch Kid
1983 (plastic, on card, color)
On Card $20
Ring Only $5-$10

Cabbage Patch
1980s (metal, cloisonne',
color)
$5-$10

Caesar (see Little Caesar)

Calgon Soap
1950s (metal)(bathtub)
$100-$200

Cameo
1930s
(metal)(white/green)
$15-$30

Cameo-Aluminum
1950s (adj.)
$15-$50

Cameo Store Card
1950s (plastic)(red/white)
$5-$10

Cameo Store Card
1950s (black)
$5-$10

Cameo Store Card
1950s (yellow)
$5-$10

Cameo Store Card
1950s (white)
$5-$10

Canada Dry (see Smilin' Jack & Smokey Stover)

Cap Gun Ring (see RinGun)

Cameo Store Card
1950s (Blue/white)
$5-$10

Capitol-Washington D.C.
1940s (Sterling, in color)
$15-$30

Captain (see Post Tin)

Cameo Store Card
1950s (plastic)(white/green)
$5-$10

Canada Dry Logo
1970s (plastic)(green, red, white)
$5-$15

Captain Action Flicker (3)
Full figure Capt. Action to full figure Batman
$20-$40

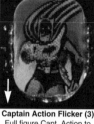

Captain Action Flicker (7
Full figure Capt. Action to full figure Green Hornet
$50-$100

Captain ActionFlicker (4)
Full figure Capt. Action to full figure Buck Rogers
$25-$50

Captain Action Flicker (8
Full figure Capt. Action to full figure Lone Ranger
$20-$40

Captain Action Flicker (5)
Full figure Capt. Action to full figure Capt. America
$20-$40

Captain Action Flicker (9
Full figure Capt. Action to full figure Phantom
$25-$50

Captain Action Flicker (1)
Full figure Capt. Action to full figure CA logo
$20-$30

Captain Action Flicker (2)
Full figure Capt. Action to full figure Aquaman
$20-$30

Captain Action Flicker (6)
Full figure Capt. Action to full figure Flash Gordon
$20-$40

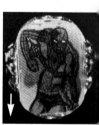

Captain Action Flicker (10
Full Figure Capt Action to full figure Spiderman
$50-$100

Captain Action Flicker (11)
Full figure Capt. Action to
full figure Steve Canyon
$15-$30

Captain Action Flicker (12)
Full figure Capt. Action to full
figure Superman
$20-$40

Captain Action Flicker (13)
Full figure Capt. Action to
full figure Tonto
$20-$40

Captain Action Flicker
1967 (silver v-base)(original
shows Hong Kong) **Note:
The modern base shows
"China"** (13 in set)
priced individually

Captain Action Doll Box
1967 (v-based rings included on inside)

Captain Action Flicker (2)

Captain Action Flicker (12)

↑ **Captain Action Flicker**
1960s (blue base)
(13 in set)
$10-$25 ea.

Captain Action Flicker (11)

Captain America
1980s (metal)(in color)
(vitamins)
$50-$125

Captain America Mood
1977 (metal)
$100-$275

Captain Bill
1940s (Hills
Brothers)(scarce)
$75-$175

Captain Caveman
1980s (metal cloisonne')
$10-$20

Captain Crunch
1970s (similar to Crazy
ring)(no indentation on side
of base)
$30-$60

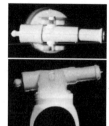

Captain Crunch Rocket Launcher
1970s (cereal)(plastic)
$75-$150

Captain Crunch Cannon
1970s (plastic)(cereal)
$30-$60

Captain Crunch Whistle
1970s (cereal)(plastic, diff. colors)(2 views)
$30-$60

Captain Crunch Compass
1970s (cereal)
$30-$60

Captain D's Seafood
1970s (plastic)(blue on white)
$2-$4

Captain Hawks Secret Scarab
Ring ad. Free w/ coupon & 2 box tops from Post's Bran Flakes)

Captain Crunch Figural
1970s (plastic)(cereal)
$150-$325

Cap'n Frosty Flicker
1960s "Cap'n Frosty" to "Dairy Clipper"
$10-$20

Captain Hawks Air Hawks
1930s (metal)(Captain Franks-Air Hawks on ring)
$50-$150

Note lustre of NM finish

Captain Hawks Sky Patrol
1930s (metal)(rare in NM)
$75-$300

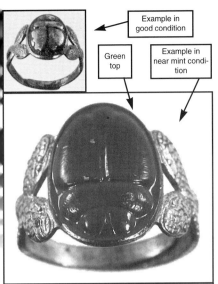

Example in good condition

Green top

Example in near mint condition

Captain Hawks Secret Scarab
1937 (rare in NM)
(Post's Bran Flakes)
(same as Melvin Purvis Secret Scarab)
(24k gold finish)(green top)
Good - $250
Fine - $500
Near Mint - $1200

Officer's Emblem Ring

Captain Midnight Flight Commander
1941 (Ovaltine)(metal)(gold color)
GD $200, FN $350, NM $500

Captain Midnight Flight Commander Signet
1957 (Ovaltine)(plastic)
(rare in VF-NM)
GD $400
FN $800
NM $1200

Top removes to reveal stamp pad for printing

Captain Midnight Initial Printing
1948 (metal)(gold color)
(Ovaltine)
GD $150
FN $325
NM $500

Compass

Captain Marvel
1940s (rare)(metal)(red/yellow)
Good - $625
Fine - $1250
Near Mint - $2500
Note: 3 versions exist, one w/Japan on compass dial, one w/Japan on back of compass & one without Japan.

Captain Midnight Flight Commander
(also see next page)

Red plastic stone symbolizes the altar of the sun god's temple

Captain Midnight Flight Commander Paper
1941
Complete $60-$80

Captain Midnight Mystic Sun-God Ring
1947 (metal/plastic)(Ovaltine)
Good $400
Fine $800
Near Mint $1600

Captain Midnight Marine Corps paper
1942 (scarce)
$100-$125

Note: A prototype exists with a stone that glows pink.

Captain Midnight Marine Corps
1942 (metal)(Ovaltine, gold color)
$150-$475

Captain Midnight Secret Compartment
1942 (metal)(Ovaltine)(also see Pilot's Sec. Compt.)
$75-$175

YOUR NEW OFFICIAL S.S. RING—

Celebrating our Secret Squadron Adventures in Mexico, Ancient Home of the Aztecs

Every organization has an official ring for its members, bearing insignia derived from campaigns or exploits in which the organization has performed outstanding service. Here is your very own official Secret Squadron ring. I hope you will wear it always as a mark of your membership in the Secret Squadron, and as a reminder of our Secret Squadron adventures in the land of the Aztecs, of which this ring is a symbol.

The Aztecs, as you may know, lived and reigned long ago in the country we now know as Mexico. Like most ancient people they worshipped many gods. Their best-known god called TONATIUH, the Sun God—is shown as the Aztecs pictured him on the side of your ring. Montezuma and other famous kings of the Aztecs worshipped this Sun God as the giver of all power and made human sacrifices to him on the high altar of the Sun God's temple.

The red plastic stone in your ring symbolizes the altar of the Sun God's temple. Its rich, brilliant color simulates the deep red glow of a genuine ruby.

Although the Aztecs were masters of such sciences as astronomy and mathematics they

believed in many superstitions which we call savage or childish today. One of their superstitious signs, the sign for "good luck" which was believed to safeguard the wearer, is shown below the picture of the Sun God on the shaft of your ring.

But your new official Secret Squadron ring is far more than simply a handsome ring with interesting Aztec designs. It contains an amazing special feature which you will find of great importance in Secret Squadron activities—an ingenious secret compartment carefully concealed so that "outsiders" cannot possibly discover it.

This secret compartment, cleverly hidden beneath the stone in your ring, can be very useful to you in carrying secret information and passing it along to friends who will seem to others to be merely examining your ring. Directions for opening this secret compartment are given on the next page. I know you will guard this secret by showing the hidden compartment only to loyal friends of the Secret Squadron.

Capt. Midnight
"SS-1"

The Story of Your SECRET SQUADRON

MYSTIC

SUN-GOD RING

by
CAPTAIN MIDNIGHT

Captain Midnight Mystic Sun-God Paper
1940s
$75-$100

HOW TO USE THE SECRET COMPARTMENT

RING OPEN

RING CLOSED

Place your thumb against the side of the stone directly above the shaft of your ring. Press gently and watch the stone slide out, revealing the hidden compartment underneath. Note how you can hide a short note written on thin paper to pass along to a friend who knows the secret of the hidden compartment and how to open it.

To close your ring, simply press the stone back in place. Be sure the edges of the stone are in the metal grooves at the sides.

Published by

SECRET SQUADRON HEADQUARTERS
360 N. MICHIGAN AVENUE
CHICAGO, ILLINOIS

Captain Midnight paper
1947
(see above)

Mailing package for Mystic Sun-god ring

Captain Midnight Skelly Oil
1940s (red V)(metal)
$75-$200

5-blade propeller-type air-turbine that whirls inside when you blow thru the holes in the top

Captain Midnight Whirlwind Whistling
1941 (Ovaltine)(metal)
$150-$525

SECRET SIGNALS

To Be Used Only By Owners of Captain
Midnight's "Whirlwind" Whistling Ring

("Whir" means a short blast. "Wheee", a long one.)

"Whit, Whit, Whit, Wheee" . . The "V" signal,
for victory.
Means "Every-
thing is Okay.
Our Side's Win-
ning!"

"Wheee, Whit, Whit!" . . . . . Danger! Watch
Out! Enemy pres-
ent!

"Wheee, Whit, Wheee, Whit!" Come here! I
need help!

"Whit, Whit, Whit, Whit!" . Hurry! Hurry!
Hurry!

"Whit, Wheee, Whit, Whit!" . Lie low! Keep out
of sight!

"Wheee, Wheee, Wheee!" . . O. K.! Come out
of hiding!

"Whit, Whit, Wheee, Whit!" . Fun! Come on out
and play!

Now remember to keep the above signals absolutely
secret! Learn them perfectly so you can use them at
any time, in any place!

P-112

THIS COUPON

With 10¢ and One Ovaltine Seal

"WHIRLWIND" Whistling Ring

IS GOOD FOR ONE

Give this coupon to some special friend of yours who would like to get a genuine Whirlwind Whistling Ring from Captain Midnight. Tell your friend that this is all he (or she) has to do to get his "Whirlwind" Whistling Ring: Simply print his or her full name and address on the back of this coupon, and put it into an envelope along with 10¢ in coin and one thin metal seal from under the lid of a can of Ovaltine. Then mail it to Captain Midnight, Chicago, Illinois. That's all! But be sure to send in right away!

Here is

YOUR OWN NEW

"Whirlwind"
Whistling Ring

from

CAPTAIN
MIDNIGHT!

Captain Midnight Whirlwind
Whistling Ring paper
1941
$80-$100
(front)

The Story Behind Your
"WHIRLWIND" Whistling Ring

THIS amazing new whistling ring is a vast improvement over any so-called whistling ring you've ever seen.

Here's how it is better. First, it is beautifully designed so that you can be proud to wear it all the time, to amaze your friends and to have always at hand when you want to give important signals. The design on the face of the ring represents a radial-type air-cooled airplane engine, and the wings on the side stand for the Spirit of Aviation.

The second advantage is the new 5-blade propeller-type "air-turbine" that whirls inside the ring when you blow into the holes in the top. This turbine is specially balanced so that it produces the same musical tone as all other rings sent out by Captain Midnight, so his friends can always recognize each other by the sound of their whistling rings. Also, this balanced air-turbine will keep whirling freely a long time after you have stopped blowing, "whirring" like a regular air raid siren!

The third special feature of this ring is that you don't have to take it off your finger to blow it! You just press against the inside edge of the ring with the tip of your thumb, so the whistling part is raised slightly from your finger, and then blow for all you're worth! For best results, be sure your lips don't close over the side vents.

So that's the story of your "Whirlwind" Whistling Ring. Now turn to the back of this folder and read about the secret signals to use in sending important messages to other friends of Captain Midnight! Learn all the signals by heart!

GIVE THIS COUPON TO A FRIEND
WHO WANTS A RING LIKE YOURS

Captain Midnight
Chicago, Illinois

Dear Sir: I am enclosing 10¢ in coin and one thin metal seal from under the lid of a can of Ovaltine. Please send me one "Whirlwind" Whistling Ring, exactly like my friend's.

(PRINT NAME CLEARLY)

Name . . . .

Address . . . .

City . . . . State . . . . .

Captain Midnight Whirlwind Whistling Paper
(see above)(back)

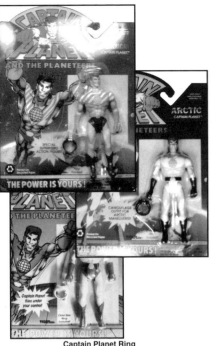

Captain Planet
1990s (on card)(all rings are
plastic with diff. designs)
On Card $8-$15
Ring Only $5-$10

Captain Planet Ring
1990s (on card, 3 diff-Arctic , Flying & All
American)
On Card - $10
Black Ring Only - $3-$6
All-American On Card $12-$25
All-American Chrome Ring Only $10-$20

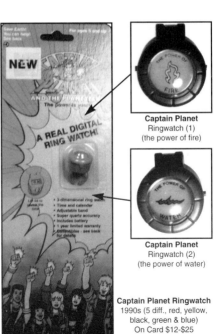

Captain Planet
Ringwatch (1)
(the power of fire)

Captain Planet
Ringwatch (2)
(the power of water)

Captain Planet Ringwatch
1990s (5 diff., red, yellow,
black, green & blue)
On Card $12-$25
Ring Only $10-$20

Captain Planet Sound Ring
1991 (on card)(gold & silver versions)
Complete - $40
Ring Only - $7-$25

Complete ring has string wrapped around top. Pulling string releases saucer to flight

Both saucers are identical except one has florescent paint on underside. Aluminum metal

Captain Video Flying Saucer
1951 (gold, aluminum & nickel base versions, 2 saucers) (one glows in dark)(two diff. saucer sets exist w/plastic glow-in-dark & metal glow-in-dark versions)(Post Toasties and Powerhouse candy premium) (rare with saucers & pull string)
Complete $750-$1500
Base Only $75-$250
Day Saucer Only $300-$425
Night Saucer Only $400-$625

Captain Video Flying Saucer
Ring paper
1951 (scarce).
$120-$150

Captain Video Flying Saucer Ring
paper
1951
$120-$150

Captain Video Pendant
1950s (rare)

Complete w/film -
Good - $500
Fine - $800
Near Mint - $1000

(Subtract $75-$100 if ring
base is missing. If picture
is missing, reduce price by
80%)

(also see Major Mars
Rocket)

Captain Video Photo
1951 (metal)
$100-$350

**Captain Video
Secret Seal**
1951 (copper top)
(gold base, metal)
GD $200, FN $410, NM $625

**Captain Video
Secret Seal**
1951 (gold)(metal)
GD $150, FN $335, NM $525

Captain Video Pendant Paper
1950s (back)

HERE'S YOUR POSITIVE IDENTIFICATION

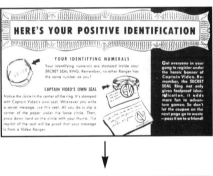

**Captain Video Pendant
Paper**
1950s (front)
$150-$200

Captain Video Secret Seal Paper
1951 (scarce)
GD $300, FN $450, NM $600

Care Bears
1983 (plastic/paper)
(yellow base)
$1-$2

Carrots, Three
1960s (3 diff.)
$5-$10 ea.

Casper Disc- Spooky
1970s (metal)(oval)
$1-$2

Casper Figure
1970 (metal, enameled)
(original in silver color, cloisonne'; repro. in gold color, enameled)
Gold version (fantasy) $1
Silver version $10-$20

Carl Barks
1995 (gold)(prototype)
(only 3 sets made)
$200

Carrots, Three 3D
1980s (metal/plastic)
$2-$5

Casper Face
1991 (plastic)(black
over white)
$2-$4

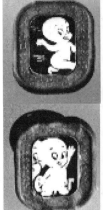

**Casper The Friendly
Ghost Flicker**
1960s (2 diff.)(blue base)
$10-$20 ea.

Carl Barks
1995 (silver)(prototype)
(only 3 sets made)
$75

Casper Disc
1970s (metal)(Harvey)
(color, many diff.)
$1-$2

Casper Figure
1950s (plastic)(cereal)
$10-$20

Carrots, Three
1960s (3 diff.)(color)
$5-$10 ea.

Casper Disc - Wendy
1970s (metal)(Harvey)
(color, many diff.)
$1-$2

Casper Figure
1960s (plastic)(black
over white)
$15-$30

**Casper The Friendly
Ghost Flicker**
1960s Casper waving to
Casper peeking from the
corner (original silver base)
$10-$40

Casper The Friendly Ghost Flicker
1960s (Casper walking to Casper flying)(original silver base)
$10-$40

Casper The Friendly Ghost
(see Universal Monster Flicker Set)(the 2 Casper flickers may have been part of this set)

Cassidy, Sean Photo
1980s (metal)
$5-$10

Cat
(see Tonka Cat)

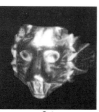

Cat
1970s
$1-$2

Cat Face
1970s (plastic, Canada, gumball, color)
$2-$4

Cat Flicker
1960s (plastic)
$2-$4

Cat Flicker
1960s (round)(color, plastic)
$2-$4

Cat Figure Flicker
1970s (plastic)(round)
$2-$4

Chandu The Magician
1940s (metal)
$75-$150

Cat & Moon to Mummy w/Hands Over Face Flicker
1980s (plastic)
$1-$2

Catwoman
1991 (metal cloisonne) (Rosecraft)
$5-$10

Chandu The Magician
1940s (metal)
$75-$150

Charles Starrett Photo
(see King Features & Real Photos)

Charlie Chaplin
1940s (rare)(metal)
$100-$300

Catwoman Party
1994 (plastic on card)(DC)(color)
On Card $8-$15
Ring Only $1

Charlie McCarthy
1940s (metal)(gold color)
$150-$325

Chief Wahoo
1941 (Goudy
Gum)(metal)
(also see Indian)
$50-$100

Chilly Willy
1980s (metal)(in color)
$5-$10

Chilly Willy Face
1970s (Canada)(plastic)
(blue over white,
& other colors)
$5-$10

Charlie McCarthy Photo
(see Real Photos)

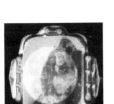

Chee-Chee Flicker
"Chee-Chee" to gorilla sitting on a log (original base)
$8-$20

Chicago White Sox
(see Baseball)

Child Jump Rope Flicker
1970s (plastic)(round)
$1-$2

Chilly Willy Buzzard
1970s (plastic)
$5-$10

Chilly Willy Face
1980s (metal)(cloisonne')
$10-$20

Chilly Willy Walrus
1970s (plastic)(Canada,
gumball)
$5-$10

Chilling Rings
1980s (in package)
$2-$5

Chick in Egg
1970s (plastic)(Canada,
gumball)
$2-$4

China Clipper
1936 (Quaker)(gold color,
metal)
$40-$120

China Luck
1940s (metal, gold color)
$50-$150

Cinderella
1960s (aluminum)(Disney)
$30-$60

Circus
(see Lucky Horseshoe)

Cisco Kid Secret Compartment
1950s (rare)(metal)
Good - $1500
Very Good - $3000
Fine - $4500
Very Fine - $6000
Near Mint - $8500

Chuck E. Cheese
980s (plastic)(small, color)
$1-$2

Cisco Kid Club
(gold & silver color
versions)(metal)
$100-$325

Chuck E. Cheese
1990s (plastic)
$1

Cisco Kid Hat
1950s (rare)
GD $200, FN $425, NM $650

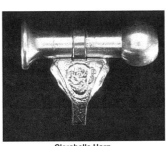

Clarabelle Horn
1950s (rare in VF-NM)(metal)(complete w/flute inside)
Good $150
Fine $325
Near Mint $500
Flute missing $75-$250

Chumley
1960s (plastic)(black
over white)
$50-$100

**Civilian Conservation
Corps.**
1930s (metal)
$20-$40

Cigar (see Garcia, Dutch
Misters & Monte Cruz)

Cincinatti Reds
(see Baseball)

Cisco Kid Saddle
1950s (rare)
GD $200, FN $425, NM $650

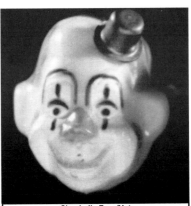

Clarabelle Face/Hat
1950s (rare)(color)
Good - $400
Fine - $800
Near Mint -$1600

Clock Flicker
1960s (Elgin)(silver base)
$10-$20

Clown
1970s (plastic) (slides onto top)
$4-$8

Clown Flicker
1950s (thick top)
$20-$60

Coca Cola with Bottle
1970s (brass, color)
$10-$20

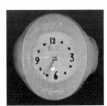

Clock Flicker
1960s (blue & yellow base versions)
$3-$5 ea.

Clock Flicker
1960s (green base)
$10-$20

Clown Face Puzzle
1970s (plasticl)(color) (several diff.)
$2-$4

Clown Face
1970s (plastic)(Canada, gumball, color)
$5-$10

Clown Face
1980s (plastic)(party, color)
$1-$2

Clown Face Flicker
(see Polly Flicker Rings)

Clown Flicker (see Polly Flicker)

Clown Flicker
1960s (gold metal)(Hong Kong star)
$10-$20

Coca Cola
1970s (metal)(brass)
Original $10-$25
1990s Repro $1

Coca Cola
1994 (metal)(gold color)
$10-$20

Coca Cola
1994 (metal, gold color) (Staber)
$10-$20

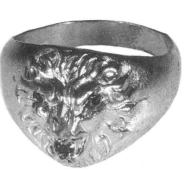

Clyde Beatty Lions Head
(Quaker Crackles)
1930s (rare)(jewel in mouth)(2 versions - green & red jewels in mouth and eyes)(ad shows without jewels)
GD $200, FN $350, NM $500

Cockatoo on Perch
1990s (plastic, color)
$2-$4

Colgate Superstar Magic Club
1970s (plastic)(blue on yellow)
$1-$2

Note unbent prongs (rare)

Compass, Cocomalt
1936 (metal)(rare example w/unbent prongs)
$60-$120

Compass
1940s (silver metal)(also see Fireball Twigg)
$20-$60

Compass, Wheaties
1940s (metal)
$20-$40

Compass
1950s (metal)
$20-$60

Compass
1950s (metal)
$20-$60

Compass
(see Black Flame, Captain Crunch, Cocomalt, Davy Crockett, Nabisco & Wheaties)

Compass, Nabisco
1950s (gold w/ red dial)
$20-$60

Compass
1960s (Generic, Large)
(metal)
$10-$20

Compass
1960s (Generic, small)
(metal)
$10-$20

Cousin Eerie
1960s (Warren) (metal)
(gold color)(also see Uncle Creepy)
$30-$60

Connestoga Wagon
1960s (metal)(stamped)
$10-$20

Count Chocula
1995 (heavy metal)
(fantasy piece)
$1

Count Chocula Flicker
(see Monster Cereal Flicker)

Count Chocula Secret Compartment
(see Monster Cereal Secret Compartment)

Cowboy Boot
1940s (Goudy Gum)(metal)
$10-$20

Cowboy Flicker
1950s (thick top)
$5-$10

Cowboy Hat
1960s (metal)(stamped)
$5-$10

**Cowboy
Riding Horse**
1950s (metal)(silver)
(gumball)
$2-$5

Cowboy Boots
1960s (metal)(stamped)
$5-$10

Cowboy Flicker
1950s (metal)(in color)
$10-$20

Cowboy Hat
1980s (metal)(silver color)
$1-$2

Cowboy Riding Horse
1950s (metal)(gold version)
(gumball)
$2-$5

Cowboy Boot
1980s (metal)(silver color)
$2-$4

Cowboy shootout flicker
1970s (plastic)
$2-$4

Cowboy Hat
1980s
(bronze)(Frontierland)
$2-$5

Cowboy Riding Horse
1950s (metal)(silver
version)(gumball)
$2-$5

Cowboy Boots
1980s
(bronze)(Frontierland)
$2-$5

Cowboy Hat (Goudy)
1940s (metal)
$10-$20

**Cowboys and Indians
Paper**
1960s (color)
$8-$15

Cowboy Riding Horse
(see Billy West Club & Tom Mix Circus)

Crackerjack Cameo

Crackerjack Diamond

Crackerjack Football

Crackerjack Knight

Crackerjack Tennis Rackets
Crackerjack
1950s (plastic)(on tree)(all on tree)(scarce on tree)
$10-$20 each

Crackerjack Army Air Corps.
1940s (plastic) (secret compartment)
$10-$30

Crackerjack Seahorse
1950s (plastic)
(scarce on tree)
$10-$20

Crackerjack Gun
1960s (plastic)(round, yellow)
$8-$15

Crackerjack Gun & Holster
1960s (plastic)
(round, yellow)
On Sprue $15-$30

Crackerjack Solar Panel
1960s (plastic)
$8-$15

Crazy Rings
(see Quaker)

Creature (see Universal Monsters)

Crest of Dracula
1995 (antique silver with carnelian agate (blood stone)).
Limited edition of 250. Came w/burnt parchment certificate in a gothic wooden coffin display case. Available in diff. sizes.
Produced by Dimensional Design.(also see Dracula)
$250

Crow Movie
1994 (metal)
(silver color)
In Box $35
Ring Only $25

Crest Gel-Man - Toothpaste
1988 (rubber)(blue)
$5-$10

Cub Scout
1950 (metal)(also see Boy Scout & Girl Scout)
$30-$75

Cupid Flicker
1960s (plastic)
$2-$5

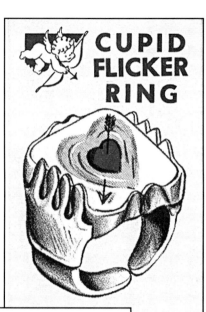

Cupid Flicker Paper
1960s (vending machine)(in color)
$8-$15

Cupid (see Heart-Arrow &
Valentine, Heart-Arrow &
Heart Throbs Flicker)

Daffy Duck (see Arby's...&
Looney Tunes)

Dagwood
1993 (Staber)(Silver(only
18 produced))
$425

Dairy Clipper Flicker
(see Cap'n Frosty)

Dancing Girl Flicker
(see Polly Flicker Rings &
Go-Go Discotheque)

Dancing Male Flicker
(see Polly Flicker Rings)

Daniel Boone
1960s (plastic)(Kellogg's)
$10-$20

Dancing Flicker
1960s (metal)(in color)
$5-$10

Dancing Flicker
(see Polly Flicker rings & A
Go-Go Discotheque Dancer
Rings)

Dancing Girl Flicker
1988 (metal)(color,
rectangle)
$2-$4

Dark Shadows
(see Barnabas Collin

Davey Adams
1940 (Lava)(siren)
(metal)(scarce)
GD $175, FN $340, NM

Davey Adams Paper
1940 (rare)
$150-$200

Davy Crockett Compass
1950s (elastic band)
$150-$375

Davy Crockett Face
1950s (metal)
$20-$60

Davy Crockett Face
1950s (green enamel)
$40-$100

Davy Crockett Figure
1950s (silver)
$20-$60

Davy Crockett Face
1950s (raised)(plastic)
(yellow, red)
$15-$40

Davy Crockett Face
1950s (metal)
$30-$80

Davy Crockett Face
1960s (raised)(silver)
$10-$40

Davy Crockett Figure
1950s (silver)(oval)
$20-$45

Davy Crockett Face
1950s (raised)
$15-$40

Davy Crockett Face
1950s (square, brass)
$20-$60

**Davy Crockett
Fess Parker head photo**
1960s
$10-$40

Davy Crockett Figure
1960s (plastic)
$10-$20

**Davy Crockett Fess
Parker figure photo**
1960s (plastic)
$15-$40

Davy Crockett Figure
1960s (plastic)
$10-$20

Davy Crockett
1960s (Fess Parker photo)
(rings on board)(24 rings)
$250-$400

Davy Crockett
1950s (blue enamel)
$50-$100

Davy Crockett Flicker,
1950s (T.V. Screen)
(scarce)
$150-$400

Davy Crockett Rifle
1950s (silver or bronze)
$15-$40

Dennis The Menace
1970s (Dairy Queen)
(rare, on tree)
On Tree $75-$100
Assembled $40-$80

Detroit Tigers
(see baseball...)

Devil Dogs
1938 (movie)(Quaker)
(gold color metal)(rare in N
$50-$200

Davy Crockett Head
1950s (gold)(plastic)
$20-$60

**Dennis The Menace
(Dennis)**
1960s (plastic)
(silver over blue)
$20-$40

Dennis The Menace (Ruff)
1960s (plastic)(Black over
yellow)
$10-$30

Devil Face
(see He-Man)

Dick Tracy
(from card)

Davy Crockett Head
1950s (bronze)(plastic)
$20-$60

**Dennis The Menace
(Joey)**
1960s (plastic)
(Black over orange)
$20-$40

Deputy Dog (1)

Davy Crockett Head
1950s (silver)(plastic)
$20-$60

**Dennis The Menace
(Margaret)**
1960s (plastic)
(silver over red)
$20-$40

Deputy Dog (2)
1970s (metal)(2
diff.)(Terrytoons)
$1-$2

Dick Tracy - Coggles
(from card)

Flat Top
(from card)

Joe Jitsu
(from card)

Dick Tracy Crimestoppers
1991
In Box game - $50
Ring Only - $20-$35

Dick Tracy Figure
1970s (plastic)(red over white)
$10-$25

Hemlock Holmes
(from card)

Prune Face
(from card)

↑ **Dick Tracy Characters**
1966 (plastic, came on card)(black, blue, green, red & yellow ring versions)
$15-$25 ea.

Hat painted green

Dick Tracy Hat
1930s (var. exists w/enamel hat)
(hat painted green)
$100-$300

Dick Tracy Card
1966 (plastic)(4 rings)(black, blue, green, red & yellow ring versions)
Complete on Card - $150
Rings Only - $15-$25 ea.

Dick Tracy Monogram
1930s (rare)(metal)
Good - $300
Fine - $600
Near Mint - $1200
Note: A prototype exists from Robbins warehouse

Dick Tracy Movie Card
1993 (plastic)(4 rings on card)(black over yellow)
Complete $20
Ring Only - $1-$2

Dino Do's Bop
1993 (metal)(color)(2 diff.)
$2-$4

Dinosaur Figure
1970s (rubber)(color, 2 diff.)
$5-$10

Dinosaur Figure
1970s (rubber)(color, 2 diff.)
$5-$10

Top of ring removes to reveal secret compartment

Dick Tracy Secret Compartment,
1940s (metal)(gold colored brass)
$150-$450

Dinosaur Figure (1)

Dinosaur Figure (2)

Dinosaur Figure (3)
1970s (rubber)(color, ? diff.)
$2-$4

Dino Do's Barney
1993 (metal)(color)(2 diff.)
$2-$4

Dino Do's On Card
1993 (metal)
On card $15

114

Dinosaurs
1970s (5 diff.)
$2-$4 ea.

Dinosaur Flicker (3)

Donald Duck

Pinocchio

Dinosaurs
1970s (5 diff.)
$2-$4 ea.

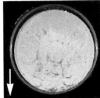

Dinosaur Flicker (4)

Dumbo

Pluto

Dinosaurs
1970s (5 diff.)
$2-$4 ea.

Mickey

Snow White

Disney (Sugerjets)
1950s (9 diff.)(plastic)
$40-$80 ea.

Dinosaur Flicker (5)

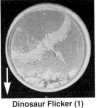

Dinosaur Flicker (1)

Minnie Mouse

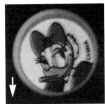

Disney Disc, Daisy

Dinosaur Flicker (6)
1980s (set of 6)(plastic)
$2-$4 ea.

Peter Pan

Dinosaur Flicker (2)

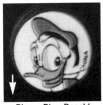

Disney Disc, Donald

Disney (Sugarjets) Ad
1950s

Disney Disc Metal
Donald

Disney Disc, Goofy

Disney Disc, Pluto

Disney Disc Plastic
1990s (plastic)(set of 6)
$1-$2 ea.

Disney Disc Metal
Mickey

Disney Disc Metal
Daisy

Disney Disc, Mickey

Disney Disc Metal
Goofy

Disney Disc Metal
Gus-Gus

Disney Disc Metal
Minnie

Disney Disc, Minnie

Disney Disc Metal
Dumbo

Disney Disc Metal

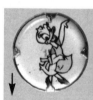

Disney Disc Metal
Daisy

Disney Disc Metal
Goofy

Disney Disc Metal
Pluto

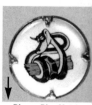

Disney Disc Metal

116

Disney Disc Metal
Pinocchio

Disney Disc Metal
Mowgli

Disney Disc Metal
Minnie

Disney Disc Metal

Disney Party Pack 1 and 2
1980s (plastic, 2 diff.)
Complete $10
Ring Only $1

Disney Disc Metal

Disney Disc Metal

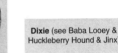

Dixie (Hanna-Barbera)
1960s (aluminum)
$15-$30

Dizzy Dean Winners
1936 (Post Grapenuts)
(metal)
$75-$250

Disney Disc Metal
Pluto

Disney Disc Metal
Donald

Dixie (see Baba Looey &
Huckleberry Hound & Jinx)

Doctor Doolittle Flicker
1970s (Dr. Doolittle to
Horse)
$20-$60

Disney Disc Metal
Baloo

Disney Disc Metal
Pete the Dragon

Disney Disc
1977 (metal)(round,
color, 21 known)
$1-$2 each

Dizzy Dean
1936 (Win With)(metal)
(Post Grapenuts).
$75-$250

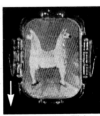

Doctor Doolittle Flicker

Doctor Doolittle Flicker
1970s (Pushmi-
pulyu)(both images
shown)
$20-$60

Dodgers (see Baseball &
Baseball, L.A. Dodgers)

Dog (see Pointer Dog)

Dog Face
1970s (plastic)(Canada,
gumball, color)
$5-$10

Don Winslow Member
1938 (Kelloggs)(metal)
(each ring carries its
own serial number)
Good - $300
Fine - $750
Near Mint - $1500

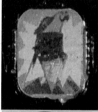

Doctor Doolittle Flicker
1970s (both images shown)
$20-$60

Doll Figure
1980s (plastic)(pvc,
color, 4 diff.)
$1-$2 each

Donald (Baby)
1984 (cloisonne', in color)
$8-$15

Donald Duck (seeDisney)

Donald Duck Dome
1970s (metal, round,
color)
$15-$30

Donald Duck Dome
1970s (metal, round,
color)
$10-$20

Donald Duck Face
1960s (3D, metal in
color)(gold & silver
versions)
$25-$50

Doctor Doolittle Flicker
1970s (Dr. Doolittle face
to "Jip" face of dog)
$20-$60

Donald Duck Face
1970s (plastic)(Canada,
gumball)
$5-$10

Donald Duck Face
1980s (gold)
$8-$15

Donald Duck Figure
1970s (metal, enameled)
$15-$30

Donald Figure
1970s (metal, painted,
color)
$10-$20

Donald Duck Face
1980s (metal)(silver & gold
variations)
$8-$15

**Donald Duck
Small Face**
1990s
$5-$10

Donald Duck Figure
1970s (metal cloisonne')
$10-$30

Donald Duck Figure
1980 (pewter)(small)
(no color))
$10-$20

Donald Duck Face
1980s (metal cloisonne')
$15-$25

**Donald Duck
Small Face**
1990s (2 diff.)
$5-$10 ea.

Donald Duck Figure
1970s (small, metal
cloisonne')
$10-$20

Donald Duck Figure
1990s (metal)
$5-$10

Donald Duck Face
1980s (red face)
(gold & silver face
versions)
$8-$15

Donald Duck Face
1980s (silver)
$8-$15

Donald Duck Figure
1935 (metal w/color)(2nd Donald
Duck ring)(Brier Mfg. Co.)
$70-$150

PEP box is a
magnet which
makes Donald
move as if he
were alive

Donald Duck Living Toy
1949 (with magnetized Pep box)
Complete $250-$400
Ring Only - $150-$250
Pep Box Only - $150

119

Donald Duck Locket
1970s (metal, round)
$15-$30

THRILLING FUN! Amaze Your Family and Friends

HERE'S HOW YOU MAKE DONALD DUCK PERFORM!

Simply hold small package of Kellogg's PEP near Donald's beak. Move it up and down slowly . . . and back and forth. WATCH his mouth open and snap shut. His head revolves. Secret magnet makes Donald *move* as if ALIVE! Try *both* ends of package. (One end attracts; other end repels.) Practice alone a few minutes before showing Ring to friends. *Note:* Try Ring on different fingers for correct fit. Plastic ring shank may be "spread" to larger sizes.

PEP'S THE DISH YOU'LL "GO FOR"!

Yep — spoon into a bowlful of sunny-golden PEP flakes. Mmm, delicious served with milk, sugar and fruit. Nourishing, too! PEP is vital whole-wheat, magically transformed into ready-to-eat flakes. Regular serving provides "Energy" vitamin B, and day's need of "Sunshine" vitamin D. Join the "Wide-awakers" . . . wake up to PEP. It's KELLOGG-GOOD AND KELLOGG-FRESH!

HERE ARE JUST A FEW OF DONALD'S AMAZING TRICKS

Donald Duck Living Toy Paper (back)

Donald Duck Locket
1970s (oval, metal)
$15-$30

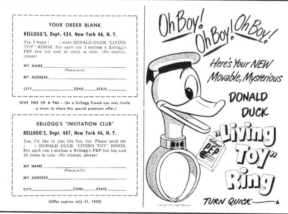

Donald Duck Living Toy Paper (front)
1949 (rare)
$125-$175

Donald Duck Locket
1970s (heart, metal)
$15-$30

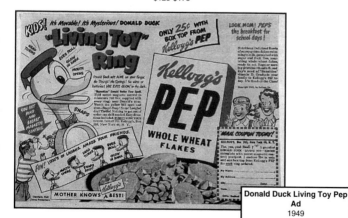

Donald Duck Living Toy Pep Ad
1949

Donald Raised Head
1960s (plastic)(in color)
$10-$20

Donald Duck 3D
1960s (large)(metal, color)
$20-$40

**Donald Duck
Good Luck Portrait**
1950s (metal)
$60-$120

Douglas MacArthur
(see Real Photos)

Dracula (see Crest of
Dracula & Universal
Monsters)

Dudley Figure
1960s (metal, painted)
$40-$80

Donald Duck 3D
1960s (small)(metal, color)
$20-$40

Donald Duck
1950s (sterling, square,
no color)
$35-$75

Donald Duck (see
Disney Disc and Ingersoll)

Dracula Crest
1972 (metal)(ad in Famous
Monsters Mag.)
$30-$40

Dudley on Horse
1960s (metal, enameled)
$20-$50

Dudley Do-Right
(see Rocky & Bullwinkle)

Donald Duck
1950s (glow-in-dark)
(square top, color & plain)
$40-$100

Door Knocker
(see salesman)

Dragon (see Figment the
Dragon)

Dukes of Hazzard
1983 (Hazzard County
Police)(plastic)
$50-$100

Dorothy Hart
1940s (metal)(rare in NM)
$150-$375

**Drug Enforcement
Admin.**
1990s (metal)(color)(U.S.
Justice Dept.)
$2-$4

Dumbo (see Disney)

Donald Duck
1950s (glow-in-dark)
(Sterling, color & plain,
round & square top)
$40-$100

Douglas DC-6
(see Kellogg's Picture)

Douglas F-3D
(see Kellogg's Picture)

Dudley Figure
1960s (metal, enameled)
$20-$50

**Dutch Misters the Mostest
Cigar**
1940s (Take off on Dutch
Masters Cigars)(metal)
(in color)
$5-$10

Dynomutt
1970s (metal, enameled)
$20-$50

Easter Secret Compartment
1995 (w/bird inside)
(plastic, color)(3 diff.)
$1-$2 ea.

Easter Secret Compartment
1995 (w/bear inside)
(plastic, color)(3 diff.)
$1-$2 ea.

Easter Secret Compartment
1995 (w/bunny inside)
(plastic, color)(3 diff.)
$1-$2 ea.

Elf (2)

Egyptian Sphinx
1940s (Smith Bros.)(metal,
gold color)(Red & green
stones)(adj.)(also see
Pharoah)
$75-$150

Elf (3)
Elf
1980s (metal, color)(3 diff.)
(foreign, silver, enameled)
$5-$10 ea.

Elsie The Cow
Store Sign
1950s (11x14", color)
$30

Eisenhower/Johnson
Flicker
1960s (black & white
flicker)(Hong Kong Star)
$15-$40

Elizabeth Taylor
(see Movie Star photo)

Elmer Fudd Flicker
(see Looney Tunes)

Elsie The Cow
1950s (plastic)(gold on
white)
$15-$30

Elvis Flicker
1960s
$60-$120

Elsie the Cow
1970s (metal, cut-out)
$25-$50

Elephant Puzzle
1970s (metal/plastic)
(Canada, gumball)
$4-$8

Elsie The Cow
1950s (plastic)
$15-$30

Elvis Flicker
1960s (metal)(Elvis Presley
to Patsy Kline)
$20-$60

Elvis Flicker
1960s (Elvis Presley
(blue) to Patsy Kline
(red))(blue)(metal)
(Hong Kong Star)
$20-$60

Elf (1)

Elvis Photo
1980s (metal)
$10-$20

Empire State Building
1930s (metal)(same base
as ROA Silver Star)
$25-$50

Erik Estrada
1980s (Chips)(plastic)
(yellow)
$2-$4

Elvis Flicker
1960s (Elvis to Pricilla
Presley)(gold base)
(Hong Kong Star)
$5-$20

Elvis Photo/Box
1980s (metal)
In Box $25

Epcot Center
1990s (metal, cut-out)
(gold color)
$4-$8

Elvis Name
1980s (metal)
$10-$20

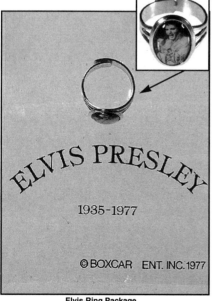

Elvis Ring Package
1977 (metal, photo)
Complete $15-$30
Ring Only - $2-$5

E.T. Face
1982 (movie,
Universal)(color)
On Card - $25
Ring Only - $10-20

ELVIS PRESLEY
1935-1977
© BOXCAR ENT. INC. 1977

E.T. and Elliot
1982 (metal, enameled,
color)(Universal)
On Card $28
Ring Only $10-$20

E.T. Face-Hat
1982 (metal, enameled,
color)(Universal)
On Card $28
Ring Only $10-$20

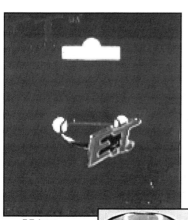

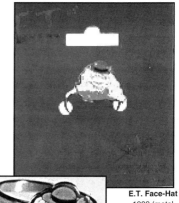

E.T. Logo
1982 (metal ,
enameled)(Universal)
On Card $25
Ring Only $10-$20

E.T. Face-Hat
1982 (metal
enameled)(universal)
On Card $25
Ring Only $10-$20

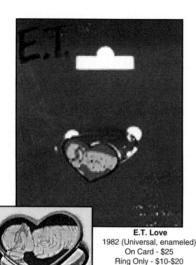

E.T. Love
1982 (Looking at planet)(metal, Universal)
$15-$30

E.T. Love
1982 (Universal, enameled)
On Card - $25
Ring Only - $10-$20

Explorer's (see Fireball Twigg)

Eye Flicker
1960s (gold metal base)
(Hong Kong Star)
$4-$10

E.T. Face
1992 (metal)(movie, Universal)(cloisonne')
$4-$10

Eye Flicker
1960s (plastic)(red & blue base versions)(B&W eye(Also see Polly Flicker Rings)
$4-$10

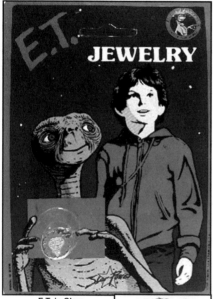

E.T. Heart
1992 (metal)(Universal)
$4-$10

E.T. in Glow
1982 (metal, enameled, color)
On Card $25
Ring Only $10-$20

E.T. Face I Love
1992 (metal cloisonne')(Universal)
$5-$10

Eye Blinking Flicker
1960s, (Picture of an eye then same eye closed as if blinking)(in color, v-base silver)
$4-$10

Eye Flicker
1960s (in color)(Hong Kong Star)(Silver base)
$4-$10

Federal Bureau of Investigation
1990s (metal, color)
$15-$30

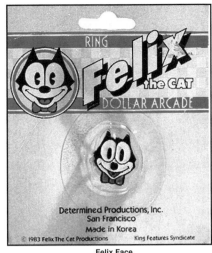

Felix Face
1970s, (in package)
In Package $30
Ring Only $10-$20

Fang
1960s (plastic)(silver over blue)
$25-$50

FDR/George Washington Flicker
1970s (Hong Kong Star)(metal)
$10-$20

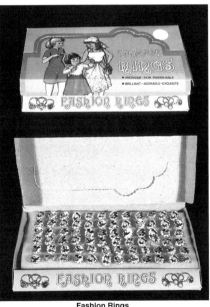

Fashion Rings
1960s (metal)
Complete In Box $25

Felix Flicker (3 diff.)
1960s (blue base)
$15-$30 ea.

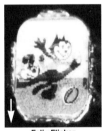

Felix Flicker
1960s Felix kicking a football (set of 3)
(silver base)
$15-$40 ea.

Felix Flicker
1960s Felix swinging a bat
(set of 3.)(silver base)
$15-$40 ea.

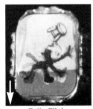

Felix Flicker
1960s Felix balancing a chair on his nose
(3 in set)(silver base)
$15-$40 ea.

127

Femforce, Ms. Victory
1994 (metal, in color)(1st comic book premium ring offer in over 4 decades)(enameled) (ad shown)
$15-$20

Femforce Ring Ads from comic book series, 1994 (shown left and below left)

Other rings in series:
Nightveil
She-Cat
Stardust
$10-$14 ea.

Fencing Flicker
1980s (plastic)
$4-$8 ea.

Fievel
1991 (metal, color) (cloisonne')
$5-$10

Figment the Dragon
1990s (metal)(gold color)
$4-$8

Fencing Flicker
1960s (metal)(Hong Kong Star)
$10-$20 ea.

Femforce, Synn
1994 (enameled metal, in color)(ad shown)
$10-$14

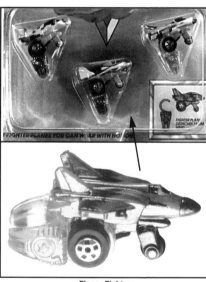

Finger Fighters
1989 (3 diff.)
Complete in Package $35
Ring Only - $4-$10

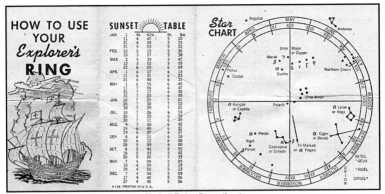

Fireball Twigg Paper (front)
1948
$75-$100

HOW TO USE YOUR EXPLORER'S RING

COMPASS: (All boys and girls)

The compass in your Explorer's Ring is a *magnetic* compass — just the same as Columbus used and sea captains and airplane pilots are still using. When you hold the ring level, the needle points to *magnetic* North. By turning the ring so that N is under the point of the needle, you can determine any other direction. You must be careful not to have any magnetic metal such as iron or steel near the compass when you are using it, or the needle will be deflected from *magnetic* north. And you will have to get off your bicycle to read it accurately. And you will have to hold it away from your pocket knife, keys, or other iron and steel.

(High school boys and girls)

Actually, there is a difference between *magnetic* north and *true* north, although in some areas it is so small that you don't have to pay any attention to it. That difference is known as *variation* and, if it is big, must be compensated for in order to get strict accuracy. Sea captains and pilots do it, and so must you. It is not hard to compensate for variation, in fact it is fun.

On the back of this sheet you will find a VARIATION MAP. In some places it is blank. If you live in such a locality, there is not enough variation for you to worry about. But in other places where the variation is greater the map will be marked W for West or E for East.

If the *variation* for your locality is listed as W, that means that *magnetic north* is slightly to the left or west of *true north*. So you turn the ring so the N is slightly to the right of the point of the needle. Then the N is more precisely at true north, the E at true east, and so on. In case the *variation* is East, turn the ring so the N is slightly to the left of the needle. If no *variation* is given, put the N right under the needle.

SUN WATCH: (All boys and girls)

Turn your Explorer's Ring so that N is under the point of the needle. Make sure you are holding it so the sun can fall on it. Then see where the shadow from the little white vane falls. This will tell you the approximate time according to the sun.

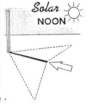

(High school boys and girls)

If you allow for the *variation* in your locality as explained above, the time will be more accurate.

However, all sun dials and sun watches tell the time *according to the sun.* This is called solar time. The kind of time we normally use in the United States is Civil Time

· 1 ·   · 2 ·

Fireball Twigg Paper (back)

Fireball Twigg Ad

Fireball Twigg
Explorer paper
1948, $25-$35

Flight Commander
1940s (generic, metal)(also
see Captain Midnight Flight
Commander)
$15-$30

**Flintstones-Barney
Rubble**
1960s (metal cloisonne')
$20-$40

Flintstones (see Hanna
Barbara)

Flintstones-Betty
1960s (plastic)(blue over
white)
$20-$40

Sundial
tells time

Flash Gordon
(see Post Tin)

Flight Commander
(see Captain Midnight)

Flintstones-Bam Bam
1960 (metal, cloisonne')
$20-$40

Fireball Twigg Explorer's
1948 (Post's Grape Nuts)
(see Sundial Shoes)(rare in
NM)(also see compass)
$50-$150

Flintstones-Dino
1960s (metal, cloisonne')
$20-$40

Fish
(see Sword in The Stone)

Flamenco Dancer
1970s (metal, die-
stamped)(color)
$5-$10

Flashihg Diamond
1993 (plastic, flashes in 2
colors)
On Card $3

Flintstones-Fred
1960s (metal cloisonne')
$20-$40

Flintstones-Fred
1960s (small, metal cloisonne')
$20-$40

Flintstones-Fred
1960s (metal, cloisonne')
$20-$40

Flintstones-Pebbles
1960s (metal cloisonne')
$20-$40

Flinstones Pebbles Crawling
1970s (metal)(cloisonne')
$15-$30

Flintstones Set
1960s (includes rings)
Set $50

Flintstones
1966 (4 rings on card)(vending machine)
(plastic figures snap on base)
$450 complete

Flintstones-Dino
1966 (set of 6)(plastic)

Flintstones-Fred
1966 (set of 6)(plastic)

Flintstones-Pebbles
1966 (set of 6)(plastic)

Flintstones-Fred Face
1970s (plastic)
$2-$4

Flintstones-Barney
1966 (set of 6)(plastic)

Flintstones-Betty
1966 (set of 6)(plastic)

Flintstones, Wilma
1966 (set of 6)(plastic)
$65-$80 ea.

131

Flintstones, Bam Bam
1970s (metal, enameled)
$20-$40

Florida Orange Bird
1970s (metal, painted)
$20-$40

Football (see NFL & Crackerjack)

Football Celestrium Rings
Made for Major League baseball, NBA, NFL and NHL by Balfour Jewelry Co., Mass. They all originally sold for $95.00 + $4.00 P&H.

Fonz, The
1970s (Happy Days TV tie-in)(metal)(photo)
$50-$125

Flintstones, Fred
1970s (metal, enameled)
$20-$40

Flying Jet
(plastic, in package)
In Package $20-$40
Ring Only $15-$30

#201—FOOTBALL RING
A heavy golden finished Football ring you'll be proud to wear. Send only 3 Touchdown wrappers and 15c to:
TOUCHDOWN, P.O. Box 239 New York 8, N. Y.

(Not valid where contrary to State laws)
Offer expires 1/31/49 ©Bowman Gum, Inc., 1948

Football
1948 (Bowman gum)(prices vary on gum cards)(also see Basketball)(Ring is in 2 variant forms; one regular weight, the other a heavier weight)
Heavier version - $100-$300

Flying Saucer
(see Capt. Video, Quisp & Wheaties)

Flying Tigers
(see Roger Wilco)

Foghorn Leghorn
(see Looney Tunes)

Football
1948 (Later issue)(Bowman gum)(regular weight version)(bronze metal)(also see Basketball)
Ring Only - $50-$100

Football, Celestrium Los Angeles Raiders
1993 (metal)(celestrium top)(Balfour)
$30-$75

Florida Orange Bird
1970s (metal, painted)
$20-$40

Fonz, The
1970s (metal, antiqued silver)(Happy Days TV tie-in)
$40-$80

Football, Celestrium Dallas
1993 (metal)(celestrium top)(Balfour)
$30-$75

Football-Chicago Bears Giant Paper Weight
1988 (metal)(Super Bowl XX)(very large)(NFL, gold w/blue top)
$20-$40

Flintstones, Dino
1970s (metal, enameled)
$20-$40

Football-Dallas
1994 (metal)(sold at Disney
World)(in color)(also see
Celestrium)
$12-$25

**Football Metal Circle,
Packers**
1970s (metal)
$15-$30

**Football Metal Disc,
Eagles (Philadelphia)**
1970s (metal, painted)
$15-$30

**Football NFL Logo
Atlanta Falcons**

Football-Giants
1991 (metal)
(Super bowl 25)
$12-$25

**Football Metal Disc,
Buffalo Bills**
1970s (metal, painted)
$15-$30

**Football Metal Disc,
Falcons**
1970s (metal, painted)
$15-$30

**Football NFL Logo
Buffalo Bills**

Football-Los Angeles
1994 (metal)(sold at Disney
World)(in color)
$12-$25

**Football Metal Disc,
Cardinals**
1970s (metal, painted)
$15-$30

**Football Metal Disc,
Kansas City Chiefs**
1970s (metal, painted)
$15-$30

**Football NFL Logo
Chicago Bears**

**Football Metal Circle,
Eagles (Philadelphia)**
1970s (metal)
$15-$30

**Football Metal Disc,
Chicago Bears**
1970s (metal, painted)
$15-$30

**Football Metal Disc,
Steelers (Pittsburgh)**
1970s (metal, painted)
$15-$30

**Football NFL Logo
Cin. Bengals**

Football NFL Logo
Cleveland Browns

Football NFL Logo
Green Bay Packers

Football NFL Logo
L.A. Rams

Football NFL Logo
New Orleans Saints

Football NFL Logo
Dallas Cowboys

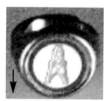

Football NFL Logo
Houston Oilers

Football NFL Logo
Miami Dolphins

Football NFL Logo
New York Giants

Football NFL Logo
Denver Broncos

Football NFL Logo
Indianapolis Colts

Football NFL Logo
Minnesota Vikings

Football NFL Logo
New York Jets

Football NFL Logo
Detroit Lions

Football NFL Logo
Kansas City Chiefs

Football NFL Logo
New England Patriots

Football NFL Logo
Oakland Raiders

Football NFL Logo Phoenix Cardinals

Football NFL Logo Washington Redskins

Football NFL Logo 1980s (28 diff.) (Kelloggs Sugar Corn Pops)(metal) $20-$45 ea.

Football-Washington Redskins 1994 (metal)(sold at Disney World)(in color)(identical to larger version) $12-$25

Football Flicker 1960s (plastic) $10-$20

Football NFL Logo Pittsburg Steelers

Football-San Francisco Giant Paper Weight 1994 (metal)(sold at Disney World)(in color) $12-$25

Football-Washington Redskins Giant Paper Weight 1994 (metal)(identical to smaller versions) $20-$40

Ford PP&K Flicker 1960s (punt, pass & kick)(rare)(aluminum) $20-$40

Football NFL Logo San Francisco 49'ers

Football-Tony's Pizza Giant Paper Weight 1990s (metal)(quota buster)(gold w/red top) $17-$35

Football NFL Logo Seattle Seahawks

Football, Toronto (see Baseball, Heavy, Toronto)

Football NFL Logo Tampa Bay Buccaneers

Football-Washington Redskins 1991 (metal)(NFL World Champions) $60-$125

Ford Magno-Power Car Paper 1950 (Complete) $75-$100

Two Finger Ring Base

Car produced in different colors; Blue, Yellow, Red, and Green known.

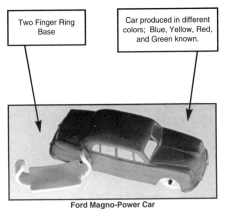

Ford Magno-Power Car
1950s (Kelloggs)(Cracker Jack's)(1950 Ford Scale Model with Mystery Control Ring)(hold magnet under a glass to move car across the top)
$200-$300

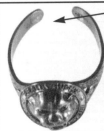

Note Rare Unbent Prongs

Frank Buck Black Leopard-Bronze
1938 (bronze)(scarce)
(note unbent prongs)
Good - $700
Fine - $1400
Near Mint - $3000

Ford Magno-Power Car ad
1950

Frank Buck Black Leopard-Silver
1938 (silver metal)(Adventurers' Club)
Good - $450
Fine - $900
Near Mint - $2000

**Frank Buck Movie
(Bring 'Em Back Alive)**
1930s (metal)
$100-$200

Note W.F. initials

Frank Buck Black Leopard-World's Fair
1939 (rare)(metal)(Jungleland)(NY)
Good - $1200
Fine - $3000
Near Mint - $6000

Hallmark

"FRANK RING"

SHOCKINGLY CHIC!

Frank Ring
1980s
(plastic)(Hallmark)(color, green)
On Card $5-$10
Ring Only $4-$8

Real ivory top

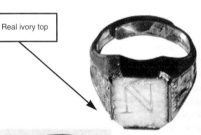

**Frank Buck
Ivory Initial**
1940s (real ivory)(gold initial)
(gold metal)
$150-$450

Frank Sinatra
(see Real Photo)

Frankenberry
(see Monster Cereal Flicker
& Monster Cereal Secret
Compartment))

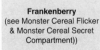

Frankenstein
1980s (metal
cloisonne)(Universal)
$10-$20

Frankenstein
1995 (heavy metal)
(fantasy piece)
$1

Freakies (Snorkeldorf)
1973-1978 (yellow plastic)
(Universal Feat.)(Ralston
Purina Co. cereal premium)
$75-$150

FUNNY RING 1

Frankenstein (see
Universal Monsters)

Freakies (Boss Moss)
1973-1978 (orange plastic)
(Universal Feat.)(Ralston
Purina Co. cereal premium)
$75-$150

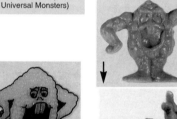

Freakies Figural
1978 (green
plastic)(Universal
Features)(two
angles shown)
$30-$60

FUNNY RING 2

FUNNY RING 3

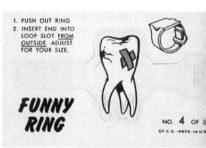

FUNNY RING 4

Freakies (Hamhose)
1973-1978 (blue plastic)
(Universal Feat.)(Ralston
Purina Co. cereal premium)
$75-$150

Frito Bandito
1969 (plastic)(in plastic
bag)(warehouse find?)
$10-$20

1. PUSH OUT RING
2. INSERT END INTO
   LOOP SLOT FROM
   OUTSIDE. ADJUST
   FOR YOUR SIZE.

FUNNY RING

NO. 5 OF 24
©T.C.G.—PRTD. IN U.S.A.

FUNNY RING 5

1. PUSH OUT RING
2. INSERT END INTO
   LOOP SLOT FROM
   OUTSIDE. ADJUST
   FOR YOUR SIZE.

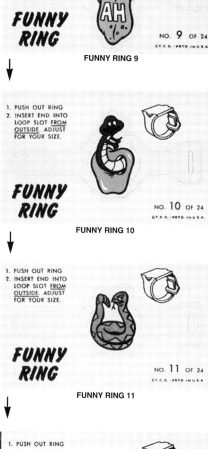

FUNNY RING

NO. 9 OF 24
©T.C.G.—PRTD. IN U.S.A.

FUNNY RING 9

1. PUSH OUT RING
2. INSERT END INTO
   LOOP SLOT FROM
   OUTSIDE. ADJUST
   FOR YOUR SIZE.

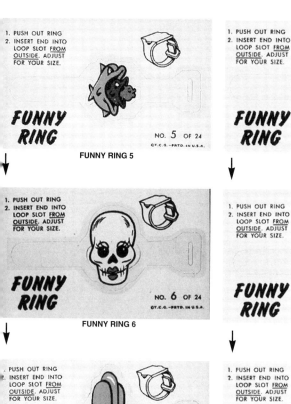

FUNNY RING

NO. 6 OF 24
©T.C.G.—PRTD. IN U.S.A.

FUNNY RING 6

1. PUSH OUT RING
2. INSERT END INTO
   LOOP SLOT FROM
   OUTSIDE. ADJUST
   FOR YOUR SIZE.

FUNNY RING

NO. 10 OF 24
©T.C.G.—PRTD. IN U.S.A.

FUNNY RING 10

1. PUSH OUT RING
2. INSERT END INTO
   LOOP SLOT FROM
   OUTSIDE. ADJUST
   FOR YOUR SIZE.

FUNNY RING

NO. 7 OF 24
©T.C.G.—PRTD. IN U.S.A.

FUNNY RING 7

1. PUSH OUT RING
2. INSERT END INTO
   LOOP SLOT FROM
   OUTSIDE. ADJUST
   FOR YOUR SIZE.

FUNNY RING

NO. 11 OF 24
©T.C.G.—PRTD. IN U.S.A.

FUNNY RING 11

1. PUSH OUT RING
2. INSERT END INTO
   LOOP SLOT FROM
   OUTSIDE. ADJUST
   FOR YOUR SIZE.

FUNNY RING

NO. 8 OF 24
©T.C.G.—PRTD. IN U.S.A.

FUNNY RING 8

1. PUSH OUT RING
2. INSERT END INTO
   LOOP SLOT FROM
   OUTSIDE. ADJUST
   FOR YOUR SIZE.

FUNNY RING

NO. 12 OF 24
©T.C.G.—PRTD. IN U.S.A.

FUNNY RING 12

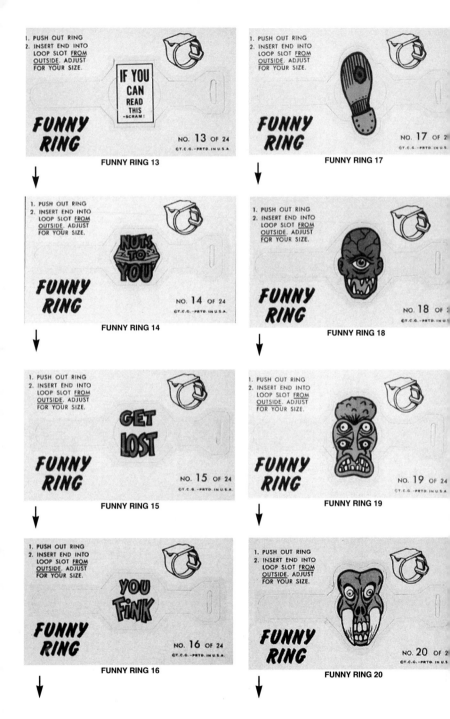

FUNNY RING 13

FUNNY RING 17

FUNNY RING 14

FUNNY RING 18

FUNNY RING 15

FUNNY RING 19

FUNNY RING 16

FUNNY RING 20

1. PUSH OUT RING
2. INSERT END INTO
   LOOP SLOT FROM
   OUTSIDE. ADJUST
   FOR YOUR SIZE.

FUNNY RING

NO. 21 OF 24
©T.C.G.—PRTD. IN U.S.A.

FUNNY RING 21

↓

1. PUSH OUT RING
2. INSERT END INTO
   LOOP SLOT FROM
   OUTSIDE. ADJUST
   FOR YOUR SIZE.

FUNNY RING

NO. 22 OF 24
©T.C.G.—PRTD. IN U.S.A.

FUNNY RING 22

↓

1. PUSH OUT RING
2. INSERT END INTO
   LOOP SLOT FROM
   OUTSIDE. ADJUST
   FOR YOUR SIZE.

FUNNY RING

NO. 23 OF 24
©T.C.G.—PRTD. IN U.S.A.

FUNNY RING 23

↓

PUSH OUT RING
INSERT END INTO
LOOP SLOT FROM
OUTSIDE. ADJUST
FOR YOUR SIZE.

FUNNY RING

NO. 24 OF 24
©T.C.G.—PRTD. IN U.S.A.

FUNNY RING 24

↑

Funny Ring
1966 (set of 24)(Topps)
$30-$60 ea.

Funny Rings
1966 (cardboard)(set of 24)(Topps)(checklist shown above)
Set $750-$1500
Ring Only $30-$60 ea.

Fuzzy Head
1980s
$2-$4

Game Ring
1940s (metal)
$50-$150

Garbage Pail Kids (1)

Garbage Pail Kids (6)

Gabby Hayes
(see Real Photos)

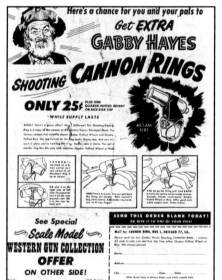

Gabby Hayes Shooting Cannon paper
1951 (metal/plastic)
$75-$100

Garbage Pail Kids (2)

Garbage Pail Kids (7)

Garbage Pail Kids (3)

Garbage Pail Kids (8)

Spring loaded to shoot
Quaker Puffed Rrice or
Wheat

Garbage Pail Kids (4)

Garbage Pail Kids (9)

Gabby Hayes Cannon
1951 (gold & silver
versions)(Quaker, metal)
$100-$250

Garbage Pail Kids (5)

Garbage Pail Kids (10)

Garbage Pail Kids
1985 (metal, color)(on card)
On Card $10

Garfield
1978 (plastic, color)
$8-$15

Garfield Flicker (3)
Round Green rings with
smiling Garfield putting
toothpaste on brush to tube
of paste exploding tooth-
paste all over him.

Garfield Flicker (3)
1978 (plastic)(large size)
(3 in set)(United Features
Synd.)(color)
$5-$10 ea.

Gary Cooper (see Real
Photo)

Garfield Flicker (1)
Garfield small mouth to
Garfield large mouth (both
versions shown)

Gene Autry Eagle
1955 (Gene Autry Dell
comic book ad premium)
(scarce)(see next page
for ad paper)
GD $250
FN $400
NM $550

Garbage Pail Kids (11)

Garcia Cigars
1930s (Brass w/plastic
covering)
$2-$5

Garfield Flicker (2)
Content looking Garfield
with eyes shut to wide eyed
surprized looking Garfield.

Gene Autry Face
1950s (copper
w/enamel coating)
$75-$150

Garbage Pail Kids (12)

Garbage Pail Kids
1985 (metal, color)
(12 known)
Ring Only $2-$4 ea.

Garfield
1970s (metal)
$5-$10

ANOTHER GENE AUTRY SPECIAL—
THE AMERICAN EAGLE RING !

This spectacular ring is yours FREE if you subscribe now to Gene Autry Comics. It's shiny golden color and the American Eagle emblazoned under a transparent setting is sure to make this ring a favorite of boys and girls everywhere. Be the first among your friends to own one. Subscribe now to Gene Autry Comics and receive this handsome ring as our FREE gift.

Think what fun it will be to have your copy of Gene Autry comics delivered right to your home each month! You'll be sure of getting every issue and receive this handsome ring FREE also. And you save money . . . 12 adventure-filled issues of Gene Autry comics costs just $1.

If you are already a subscriber you can still take advantage of this great FREE offer because we'll send you your ring now and start your new subscription when your present one expires.

CUT ON DOTTED LINE. PLEASE PRINT PLAINLY.

SUBSCRIPTION RATES: ☐ 1 year-12 issues $1.00
☐ 2 yrs.-24 issues $1.85 ☐ 3 yrs.-36 issues $2.70
Canada: ☐ 1 yr. $1.20; ☐ 2 yrs. $2.00; ☐ 3 yrs. $3.00

A PLEDGE **DELL** TO PARENTS

The Dell Trademark is, and always has been, a positive guarantee that the comic magazine bearing it contains only clean and wholesome juvenile entertainment. The Dell code eliminates entirely, rather than regulates, objectionable material. That's why when your child buys a Dell Comic you can be sure it contains only good fun. "DELL COMICS ARE GOOD COMICS" is our credo and constant goal.

Mail To: DELL PUBLISHING CO., INC. DEPT. 5GA
10 W. 33rd St., New York 1, N. Y.

Please enter subscription to Gene Autry Comics. Include special offer of Free American Eagle Ring and Dell Comics Club Membership Certificate.

Name .... Age ....
St. and No. ....
City .... Zone ..... State .....
I am enclosing remittance for $ ...... in full payment.
(If this is a gift subscription please fill in below. List any additional names on separate sheet)
ENCLOSE GIFT CARD TO READ FROM:
Donor's Name ....
St. and No. ....
City .... Zone ..... State .....

Gene Autry Eagle Ad
Ad From Gene Autry Comics #99, May 1955
paper (price based on value of comic book)(see
the Overstreet Comic Book Price Guide)

Gene Autry Flag
1950s (Dell, gold
& silver versions)
$100-$200

Gene Autry Museum
1995 (metal)
$4-$8

Wear my
Horseshoe Nail
RING
FOR GOOD LUCK
Gene Autry

Gene Autry Nail
1950 (on card)(metal)(also s
Tom Mix Nail)(nail signed)
On Card - $250
Ring Only $20-$40

Gene Autry Face
1950s (copper)
$75-$150

Gene Autry Face
1950s (silver)
$75-$150

Gene Autry Face
1950s (aluminum
w/gold face)
$75-$150

Gene Autry Photo
(see Real Photos)

Gene Kelly
(see Movie Star photo)

Ghost Busters
1992 (movie)(metal
cloisonne')
$4-$8

General Insignia Pack
1960s (metal)(gold/green top)
On Card $8-$15
Ring Only $5-$10

Generic Doll
1980s (plastic)
$1-$2

Genie
1950s (metal w/plastic eye)
$20-$40

Ghostbusters-Slimer
1992 (metal, cloisonne')
$4-$8

G. I. Joe Artic Force
1980s (plastic)
$5-$10

Genie Squirt
1990s Ring
$2-$4

Generic
1960s (on card)
$10-$20

Gerber Baby Food
1940s (metal)
$50-$100

G.I. Joe Artillery
1980s (plastic)
$5-$10

G.I. Joe Seal
1980s (plastic)
$5-$10

G.I. Joe Target
1980s (plastic)
$5-$10

G.I. Joe Shuttle
1980s (plastic)
$5-$10

G.I. Joe
1982 (came on card dis
with pinback)(meta
On Card - $100
Ring Only - $40-$7

G.I. Joe Tank
1980s (plastic)
$5-$10

G.I. Joe Coin
1964-1994 (30th salu
1994
Gold - $400
Silver - $200
Bronze - $100

G I. Joe® Command Rings are worn by Joe™ and Cobra™ forces to signify their combat speciality. Never before have these rings been available to you. Now, you can collect all 8 and show your friends that you're a member of the elite G.I. Joe Forces!

COLLECT ALL 8

AIRBORNE   ARTILLERY FORCE

ARCTIC FORCE   INFANTRY   S.E.A.L.

SHUTTLE CREW   T.A.R.G.A.T.   TANK CORPS

G.I. Joe Paper
1980s
$10-$20

G.I. Joe Sgt. Savage Compass
1996 (with figure)
On Card $10

G.I. Joe Sgt. Savage Decoder
1996 (with figure)
On Card $10

G.I. Joe Sgt. Savage Squirt
1996 (with figure)
On Card $10

G.I. Joe action figure
and ring

G.I. Joe
Tank Commander
1994 (Only 275 given away)
Complete $50

G.I. Joe Special Forces
1994 (metal)
Blue stone - $250
Black stone - $400

Giant (see Lucky Horse Shoe) Note: All Giant rings that follow are large over-sized rings.

Giant -Circus
1940s (scarce)(Thompson)
(several diff.)(also see
Lucky Horse Shoe)
$25-$50

Giant- Circus Hall of Fame
1950s (metal, gold color)
$25-$50

Giant -petursson, Johann K.
(Scene from movie "David & Goliath" w/Petursson starring as
Goliath. Born 1913, 8'8 " tall, 425 lbs, size 24 shoe).
Postcard $5

Giant- Earl, Jack
1950s (metal, dark color)
Original (dark) $15-$30
Repro (shiny) $1

Giant-Petursson, Johann
1950s (plastic, photo)
(green)
$5-$10

Giant -Earl, Jack
1950s (metal, silver color)
Original $15-$30
Repro (shiny) $1

Giant-Petursson, Johann
1940s, (metal, gold color)
$5-$10

Giant-Petursson, Johann
1950s (plastic, photo)
(yellow)
$5-$10

**Giant-Tallest Married
Couple**
1950s (metal, gray color)
$25-$50

Giant, J.G. Tarver
1950s (Texas Giant)(metal
dark color)
$25-$50

Giant, Tomaini, AL
1950s (metal, silver color)
$25-$50

Girl and Bell Flicker
1970s (plastic)(round)
$2-$4

Girl Scout
1930s (10k gold
filled)(green stone)
$140-$275

Girl Scout
1950s (silver)(cut-out)
$20-$40

Girl Scout
1950s (metal)(sterling)
$20-$40

Black
color

Gold color
(scarce)

G-Man Club
1930s (gum ball)(black &
gold versions)
Original $2-$5
Repro. - no value

G-Men
1930s (metal)(name in G)
$20-$60

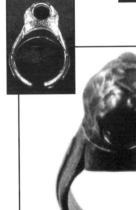

Gleason, James Photo
1940s (metal)
$50-$100

G-Men
1930s (metal)(name
below G)
$20-$75

**Go-Go Discotheque
Dancer Rings**
1960s (Flickers)(plastic)
(8 rings on card)
Set $40-$80
Ring Only $5-$10 each

Golden Nugget Cave
1950s (casino)(rare)(less than 10 known)(see
Straight Arrow Nugget)
GD $400, FN $575, NM $750

**Goldilocks & the
Three Bears**
1980s (secret compartment)
(Plastic, color)
$1

Good Luck Initial Ring Ad
1952 (24k gold-plated)
(Smith Brothers Cough Drops)
Ring $25-$60

Golf Flicker
1970s (plastic, color)
(see Rabbit)
$2-$5

Goofy Face
1970s (plastic, Canada,
gumball)
$4-$10

Goofy
3D figure (in color)
$25-$50

Goofy
1994 (sterling)
$17-$35

Hologram Ring

Goosebumps (1)
(The Curse of The Mummy's Tomb)

150

Hologram Ring

THE HAUNTED MASK

Goosebumps (2)
(The Haunted Mask)

Hologram Ring

NIGHT OF THE LIVING DUMMY

Goosebumps (4)
(Night Of The Living Dummy)

Hologram Ring

MONSTER BLOOD II

Goosebumps (3)
(Monster Blood II)

Hologram Ring

ONE DAY AT HORRORLAND

Goosebumps (5)
(One Day At Horrorland)

Hologram Ring

Goosebumps (6)
(Say Cheese And Die)

Goosebumps
1996 (TV)(metal w/hologram)(set of 12)
(each ring is tagged with a number)
On Card $5 ea.

Green Giant
1980s (rubber)
$25-$50

Green Hornet
1970s (plastic, gumball, large)
$7-$15

Green Hornet
1970s (plastic, gumball, small)
$10-$20

Green Hornet
1960s (plastic)
$8-$15

Goudy Gum Cowboy Boot
(see Cowboy Boot)

Granger, Farley
(see Movie Star Photo)

Green Hornet
1970s (plastic)
$2-$4

Green Hornet
1930s (plastic)(rare)(only 10 known)
Good - $600
Fine - $1500
Near Mint -$3000

Goudy Gum Cowboy Hat
(see Cowboy Hat)

Goudy Gum Indian
(see Indian)

Green Beret
1970s (plastic, movie)
$20-$40

Green Hornet
1966 (rubber)
$5-$10

Green Hornet Flicker (1)
"The Green Hornet" to sma
silhouette of the Green
Hornet firing hornet gun
next to car.

Green Hornet Action Flicker Rings
1960s (on card)
On Card $150

Green Hornet Flicker (6)
Full figure of Kato as butler to full figure Kato in front of car.

Green Hornet Flicker(7)
Full figure of the Green Hornet running from car with sting gun to Hornet rescuing a woman.

Green Hornet Flicker (10)
Picure of a couple kissing to black beauty driving thru a wall.

Green Hornet Flicker (11)
Hornet sting weapons to "Sting".

Green Hornet Flicker (2)
Picture of A Green Hornet to face of the Green Hornet with mask.

Green Hornet Flicker (3)
"Green Hornet Action ring" to full figure of the green hornet holding sting gun.

Green Hornet Flicker (5)
Face of Britt Reid to face of the Green Hornet.

Green Hornet Flicker (12)
"Hornet Gun" to a man
getting gassed.

↑ **Green Hornet Flicker**
1960s (silver)(set of 12)
$10-$20 ea.

Green Hornet Flicker (4)

Green Hornet Flicker (6)

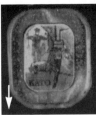

Green Hornet Flicker (8)

Green Hornet Flicker (1)

Green Hornet Flicker (5)

Green Hornet Flicker (7)

Green Hornet Flicker (9)

Green Hornet Flicker (2)

Metal top swivels open to
reveal secret compartment

(also see Knights Of Columbus
which uses same ring base)

Glow-in-dark
secret compart-
ment

Green Hornet Seal
1947 (General Mills)(Secret Compartment)(Base glows-in-dark)
Good - $250
Fine - $600
Near Mint - $1000

Green Hornet Flicker (3)

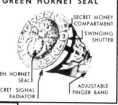

Green Hornet Seal Paper
1947 (complete)
$100-$150

Green Hornet Seal
1966
$10-$20

Green Lantern Glow-in-dark
1992 (DC Comic giveaway)
$1-$2

Note: Marty Nodell, creator of Green Lantern has given away examples of this ring autographed. $4 ea.

Green Hornet Stamp
1960s (plastic)
$20-$40

Gremlin
1980s (metal, painted)
$8-$15

Green Hornet Flicker (10)

Green Hornet Flicker (12)

Green Hornet Flicker
1960s (set of 12)
(plastic)(blue base)
$8-$15 ea.

Green Hornet Flicker (11)

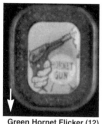

Green Hornet Logo
1990s (metal, color)
(fantasy)
$1

Green Lantern Water Jet
1980s (squirt)
On Card $35
Ring Only $8-$16

Gumball-Dice
1930s
$7-$15

Guitar Player Flicker
1960s (metal, color)
$5-$10

Gumball-Indian
1930s
$8-$20

Guitar Player Flicker
1980s (plastic, color)
$2-$4

Gumball
1970s (plastic, Canada)
$5-$10

Gumball-Arrow
1930s
$7-$15

Gumball set
1960s (18 in set)
$4 each

Gumby (7 diff.)
1980s (plastic)
$3-$6 ea.

Gumby
1980s (set with paper)(7 diff.)
Set $50

Hanna Barbera (1)
Dynomutt

Hanna Barbera (3)
Grape Ape

Hanna Barbera (2)
Fred Flintstone

Hanna Barbera (4)
Huckelberry Hound

Gun & Holster
(see Crackerjack--)

Gun & Holster
1995 (metal)(nice
detail)(fantasy piece)
$1

Gun & Hunting Ring
(see Official--)

Hagar The Horrible
1993 (silver metal)(Staber)
Silver (46 made) - $200
Gold (12 made) - $650

**Halloween packaged
set of 24 rings**
1990s
In Package $4

Hanna Barbera (5)
Magilla Gorilla

Hanna Barbera (6)
Pebbles Flintstone

Hanna Barbera (7)
Quick Draw McGraw

Hanna Barbera (8)
Scooby-Doo

Hanna Barbera (9)
Underdog

Hanna Barbera (10)
Yogi Bear

Hanna Barbera Disk
1977 (metal, color,
10 diff.)
$1-$2 ea.

Hans (see Post Tin)

Hansel and Gretel
1992 (secret compartment)
(red plastic)
$1

Happy Face (see Smile)

Happy Face
1970s (metal,
enameled)(yellow
face over gold color)
$4-$8

Happy Face
1990s (metal)(fantasy)
$1

Hardy Boys
1960s
$75-$150

Harold Teen (see Post Tin)

Have Gun Will Travel
1960s (Paladin)(white &
black top versions)(T.V.)
On Card $75
Ring Only $25-$50

Have Gun Will Travel
1960s (Paladin)(plastic,
gold base)
$15-$25

Hearst Castle
1990s (metal)(San
Simeon, CA)
$4-$8

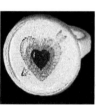

Heart-Arrow Flicker
1960s (plastic)(Cupid)(see
Valentine)
$3-$6

Heart Throb Flicker
1960s (silver base)
$10-$20

Heckle and Jeckle Dis
1977 (metal, color)
$2-$4

Heckle and Jeckle Dis
1977 (metal, color)
$2-$4

He-Man Secret
Compartment (open)

He-Man Secret
Compartment (closed)
1980s (plastic)
$15-$30

Hiawatha Flicker
1970s
(modern "v" base)
$2-$5

Hockey NHL Philly Flyers
1970s (metal, color)
$10-$20

Hockey NHL Texas Rangers
1970s (metal, cloisonne' band)
$10-$20

High School
1950s (metal, gumball, gold color)
$5-$10

Hill Valley High
1994 (Hill Valley High class ring)(red, green & blue birthstones)(gold and silver color versions)
(6 rings in set)(Universal Studios)
$20 ea.

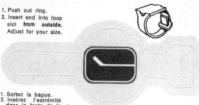

1. Push out ring.
2. Insert end into loop slot **from outside.** Adjust for your size.

1. Sortez la bague.
2. Insérez l'extrémité dans la fente de la boucle **à partir de l'extérieur.** Ajustez-le pour votre doigt.

NO. 1 OF 17
© O.P.C.   PRINTED IN CANADA

HOCKEY RING 1

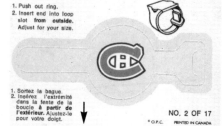

1. Push out ring.
2. Insert end into loop slot **from outside.** Adjust for your size.

1. Sortez la bague.
2. Insérez l'extrémité dans la fente de la boucle **à partir de l'extérieur.** Ajustez-le pour votre doigt.

NO. 2 OF 17
© O.P.C.   PRINTED IN CANADA

HOCKEY RING 2

Hockey NHL Chicago Blackhawks
1970s (metal, color)
$10-$20

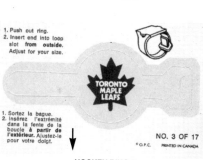

1. Push out ring.
2. Insert end into loop slot **from outside.** Adjust for your size.

TORONTO MAPLE LEAFS

1. Sortez la bague.
2. Insérez l'extrémité dans la fente de la boucle **à partir de l'extérieur.** Ajustez-le pour votre doigt.

NO. 3 OF 17
© O.P.C.   PRINTED IN CANADA

HOCKEY RING 3

Hockey NHL Boston Brewers
1970s (metal, cloisonne' band)
$10-$20

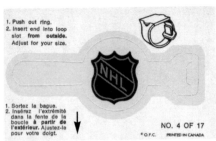

HOCKEY RING 4

HOCKEY RING 8

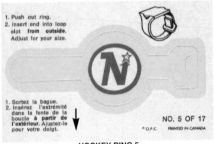

HOCKEY RING 5

HOCKEY RING 9

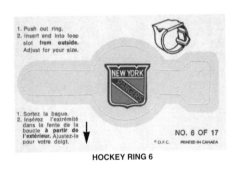

HOCKEY RING 6

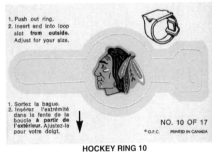

HOCKEY RING 10

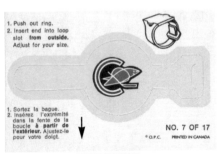

HOCKEY RING 7

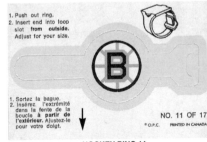

HOCKEY RING 11

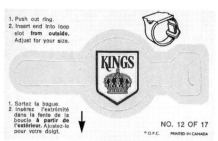

© O.P.C.   PRINTED IN CANADA

HOCKEY RING 12

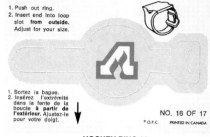

© O.P.C.   PRINTED IN CANADA

HOCKEY RING 16

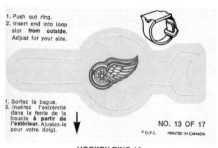

© O.P.C.   PRINTED IN CANADA

HOCKEY RING 13

© O.P.C.   PRINTED IN CANADA

HOCKEY RING 17
Hockey Rings
1960s (cardboard)(set of 17)
$25 ea.

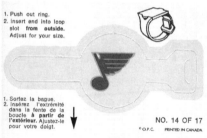

© O.P.C.   PRINTED IN CANADA

HOCKEY RING 14

Holly Hobby
1970s (metal cloisonne')
$25-$50

Hopalong Cassidy Bar 20
1950s (brass)
$20-$60

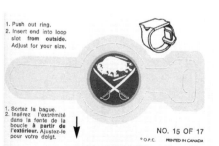

© O.P.C.   PRINTED IN CANADA

HOCKEY RING 15

Hoover/Wilson Flicker
1960s (metal)(Hong Kong
Star)
$20-$35

**Hopalong Cassidy
Bar 20**
1950s (silver)(metal)
$20-$60

HOPALONG CASSIDY
ADJUSTABLE RING & BADGE

Wear Hoppy's official badge and ring to identify yourself as a real range rider. Both in handsome silver colored finish embossed with Hoppy's picture. Ring adjustable to any size. Mail 2 Box Top Coupons and 25c in coin to H. C. Badge & Ring Dept.

Hopalong Cassidy Ring Paper w/ cut-outs,
1950s,
$75

HOPPY'S DICTIONARY OF WESTERN HORSES

MUSTANG   BRONCO   QUARTER HORSE   PINTO OR PIEBALD   PALOMINO

KIDS — This is one of 4 Different HOPPY "WESTERNS" Packed in DELICIA Cone Cup Packages. Get 'Em All!

STRIP No. 4

Hopalong Cassidy Compass/Hat
1950s (metal)(hat fits over compass base)
$100-$200

Hopalong Cassidy Steer Head paper
1950s
$30-$50

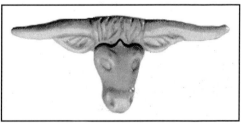

Hopalong Cassidy Steer Head
1950s (Conchos or ring slide)(rare)(mouth opens so teeth can punch brand on inserted paper)(Grape-Nuts Flakes box-top premium)
$100-$250

Horror Ring Paper
1950s (vending machine paper)(in color)(rare)
$15-$25

Horror rings boxed set
1960s (metal)(ring design different than other boxed set)
Set $170
Ring Only $2-$4

Horror Rings Boxed Set
1960s (rings different than boxed set on next page)
Set $150
Ring Only $2-$4

Horse Head
1960s (plastic)(gumball, square)
$4-$8

Horseshoe and Boot
1980s (bronze)
(Frontierland)
$5-$10

Horse Head
1980s (bronze)
(Frontierland)
$5-$10

Horseshoe and Cowboy
1980s (bronze)
(Frontierland)
$5-$10

Horseshoe and Gun
1960s (plastic)(silver color)
$4-$8

Horseshoe Good Luck
1950s (plastic)(gumball)
$4-$8

Horseshoe (see China
Luck & Tiger Eye)

Horseshoe Nail (see Gene
Autry & Tom Mix)

Hot Dog
1960s (plastic)
$2-$4

Hot Wheels Flicker
1970s (plastic)(black, blue
& yellow base colors
known)
$12-$20

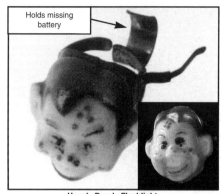

Holds missing
battery

Howdy Doody Flashlight
1950s (metal/plastic, color)
Complete w/Battery $75-$200
Battery Missing $55-$180

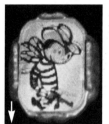

Buffalo Bee Flicker

Chief Thunderthud Flicker

Buffalo Bob Flicker

Clarabelle Flicker

Flubadub Flicker

Howdy Doody Flicker

Mr. Bluster Flicker

Princess

Howdy Doody Flicker
1950s (set of 8)(Nabisco
Rice Honeys cereal
premium)(gray bases)
$15-$30 ea.

Howdy Doody
1976 (metal/plastic)
$50-$100

Howdy Doody Glow Photo
1950s (metal base)
$125-$250

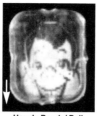

Howdy Doody/ Poll Parrot Flicker
1950s (Howdy Doody to Poll Parrot flying)(Thick top lens held on by four prongs)
$50-$100

Howdy Doody Raised
1950s (Face)(white base)
$75-$150

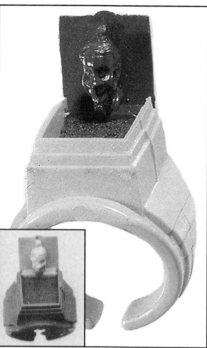

Howdy Doody Jack in Box
1950s (rare) (red & yellow plastic) (two color versions exist)
Good - $1735
Fine - $3470
Near Mint - $5500

Howdy Doody /Poll Parrot T.V. Flicker
1950s (scarce)(blue or orange bases)(showing Poll Parrot & Howdy)
$100-$200

Howdy Doody Poll Parrot
(see Poll Parrot)

Howie Wing Weather
1940s (scarce)(metal)(also see Lone Ranger & Peter Paul Weather)
GD $250
FN $400
NM $550

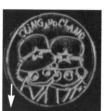

H.R. Puf'n Stuf (Cling & Clang)

H.R. Puf'n Stuf (Puf'n Stuf)

Howdy Doody Insert
1950s (red base)
$75-$150

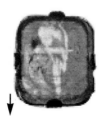

Howdy Raised Face
1950s (silver base)
$75-$150

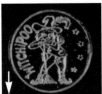

**H.R. Puf'n Stuf
(Witchipoo)**

H.R. Puf'n Stuf
1970s (7 diff.)
$20-$40 ea.

Huckleberry Hound Club
1960s (2 variations exist,
metal cloisonne' & plain)
$30-$100 each

Huckleberry Hound (see
Baba Looey, Dixie & Quick
Draw McGraw)

Huck Finn Flicker
1950s (shows both images)
$20-$40

Humpty Dumpty
1970s (plastic)(red over
white)(Canada)
$5 - $10

Huckleberry Hound
1960s (aluminum)
$15-$30

(cloisonne')

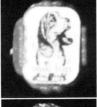

Hush Puppies Flicker
1960s "Hush Puppies" pic-
ture of the dog to "casual
shoes" picture of dog
looking other way.
$20-$40

Huskies Club
1936 (rare)(metal)
(cereal, gold color)
GD $300
FN $450
NM $600

Icee Bear
1970s (plastic)
$25-$50

Ice Maiden Magnet
1990s
$3-$6

Incredible Hulk
1980s (metal)(vitamins)
(also see Captain America
& Spiderman)(Marvel
Entertainment Group)
(in color)
$50-$150

Indian (see Gumball-)

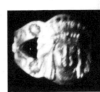

Indian
1950s (gumball)(metal)
$20-$40

Indian Chief
1980s (bronze)
(Frontierland)
$5-$10

Indian Chief
1970s (metal)
(stamped, color)
$4-$8

Indian Chief
1970s (metal)(silver color)
$5-$10

Indian, Goudy Gum
1940s (silver colored metal)(5 box tops from Indian chewing
gum to get ring)(also see Chief Wahoo)
$75-$150

Indianapolis Speedway
1960s (metal)(round,
cloisonne')
$10-$20

Indian Chief
1960s (plastic)(gumball,
white)
$4-$8

Indian Chief
1960s (plastic)(gumball,
square)
$4-$8

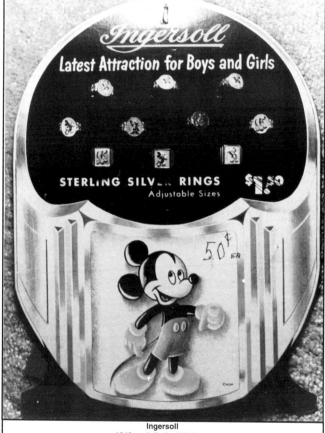

Ingersoll
1948 card display (10 rings)
(individual rings are listed and priced
under the character names)
Complete $2000

Indian Chief
1970s (metal)(color)
.50-$1

Initial (Generic)
1950s
$5-$10

Inspector (see Post Tin)

Jabber Jaws
1990s (metal, cloisonne')
$2-$4

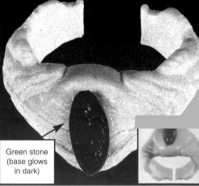

Green stone
(base glows
in dark)

Jack Armstrong Dragon's Eye
l940s (green stone)(also see Buck Rogers Ring of Saturn &
Shadow Carey Salt)(rarest in high grade of the
crocodile set)
GD $300, FN $750, NM $1200

Initial (Generic)
1940s (metal)
(premium)(scarce)
$100-$200

Initial Ring (see Good
Luck--, Quaker, Radio
Orphan Annie & Signet
Ring)

Jack and the Beanstalk
1990s (plastic, color)
$1

FOLLOW JACK ARMSTRONG'S TRAINING RULES
Here's the special training program designed for young athletes and
recommended by nationally famous coaches and players. Follow these
rules regularly and you're helping yourself to deliver better performance
at your favorite sports.

1. Get plenty of fresh air, sleep and exercise
every day. These are basic training require-
ments needed to help put you in condition for
fast, strenuous play.

2. Make a friend of soap and water. Dirt breeds
germs, and germs can very easily undermine
an athlete's condition. Good health is vital to suc-
cess in sports.

3. Eat a "Breakfast of Champions" every
morning! Treat yourself to a big bowlful of
nourishing whole wheat, Wheaties, with lots of
milk and fruit. Probably more great athletes eat
this training breakfast than any other dish of its
kind.

YOURS! THIS MYSTERIOUS RING THAT GLOWS IN THE DARK!

MAIL THIS COUPON TODAY

Jack Armstrong Baseball Centennial
(1839 - 1939) 1939 (metal)(rare)
GD $325, FN $480, NM $650

**Jack Armstrong
Dragon's Eye Paper**
1940s (rare)
$125-$175

**SPECIAL ORDER BLANK FOR
ADDITIONAL DRAGON'S EYE RING**

If you want to get another dragon's eye ring, (or several
rings) for yourself or to give to your friends for Christmas, send the order blank below to "Jack Armstrong,
Dept. 494, Minneapolis, Minn." Be sure to enclose 10
cents and a Wheaties boxtop for *each* ring you order.

I want____rings. Enclosed is____cents and____Boxtops.

My name is_____

I live at_____
                    (Street)

_____ • _____
(City)   (State)
(This offer expires January 2, 1941.)

B1090

IMPORTANT!

**HOW TO "CHARGE" YOUR LUMINOUS
DRAGON'S EYE RING TO MAKE IT
GLOW IN THE DARK!**

Hold your dragon's eye ring up close to
a lighted electric bulb for one half minute or more. This "charges" your dragon's eye ring so it will glow in the dark
—the longer you hold your ring to the
light, the brighter and longer it will glow. You may "charge" your
ring this way as often as you wish. You can also "charge" your
dragon's eye ring by holding it in the sunlight. *But be sure you
do not expose your ring to the direct rays of the sun for too
long a time!*

IF YOU WANT TO MAKE YOUR RING LARGER: (1) Place
it in hot water (not boiling) for about five minutes. (2) Take
it from the water and put it on your finger, bending it to the
right size. (3) When you have bent it so it fits, put it in cold
water for a minute. (4) Your ring should now fit perfectly.

(Special Order Blank on other side)

Jack Armstrong Egyptian Whistle
1940s (metal)(gold color)(also see Tom Mix Musical)
$40-$150

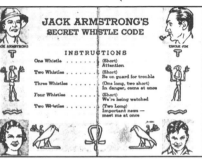

Jack Armstrong Egyptian Whistle Paper
1940s (beware of repro. paper which is on cardboard; original on paper)
$60-$80

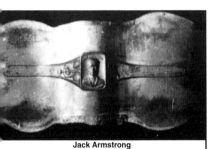

Jack Armstrong Lead Proof
1939 (Ring was never issued)
Estimate $2000

Jack Benny Photo (see Real Photos)

Jackie Kennedy Photo (see Real Photos)

Jackie Gleason Photo (see Real Photos)

James Bond (see Agent 007)

Jasmine (see Aladdin)

Jaws (see Shark)

Jaws
1975 (movie, Universal Pics.)(plastic)(green/gold)
$2

Jaws
1975 (plastic, green/silver)(Universal movie pics)
$2

Jerry (See Tom & Jerry)

Jerry's Restaurants Flicker
1960s "Jerry's Restaurants" to cartoon figure of a chef.
$15-$30

Jester Face
1960s (metal, color)
$2-$4

Jesus Flicker
1960s (metal)(round, large, color)
$10-$20

Jesus Flicker
1960s (metal)(round, small, color)
$10-$20

Jesus Flicker
1960s (plastic) (rectangle, color)
$10-$20

Jesus Flicker
1970s
$10-$20

Jet Pilot
1950s (metal)(see also
Junior-)
$20-$40

Jet Plane (see Super Jet)

Jet Stewardess
1950s (metal)(Red Goose
shoes)
$25-$50

Jetsons, Judy
1980s (metal cloisonne')
$10-$25

Jiggs (see Post Tin)

Jimmy Allen Flying Clu
1930s (metal)
$50-$100

Jimmy Durante Photo
(see Real Photos)

Jinks (Hanna-Barbera)
1960s (aluminum)
(also see Dixie)
$15-$30

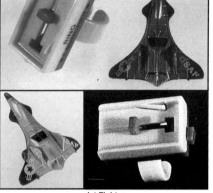

Jet Fighter
1978 (with launching base)(plastic)
$5-$10

Jet Ring Squadron
1989 (plastic)(4 diff., blue, black, yellow & red)
On Card $15
Ring Only $2-$4

Jimminy Crickett
1960s (aluminum)
$20-$35

Jimminy Crickett
1970s (plastic)(red over
white)(Canada)
$5-$10

Joe Dimaggio club
1940s (metal)
$200-$400

Joe E. Brown
1940s (metal)
$50-$150

170

John Deere
1970s (aluminum)(color)
$5-$10

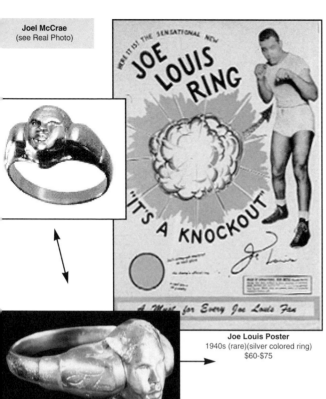

Joe Louis Poster
1940s (rare)(silver colored ring)
$60-$75

John F. Kennedy Photo
(see Real Photos)

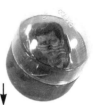

John F. Kennedy Flicker
1960s (in vending machine container)
$10-$20

Joe Louis Face
1940s (rare)(nickel metal)
GD $1000, FN $1800, NM $2600

Joe Louis Photo
(see Real Photos)

Joe Penner Face Puzzle
1940s (rare)(radio)(metal)
(less than 10 known)
GD $300
FN $475
NM $650

John F. Kennedy Flicker
1960s John F. Kennedy
35th president 1917-1963
picture of American Flag to
face of JFK. (metal)
$10-$20

Joe Louis Figural
1940s (scarce)(Metal)(2 color variations)
GD $500, FN $1000, NM $1500

John F. Kennedy Flicker
1960s (gold metal
base)(oval)
$10-$20

**Jungle Jim's
Playland**
1980's (plastic)
$1-$2

Junior Fire Marshal
1950s (metal)
$20-$40

Kangaroo (see Looney
Tunes)

Kazoo (1)

John F. Kennedy Flicker
1960s (gold metal
base)(Hong Kong Star)
$10-$20

Kazoo (2)

Kazoo (3)
1960s (plastic, 3 diff. colo
variants, gumball)
$10-$20 ea.

John F. Kennedy Flicker
1970s (oval)(plastic)
$5-$10

John Wayne Photo
(see Movie Star Photo &
Real Photo)

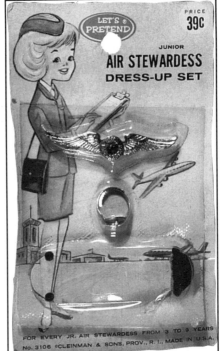

Junior Air Stewardess
1970s (on card)
Complete $10

Keebler Elf
1970 (plastic, white & pink
$30-$60

Joker Disc
1960s (plastic, red on
white paper)(red & green
base variations)
$12-$25

Junior Pilot
1955 (American
Airlines)(metal)
(also see Jet-)
$20-$40

Junior Stewardess
1955 (American
Airlines)(metal)
$20-$40

Keep On Trucking (see
Turtle-)

Kellog's Picture Rings

Kellogg's Picture Ring Ad

Kellogg's Picture Republic XF-91 Thundercepter
1950s (plastic)
$20-$40

Sitting Bull
1950s (Kelloggs)(plastic)
$10-$20

Airplanes

Kellogg's Picture Douglas DC-6
1950s (plastic)
$20-$40

Kellogg's Picture Pan American Clipper
1950s (plastic)
$20-$40

Kellogg's Picture Douglas F-3D Sky Knight
1950s (plastic)
$20-$40

Kellogg's Picture Republic F-84E Thunderjet
1950s (plastic)
$20-$40

Cowboys

Buffalo Bill
1950s (plastic)
$15-$30

Dennis O'Keefe Photo
1950s
$10-$20

Indians

Pocahontas
1960s (plastic)
$10-$20

Movie Stars

Burt Lancaster
1950s (Kellogg's)
$10-$20

Joanne Dru
1950s (plastic)
$10-$20

Wanda Hendrix
1950s (Photo)(plastic)
$10-$20

Baseball, Babe Ruth
1949 (plastic) Kellogg's
$25-$60

Kewpie Kid
1940s (metal)(scarce)
$150-$300

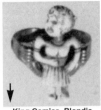

King Comics, Blondie

King Comics, Fritz

Gene Tunney
1950s (plastic)(Kellogg's)
$20-$40

**Kill the Jinx Good Luck
Signet Ring**
1929 (metal)
(sold in Johnson Smith &
Co. catalogue for $1.00)
(Also see Swastika &
Navajo Good Luck)
(used as Paul Whitman)
$125-$250

King Comics, Captain

King Comics, Hans

Jack Kramer
1950s (plastic,orange top,
brown base) & (blue top,
green base)
$20-$40

Kilroy is Back
1970s (plastic)(Canada,
gumball)(yellow & silver on
blue versions known)
$5-$10

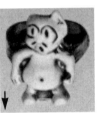

King Comics, Felix

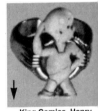

King Comics, Henry

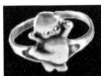

Kewpie Figure
1970s (metal)(adj.)(gold
color)(fantasy)
$1

King Edward VIII
1940s (metal)(British)
$20-$40

**King Comics, Flash
Gordon**

King Comics, Inspector

Kewpie Figure
1930s (sterling)(not adj.)
$75-$150

King Comics, Jiggs?

King Comics, Olive Oyl

King Comics Set on card (36 rings),
1953 (each ring occurs in diff. colors)
(Note: most cards have multiple rings of same characters)
Complete Card Set $550

King Comics, Little Lulu

King Comics, Snuffy
Smith

King Comics, Maggie

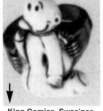

King Comics, Swee'pea

**King Features
Comics**
1953 (set of 20
known)(ceramic
material in color)
(each ring occurs in
diff. colors; Phantom
ring has never
been verified)
$10-$15 ea.

King Features
1980s (metal cloisonne')(TV)
$5-$10

King Features
1950s (Mandrake)(in
color)(plastic)
$25-$75

King Comics, Mama

King Features
1950s (Lone Ranger)(in
color)(plastic)
$25-$75

King Features
1950s (Phantom)(thick top)
(in color)(plastic)
$25-$75

King Features
1950s (Prince
Valiant)(thick top)
(in color)(plastic)
$25-$75

King Features
1950s (Tonto)(in
color)(plastic)
$25-$75

Kissing Flicker
1960s (gold metal bas
(Hong Kong Star)
$10-$20

King Features
1950s (Charles Starrett)(in
color)(plastic)
$25-$75

King Kong
1962 (gumball)(plastic)(base comes in
pink, red, yellow, orange, green)
In Package - $10
Repro $1

Kit Carson T.V.
1950s (scarce)(metal)
$200-$350

Kix Rocket (see Rocket-
The-Moon)

KKK (see USA/KKK)

King Features
1950s (Tillie the Toiler)
(thick top, in color)(plastic)
$25-$75

Knot Hole Gang
1940s (metal)
$20-$60

King Features
1950s (Sweeney)(thick top)
(in color)(plastic)
$25-$75

King Vitamin Disc
1970s (plastic)
$2-$4

King Vitamin Hologram
1970 (1st hologram
ring)(plastic)
$12-$25

Top pivots to reveal glow-in-dark secret compartment with a wax seal over bottom concealing secret message

Krazy Kat
1940s (metal cloisonne')
$50-$150

Lake Winepesauka
1980s (metal)(Chatt., TN.)
$2-$4

Lassie Friendship
1950s (metal)(20 carat
gold plated)
$90-$180

Knights of Columbus
1940s (radio)(rare)(less
than 10 known)
View of base used from Green
Hornet ring. "G H" (Green
Hornet) initials on side of base
changed to mean "Holy
Ghost."
Good - $750
Fine - $2000
Near Mint - $3750

Kolonel Keds
1950s (see U.S.
Keds)(paper disc)
$30-$60

Kool Aid Aztec Treasure
1930s (metal)
$100-$200

Land of the Lost Pop-Up Ring
1991 (plastic)(color, 3 diff.)
On Card $25
Ring Only $5-$10 each

Lassie Friendship Ring Paper
1950s (Rare)
$125-$175

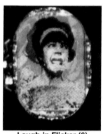

Laugh-in Flicker (5)
(16 diff.) Henry Gibson as
Indian to Henry Gibson
as a priest
$10-$20 ea.

Laugh-in Flicker (8)
(16 diff.) Artie Johnson as
German soldier "Very
Interesting" to "But Stupid"
$10-$20 ea.

Laugh-in Flicker (6)
(16 diff.) JoAnn Worley sad
face to JoAnn Worley
screaming
$10-$20 ea.

Laugh-in Flicker(9)
(16 diff.) "Here Comes the
Judge" to Black Man
$10-$20 ea.

Laugh-in Flicker (1)
(16 diff.) "Laugh-in" to
Dan & Dick
$10-$20 ea.

Laugh-in Flicker (3)
(16 diff.) Goldie Hawn figure
in bikini dancing
side to side.
$10-$20 ea.

Laugh-in Flicker (7)
(16 diff.) Beauty (Ruth
Buzzi w/bonnet) to Beast
(Dan Rowan profile)
$10-$20 ea.

Laugh-in Flicker (10)
(16 diff.) "Here Comes the
Judge" to cartoon judge
jumping out of circle
$10-$20 ea.

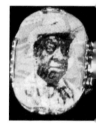

Laugh-in Flicker (2)
(16 diff.) Goldie Hawn to
Goldie dancing in bikini
$10-$20 ea.

Laugh-in Flicker (4)
(16 diff.) Ruth Buzzi w/hair-
net to Ruth Buzzi w/bonnet
$10-$20 ea.

Laugh-in Flicker (11)
16 diff.) "The Hymns for
oday are 76, 81, 92, 85,
2..."to Dick Martin cartoon
yelling "Bingo"
$10-$20 ea.

Laugh-in Flicker (14)
(16 diff.) Circle psychedelic
design to square
psychedelic design.
$10-$20 ea.

Laugh-in Flicker (1)

Laugh-in Flicker (13)
1968 (16 diff.)(blue base)
$10-$20 ea.

Laugh-in Flicker (12)
(16 diff.) "Fickle Finger of
Fate Award" to picture of
finger of Fates Award
$10-$20 ea.

Laugh-in Flicker (15)
(16 diff.) "Goodnight Dick"
to "Who's Dick"
$10-$20 ea.

Laugh-in Flicker (4)

Laugh-in Flicker
1968 (Square variant)
(Goldie Hawn to Goldie
dancing in bikini)
$40-$75 ea.

Laugh-in Flicker (13)
16 diff.) If Minnehaha married Don Ho" to "She'd be
Minne Ha Ha Ho"
$10-$20 ea.

Laugh-in flicker (16)
1968 (16 diff.)(original
silver base)(vending
machine ring)
$10-$20 ea.

"Sock it to me" to
Judy Carne
in a striped sweater
leaning w/hat

Laugh-in Flicker (6)

Laugh-in T.V. Metal
1960s (here comes the
judge)
$20-$40 ea.

Laugh-in T.V. Metal
1960s (luv)
$20-$40 ea.

Laugh-in Flicker (11)

Laugh-In Vending Machine Display Ring Card
1968 (cardboard, holds 6 Laugh-In rings)(rare)
$50

Laugh-In Case
1960s (includes rings)
$50

Laugh-in Package
1960s (plastic)
In Pkg. $20
Ring Only $8-$15

Laugh-in T.V. Metal
1960s (very interesting)
$20-$40 ea.

Legion Of Super Heroes Flight
1994 (gold, 16 made)(ri
engraved with a diff. Leg
character optional)
$200 ea.

Laugh-In "Sock it To Me"
1960s (plastic)(gumball, red/silver)
$4-$8

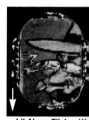

Lil Abner Flicker (1)

Laurel & Hardy
1980s (metal cloisonne')(Hardy)
$20-$40

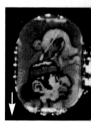

Lil Abner Flicker (2)

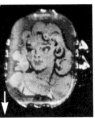
Lil Abner Flicker (3)

Lil Abner Flicker (3)

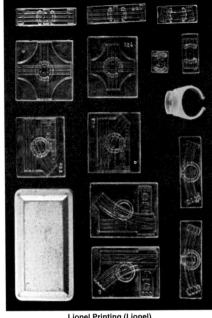
Lionel Printing (Lionel)
1950s (box)(w/stamp pad)(15 pieces)
$175-$225 set

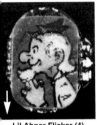
Lil Abner Flicker (4)
1960s (silver base)(set of 4)
$8-$15 ea.

Lil Abner Flicker (4)
1960s (blue base)(set of 4)
$5-$10 ea.

Lillums (see Post Tin)

Lil Abner Flicker (1)

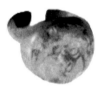
Lion Face
1960s (plastic)
$2-$5

Lion King Dome
1994 (metal/plastic)
On Card $3-$5
Ring Only $1-$2

Lion King Party (1)

Lil Abner Flicker (2)

Lion
1960s? (plastic)(large)
$2-$5

Lion King Dome (Simba)
1994 (metal/plastic)
On Card $3-$5
Ring Only $1-$2

Lion King Party (2)

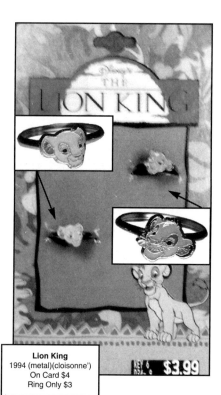

Lion King Party (7)

Little Caesar's Pizza Man
1980s (plastic)
$4-$8

Little King (see Post Tin

Lion King Party (8)
1994 (plastic)(8 diff.)
On Card $2
Ring Only .50 each

Lion King
1994 (metal)(cloisonne')
On Card $4
Ring Only $3

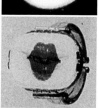

Little Mermaid (Flounder)
1990s (rubber)(color)
$2-$4

Lips Kiss Flicker
1970s Cloverleaf Milk
picture of red lips to same
lips puckering for akiss.(also
exists in oval form)(plastic)
$5-$10

Lion King Party (3)

Little Mermaid (Sebastian
1990s (rubber)(color)
$2-$4

Lion King Party (5)

Lion King Party (4)

Lion King Party (6)

Little Caesar's Pizza Secret Compartment
1980s (plastic)
$10-$20

Lone Ranger (see Tonto)

uminum warhead

Bombardier's insignia on top of ring

secret message compartment in tail fin

4-pronged Red tail fin removes from bomb to show atoms smashing inside (magnified radium)

All rings have gem stone insets on base and gold plated lightning bolts

Interchangeable bullets slide on/off shank

Lone Ranger Bullet Ring (38 Caliber)
1992 (w/2 bullets that interchange, a Tonto and a Lone Ranger bullet) (solid silver, 30 made)
$300

Lone Ranger Atomic Bomb
1946 (Kix cereal) (one of the most popular rings ever given away)(also see Whistle Bomb)
$50-$150

Lone Ranger Bullet Ring (22 Caliber)
1992 (same as 38 caliber, but smaller 22 caliber) (w/ 2 bullets that interchange, a Tonto and a Lone Ranger bullet)(solid silver, 30 made)
$300

NOTICE
★

You May Have to Wait A Few Minutes Before You Can See the Atomic Display Inside Ring

Do Not Remove Tail-Fin in Bright Light

Keep red tail-fin on ring until you are in the dark. Otherwise you will be unable to see atomic display for approximately half an hour. Removing tail-fin in bright light results in a steady glow inside the atom chamber instead of frenzied flashes.

HERE'S HOW RING WORKS

1. Take ring into dark room or closet. Close door so that no light can enter.

2. Wait until pupils of eyes dilate—this may take from 2 to 10 minutes. Best and quickest results are obtained at night.

3. Twist red tail-fin on ring until it slides off "bomb".

4. Hold ring close to your eyes. Look into Observation Lens which seals the atom chamber.

5. Keep your eye glued to Observa-

tion Lens. As soon as your eye becomes accustomed to the dark you'll see the thrilling spectacle of atomic energy in action.

HERE'S WHAT YOU'LL SEE—You'll see brilliant flashes of light in the inky darkness inside the atom chamber. These frenzied, vivid flashes are caused by the released energy of split atoms.

PERFECTLY SAFE—We guarantee you can wear KIX Atomic "Bomb" Ring with complete safety. The atomic materials inside the ring are harmless.

Lone Ranger Atomic Bomb Paper
1946 (Kix cereal)
$60-$75

bulb flashes on and off

Lone Ranger Flashlight
1948 (w/battery)(gold color metal)(Cheerios cereal premium)
Complete $125
Battery $10

Lone Ranger Disc
1966 (plastic)
$2-$5

HOW TO PUT
BATTERY IN RING

1. Slide battery into opening at bottom of ring band (see picture).

2. Wire "A" should not quite touch button on end of battery.

3. Press Wire "A" lightly against button on battery to light bulb.

Good Deed Order Blank on Other Side

You'll have double fun if you can get your friends to order a Lone Ranger Flashlight Ring, too. Then you can send flash signals back and forth—organize night patrols—play hide and seek in the dark—and lots more things that are big fun. So give the Good Deed Order Blank on opposite side to your best pal and tell him to send for his Lone Ranger Flashlight Ring quick.

HOW TO GET
EXTRA BATTERIES

For only 10¢ and one Cheerios Boxtop you can get 2 additional batteries. Use Battery Order Blank on opposite side to order.

482   © T.L.R, INC.   (USE BATTERY ORDER BLANK ON OTHER SIDE)

GIVE THIS *Good Deed Order Blank* TO A FRIEND

MAIL TO: LONE RANGER, BOX 1600, MINNEAPOLIS, MINNESOTA

Here's 25¢ and one Cheerios boxtop. Please send my Official Lone Ranger Flashlight Ring complete with 2 batteries and bulb. (DO NOT SEND STAMPS)
Offer expires June 1, 1949

[Print your name here]

[Print your street address here]

(TOWN)   (ZONE)   (STATE)

USE THIS BLANK TO ORDER
Extra Batteries

MAIL TO: LONE RANGER, BOX 1700, MINNEAPOLIS, MINNESOTA

Here's 10¢ and one Cheerios boxtop. Please send my 2 extra batteries. (DO NOT SEND STAMPS)
Offer expires June 1, 1949

[Print your name here]

[Print your street address here]

(TOWN)   (ZONE)   (STATE)

Lone Ranger Flashlight Paper
1947
Complete $50-$60

Real gold ore sealed under clear plastic top

Lone Ranger Gold Ore
1940s (rare)(Kellogg's, scarce)
Good - $1175
Fine - $2350
Near Mint - $5000

Lone Ranger Ice Cream
1938 (plastic)(Advertised in 1938 Lone
Ranger comic book)(rare)
(less than 10 known)(see Tonto)
Good - $1000
Fine - $2000
Near Mint - -$4000

Ad from back cover of 1938 Lone Ranger Ice Cream comic book

**Lone Ranger
Ice Cream paper**
1938 (Coupon(s) required when ordering
premiums)(ring)(also see Tonto Ice Cream ring)
(100 coupons complete with envelope)(Beware
of repros made of cardboard; original coupons
are paper)
Complete $300

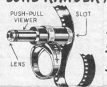

Lone Ranger Movie Film Ring Paper
1949
Complete $50-$75

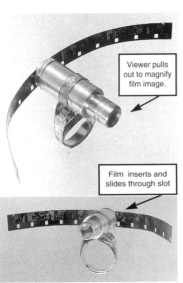

Viewer pulls out to magnify film image.

Film inserts and slides through slot

Lone Ranger Movie Film Ring
1949 (gold, silver color metal)
Complete w/film
$75-$175
Ring Only $50-$125
Film Only $25-$50

Has photo of the Lone Ranger in the roof of sec. compt. area	top fits over base

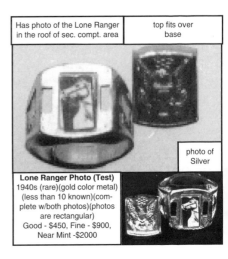

photo of Silver

Lone Ranger Photo (Test)
1940s (rare)(gold color metal) (less than 10 known)(complete w/both photos)(photos are rectangular)
Good - $450, Fine - $900, Near Mint -$2000

Lone Ranger Plastic
(see King Features)

Saddle slides back to reveal glow-in-dark base that will illuminate film for night viewing

contains diagonal mirror for seeing at a 45 degree angle

Lone Ranger National Defenders Look Around
1940s (same as Radio Orphan Annie)(metal, gold color)
$75-$150

Film slides through saddle

Lone Ranger Saddle w/film
1950 (gold color metal)
Complete w/film $100-$200
Ring Only $75 - $150
Film Only $25-$50

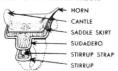

PARTS OF A WESTERN SADDLE

- HORN
- CANTLE
- SADDLE SKIRT
- SUDADERO
- STIRRUP STRAP
- STIRRUP

★ INSTRUCTIONS ★
HOW TO HAVE FUN WITH YOUR SADDLE RING

REMEMBER | **LIGHTS ON** ...to charge paper or erase pictures and signs.
| **LIGHTS OUT** ...to view pictures and make code signs glow.

To View Film Strip Pictures in the Dark...

1. Remove saddle by sliding backwards. The pale green area under saddle is specially prepared to glow in the dark after exposure to light. This material is harmless.

2. Hold the ring near a lightbulb (don't come too close as most lightbulbs become hot) or point it towards the sun. This charges the luminous paper.

3. Slide film strip into guide from the side of ring.

4. You can now observe the silhouette pictures in a dark room.

To Send Blinker Signals in a Dark Room...

1. Directly expose entire area of luminous paper to light, then completely darken room.

2. Repeatedly cover and uncover the charged luminous paper in darkness.

NOTE: For bright signals, re-charge luminous paper in film-guide after about four minutes.

To Carry Concealed Messages...

1. Write your secret message on a small piece of tissue paper.

2. Fold compactly so that it rests well within the emptied frame of the film-guide.

3. Slide saddle seat back over the film-guide which now serves as a cleverly concealed compartment.

FASCINATING EXPERIMENTS!

A. After sliding back saddle, insert film evenly into film-guide over luminous paper. Then hold loaded ring up to light, being careful not to move film. Next remove film from its position over luminous paper. Pictures will mysteriously glow in the darkness.

NOTE: Picture can be instantly erased by direct exposure to light.

B. See how many code signs of your own you can work out. Cut out a triangle, bull's-eye or some such sign from heavy black paper, clipped to fit the film-guide. Expose, then snap out lights, and see your own secret code sign glow through! For dark signs against glowing background heavily mark a piece of tissue paper, and use in same manner as film.

C. After exposing luminous paper in usual manner, allow it to glow in darkness through scene from film strip which you slide back and forth over glowing paper. Note quivering "television effect."

Tell your friends to get a Saddle Ring!
Order another for yourself!

USE THIS HANDY ORDER BLANK
Send with 20c in coin and boxtop from Cheerios to:
CHEERIOS, Box 200, Minneapolis, Minnesota

Name _____

Address _____

City or Town _____ State _____

OFFER GOOD ONLY WHILE SUPPLIES LAST
PLEASE PRINT CLEARLY

A-5991

Lone Ranger Saddle film paper
1950 (printed on thin unstable paper, scarce)
$125-$150

HERE'S WHAT YOU DO IN AN AIR RAID
1. KEEP COOL—Don't lose your head. Don't crowd the streets and create mob violence. If planes come over, stay where you are.
2. STAY HOME—The safest place in an air raid is at home. If you are away from home, get under cover in the nearest shelter. Avoid crowded places—stay off the streets.
3. PUT OUT THE LIGHTS—If planes come over, put out or cover all lights at once—don't wait for the blackout order.
4. LIE DOWN—If bombs start to fall near you, lie down. You will feel the blast least that way. The safest place is under a stout table.
5. STAY AWAY FROM WINDOWS—Glass shatters easily. Besides anti-air craft fire means shrapnel—and you are safest away from windows.
6. YOU CAN HELP—Strong, capable, calm people are needed. If you want to help, volunteer at the Civilian Defense Office in your community.

DO YOU KNOW THE PLEDGE OF ALLE-GIANCE? STUDY IT! LEARN IT BY HEART!
Here is the official Ritual when reciting the Pledge: Stand at attention. When you say, "to the Flag," extend your right hand, palm upward, toward the Flag. After the words, "justice for all," have been spoken, let your hand fall to your side and pause for one second.

★ ★ ★

"I pledge Allegiance to the Flag of the United States of America and to the Republic for which it stands, one nation indivisible, with liberty and justice for all."

≡ ★ ≡ ★ ≡ ★ ≡
AMERICA NEEDS YOU!
Yes, America needs you . . . the help of every boy and girl . . . in our mighty effort of defense.
You are the new "Minute Men" of Liberty. Soon you will inherit . . . as full grown men and women . . . this great land and the full Liberty for which it stands.
Learn how you can help defend your Heritage.
There are many things you can do. Co-operate with Civilian Defense agencies by spreading blackout news, and other necessary information. Or you can write to the boys in the Service. Send papers and magazines to Military Camps. Urge your parents to buy Defense stamps.

America Needs You in Her Defense!

GETTING THE MOST FUN OUT OF YOUR...

"SECRET COMPARTMENT" RING

HOW YOUR RING WORKS
The sliding top of the ring moves to the side . . . revealing the picture hidden inside.
Substitute your own pictures. Your friends in Military Service—movie stars—baseball heroes—secret messages and codes—passwords—or patriotic slogans.
TO INSERT PHOTOS: First slide off the insignia top. Now turn the top over . . . and either remove the picture already in the top inside or slide the place your own picture (cut to size) over the picture now inside.
To replace pictures in the ring part push downward the frame holding the picture now inside.
The Men in Military Service take pride in caring for . . . in keeping bright and un-spotted their brass buttons and other "insignia." You should be proud to keep your "Secret Compartment" Ring shining.
WARNING: DO NOT WASH YOUR RING WITH WATER OR SOAP . . . AS IT WILL SPOIL YOUR PICTURES.

"BUT . . . I WAS UNABLE TO LIFT THE OTHER FOOT!"
That's what tiny Vita Roth recalled of her first parachute jump. Since then she has made 263 jumps . . . holds the altitude record of 19,600 feet for one jump!
Today . . . Mrs. Roth is organizing the Women Flyers of America . . . to serve Our Country in defense work. Truly, she is one of those people who do things!
This brave woman says: "It's a thrill to make a parachute jump. But it was a thrill, too, to have discovered KIX!"

[KIX box image]

Follow this excellent suggestion of people who do things. Fellas and girls, America needs healthy bodies and active minds. So you want to be sure to eat foods with plenty of real nourishment. No ready-to-eat cereal we know of can top KIX in this respect.
"KIX" is copyrighted by General Mills, Inc.

★
LET YOUR PALS IN ON IT!
Everyone of your pals . . . every member of your club . . . should wear a "Secret Compartment" Ring . . . to show loyalty to our Country. Tell them how to get theirs!
And did you ever think that your friends or relatives in the Army, Navy, Marines or Air Corps might like to have just such a ring? He can put pictures of those at home in . . . and have them "near" him always. Why not send him one of these rings! / Remember: They fit any size finger. Truly, they make "perfect" gifts. Use the handy order blank on the next page — for more "Secret Compartment" Rings!

HERE'S ALL YOU HAVE TO DO TO GET MORE "SECRET COMPARTMENT" RINGS
Order as many rings as you like . . . but be sure you enclose 10c (in coin) and one KIX box top for each one you want. Send to KIX, Minneapolis, Minnesota, and the ring (or rings) will be sent to you immediately!

KIX, Minneapolis, Minn.
Please send me .... "Secret Compartment" Rings at once!
(Put "X" mark after Military design, or designs, you desire)
Army? .... Marines? ....
Navy? .... Air Corps? ....
NAME: ....
ADDRESS: ....
CITY: .... STATE: ......

*Long Ranger Secret Compartment-paper
1940s (both sides shown)
$125-$150

*Lone Ranger Secret Compartment-Marines
1940s (metal)(scarce)
with photos(2)
GD $400, FN $625, NM $850

Lone Ranger Sec. Compt.
(All above rings were issued later without the photos) Value would be 60% less)

*Lone Ranger Secret Compartment rings—Includes photos of Silver & Lone Ranger. Beware of repro photos.

*Lone Ranger Secret Compartment-ad
1940s (both sides shown)

Lone Ranger Seal Print Face
1940s (metal)
$150-$300

contains flint that emits sparks when spinned

*Lone Ranger Secret Compt.-Army Air Corps.
1942 (metal)(scarce)
(with a Lone Ranger photo & a Silver photo)
GD $375, FN $590, NM $800

*Lone Ranger Secret Compartment-Army
1940s (metal)(scarce)
with photos (2)
GD $400, FN $625, NM $850

Enlargment of Silver's photo that appears under top of all military rings

*Lone Ranger Secret Compartment-Navy,
1940s (metal)(scarce)
with photos (2)
GD $500
FN $750
NM $1000

Lone Ranger Six Shooter
1947 (metal)(silver color handles)
$60-$125

Looney Tunes
1995 (Bugs Bunny)
(on card)(color)
(Warner catalog)
On Card $5

WARNING!

ALWAYS TAKE THIS RING OFF YOUR FINGER BEFORE WASHING YOUR HANDS! The reason for this is because the special indicator material in the ring is very sensitive! But . . . if you do get it wet, replace the indicator material in the ring with some of the extra material which we enclose in this package.

To replace the indicator material in your Weather Ring, simply use the point of a pin to pull out the old indicator . . . being careful not to raise the plastic setting. Then trim a piece of the extra indicator material to proper size and carefully slide it into position.

REMEMBER : . .

Don't expect this ring to change with the weather while you are inside the house! For most satisfactory results, always notice the color of the ring after you have been outside for thirty minutes. When your ring turns from blue to pink that is an indication that it may rain or snow. When it turns from pink to blue that is an indication that it may clear.

Lone Ranger Weather envelope/paper
1947
$75-$85

Clear plastic top

Lone Ranger Weather
1947 (metal)(paper changes color)(also see Howie Wing and Peter Paul Weather)
$60-$125

Lone Wolf
(see Thunderbird)

Lone Wolf Tribal
1932 Wrigley (sterling silver)(radio) (the first radio premium ring)
$100-$200

Looney Tunes
1995 (Sylvester)
(on card)(color)
(Warner catalog)
On Card $5

Looney Tunes
1995 (Tweety)(on card)
(color)(Warner catalog)
On Card $5

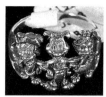

Looney Tunes
1995 (Animaniacs)(metal)
(Warner catalog)
$24

Looney Tunes
1995 (silver)(Warner)
$24

**Looney Tunes Flicker
Daffy Duck**
jumping and flapping
his wings

**Looney Tunes Flicker
Elmer Fudd**
firing his rifle

Looney Tunes - Tweety
1992 (on card)(color)
On Card $15
Ring Only $5-$10

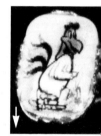

**Looney Tunes Flicker
Boxing Kangaroo**

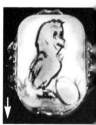

**Looney Tunes Flicker
Foghorn Leghorn**
walking

**Looney Tunes Flicker
Bugs Bunny**
eating a carrot

**Looney Tunes Flicker
Henry the Chicken Hawk**
kicking an egg

Looney Tunes Flicker
PePe LePew
pinching his nose

Looney Tunes Flicker
Sneezy Mouse
turning his head raising his
hand to his ear

Looney Tunes Flicker
Wile E. Coyote
howling

Looney Tunes Flicker
Foghorn (modern)

Looney Tunes Flicker
Porky Pig
tipping his hat

Looney Tunes Flicker
Speedy Gonzales
arms outstretched, then
points to himself, then he's
gone. Only his hat remains.

Looney Tunes Flicker
Yosemite Sam
shooting his guns

Looney Tunes Flicker
Henry Hawk (modern)

Looney Tunes Flicker
1970s (set of 16)(plastic)
(Original flickers on original
bases)
$8-$15 ea.

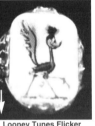

Looney Tunes Flicker
Road Runner
running

Looney Tunes Flicker
Sylvester
tip-toeing

Looney Tunes Flicker
Porky Pig (modern)

Looney Tunes Flicker
1990s (modern "v " base)
$2-$5 ea.

Los Angeles Olympics
(see Olympic Sam the
Eagle)

Looney Tunes Flicker
Elmer Fudd (modern)

L.A. Dodgers
(see Baseball)

Looney Tunes Flicker
Sam the Sheepdog
dancing around

Looney Tunes Flicker
Tweety Bird
looking side to side

Love
1960s (metal)(oval, gold color)
$2-$5

Lucky Charms Horseshoe
1985 (boys)
(warehouse find?)
$10-$20

Mac (see Post Tin)

Mack
1940s (bronze metal)
(Mack Truck)
$40-$75

Macy's Santa Flicker
1960s (plastic)(Santa Claus to "Macy's Santa Knows")
$15-$25

Maggie (see Post Tin)

Love
1960s (plastic, round)(gumball)
$2-$4

Lucky Charms Horseshoe
1985 (girls)
(warehouse find?)
$15-$30

Magic Glow
1995 (store)(glows in dark)
In pkg. $3

Love Is
1980s (metal cloisonne')(L.A. Times)
$6-$12

Lucky Horse Shoe
1940s(scarce)(large)
(plastic)(circus)(see Giant)
$20-$40

Lucky Skull
(see Montrose)

Magic Mountain
1970s (metal cloisonne')
$10-$20

Magic Pup (see Pet Parade)

Magic Ring
1995 (knife thru finger)(plastic/metal)
(gumball)
$1

Lucky Buddha
1940s (metal)
$25-$50

Lucy
1980s (from Snoopy)
(metal cloisonne')
$20-$35

Magnum P.I.
1981 (plastic)(came on card
with sun glasses,
wallet or pistols)
Card with Ring $35
Ring Only $15-$25

Majestic Radio
1930s (Bakelite plastic)(made in regular
jewelers ring sizes including adult)
$75-$150
Note: "Majestic" was the trade name of the
Grisgsby-Grunow Co. from the late 1920s
until the company failed in 1934. The
Majestic Radio and Television Corp. carried
on the Majestic name beginning in 1937
with many advertising devices including this
ring and the 1938 vintage Charlie McCarthy
novelty radio show to try and regain the
share of the market it once held.

Major Mars Rocket
ad from Action Comics #170, 1952

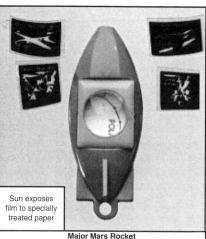

Sun exposes
film to specially
treated paper

Major Mars Rocket
1952 (w/ 4 negatives & 12 printing papers)
(Popsicle premium)(sun exposes film to paper)(also see
Captain Video Pendant)
Complete $1200

Mandrake Face
(see King Features)

**Man From U.N.C.L.E.
Flicker (1)**
1960s "U.N.C.L.E." logo to
waist up picture of solo
blowing smoke off gun
(black & white)
$50-$75

**Man From U.N.C.L.E.
Flicker (2)**
1960s "U.N.C.L.E." smaller
logo with picture of three
men to full figure being
shot through glass
(black & white)
$50-$75

THE MAN FROM U.N.C.L.E.

Man From U.N.C.L.E. Card
1960s (with flicker rings)
Complete $300

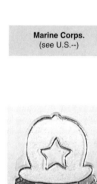

Marilyn Monroe
1950s (Possible gas
station premium?)
$30-$50

Marine Corps.
(see U.S.--)

Martian Finks (1)
1950s (plastic)(diff. colors)
$5-$10 each

Martian Finks (2)
1950s (plastic)(diff. colors)
$5-$10 each

Mario
1970s (based on game
Super Mario Brothers)
$5-$10

**Man From U.N.C.L.E.
Flicker (3)**
1960s (Face of Solo to
face of Ilya)
Silver version $10-$20
Blue version $8-$15

**Man From U.N.C.L.E.
Flicker (4)**
1960s (Face of Solo
to face of Ilya)
(square version)
$10-$20

Mario Disc
1980s (plastic, paper, color)
$2-$4

Martian Finks (3)
1950s (plastic)(diff. colors)
$5-$10 each

**Martin Luther King, Jr.
Flicker (2)**
"I Have Climbed The
Mountain" to Face (profile)

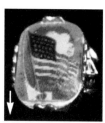

**Martin Luther King, Jr.
Flicker (4a)**
Picture of American Flag to
Face (front view)

Martian Finks
1950s (on card)(4 rings)
Card set Complete $50

**Martin Luther King, Jr.
Flicker (3a)**
"Free at Last" to Face (front
view)

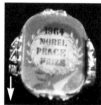

**Martin Luther King, Jr.
Flicker (5a)**
"1964 Nobel Peace Prize" to
Face (profile)

**Martin Luther King, Jr.
Flicker (1)**
"Martin Luther King"
1918-1968
to Face (front view)

Martian Finks (4)
1950s (plastic)(diff. colors)
$5-$10 each

Martin Luther King, Jr.
1964 (flicker picture rings on card)
Complete w/rings $125

Martin Luther King, Jr. Flicker (6a)
"I Have A Dream" to Face
(front view)

Martin Luther King, Jr. Flicker
1964 (set of 6)(plastic)
(silver base)
$15-$25 ea.

Marvel (see Amazing--)

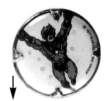

Marvel Disc Captain Marvel

Marvel Disc Dr. Strange

Marvel Disc Ghost Rider

Marvel Disc Hulk

Marvel Flicker (1) Marverl Super Heros
"Marvel Super Heroes Ring Club" to 4 faces-Spiderman Capt. America, Thor, Thing

Marvel Flicker Ring Card
1966 (Jack Kirby art)
Card Only $40-$75
With (3) Rings $150

Marvel Disc Spider-Man

Marvel Disc Spider Woman
Marvel Disc
1977 (set of 6: Captain Marvel, Dr. Strange, Ghost Rider, Hulk, Spider-Man, Spider Woman)
(gumball)(metal)
$2 each

Marvel Flicker (2) Captain America
"Captain America" face to "WUM" Captain America punching enemy

Marvel Flicker (3) Dr. Strange Flicker
Dr. Strange face to full figure Dr. Strange w/arms outstretched

Marvel Flicker
1966 (plastic silver base)
(Marvel Entertainment
Group)
$10-$20 ea.

Marvel Flicker (10)
Sub-Mariner
"Sub-Mariner" full figure to
"Kop" full figure left handed
punch

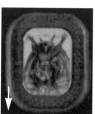

Marvel Flicker (3)
Dr. Strange

Marvel Flicker (7)
Iron Man
"Iron Man" face to "Conk"
Iron Man punching enemy

Marvel Flicker (11)
Thing
"Thing" face to full figure
Thing w/arms in the air

Marvel Flicker (4)
Fantastic Four

Marvel Flicker (4)
Fantastic Four
"Fantastic" faces to "Four"
2 faces

Marvel Flicker (5)
Hulk
"Hulk" face to "PAM" Hulk
fist slamming a wall

Marvel Flicker (8)
Spider-Man
"Spider-Man" face to full
figure running

Marvel Flicker (6)
Human Torch

Marvel Flicker (6)
Human Torch
"Human Torch" face to "Dr.
Doom" face

Marvel Flicker (9)
Spider-Man
"Spider-Man" full figure on a
web to "Pow" throwing a
punch

Marvel Flicker (12)
Thor
"Thor" face to full figure
Thor swinging hammer

Marvel Flicker (7)
Iron Man

Marvel Flicker (8)
Spiderman

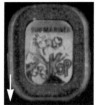

Marvel Flicker (10)
Sub-Mariner

Marvel Flicker (9)
Spider-Man

Marvel Flicker (11)
Thing

Marvel Super-Hero Rings
1980s (on Card)(3 card sets with 2 rings per card)
Complete $75

Marvel Super-Hero Rings
1980s (3 card sets with 2 rings per card)
Complete $75

Marvel Super-Hero Rings
1980s (on card)(3 card sets with 2 rings
per card)
Complete $75

Marvel Flicker (12)
Thor

Marvel Flicker
1970s (set of 12)(blue base)
(two diff. blue base versions
shown)(Marvel Ent. Group)
$10-$15 ea.

Mask Flicker (3)
(red plastic base, blue
flicker)

Mask Flicker (4)
(yellow plastic base, blue
flicker)

Marvel (Captain Marvel)
1970s (plastic, round)
$1-$2

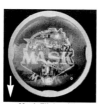

Mask Flicker (5)

Mask Flicker
1985 (set of 5)(plastic)
(TV ring giveaway
with card)
$20 ea.

Mask Flicker (1)
(yellow plastic base, blue
flicker)

Mask Flicker (2)
(yellow plastic base, blue
flicker)

Mask Movie Ring
1994 (w/card)
$20

Mask Movie
1994 (plastic, color)(on card)
On Card $50
Ring Only $25

McDonald's Character
Big Mac
1970s (plastic)
$5-$10

McDonald's Character
Ham Burgler

McDonald's Character
Grimace

McDonald's Character
McBird

McDonald's Character McHook

McDonald's 500 Smile Race Car
1985 (top & bottom shown)(plastic)
$7-$15

McDonald's Flicker (4)
Ronald juggling balls to same face moving side to side

McDonald's Flicker
1970s (original silver base)
$12-$25 ea.

McDonald's Flicker (4)

McDonald's Flicker
1970s (set of 4)(blue base)
$8-$15 ea.

McDonald's Character Ronald McDonald

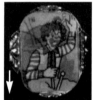

McDonald's Flicker (1)
Ronald waving to Ronald on flying hamburger

McDonald's Flicker (1)

McDonald's Friendship Space Shuttle
1985 (plastic)
$7-$15

McDonald's Character Hamburglar
1970s (plastic)(black on yellow)

McDonald's Character
1970s (plastic)
$5-$10 ea.

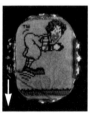

McDonald's Flicker (2)
Ronald on diving board to Ronald splashing as he dives into pool

McDonald's Flicker (2)

McDonald's McFries
1970s (metal)(enameled)
$15-$30

McDonald's 500 Smile Race Car

McDonald's Flicker (3)
Ronald standing with jump rope to Ronald jumping rope

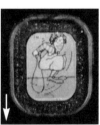

McDonald's Flicker (3)

McDonald's McFries
1975 (metal, enameled)(red & yellow versions)
$15-$30 ea.

McDonald's Easter Bunny
1970s (plastic)(blue, green, pink & yellow known)
$5-$10

McDonald's Halloween Flicker (side 2)

McDonald's Halloween Flicker
1970s (plastic)("McDonald's Halloween to McBoo)
$8-$15 ea.

McDonald's McKids From Sears
1970s (plastic)(red on yellow)
$15-$30

McDonald's Grimace with Hat
1970s (plastic)
$5-$10

McDonald's Halloween Pumpkin
1994 (red plastic)
$2-$4

McDonald's Polly Pocket
1994 (plastic in bag)
$4

McDonald's Grimace
1970s-80s? (metal) (enameled)
$15-$30

McDonald's Horn
1980s (plastic)
$30-$60

McDonald's QSC Employees
1980s (Balfour stainless steel)
$100

McDonald's Halloween Flicker (side 1)

McDonald's Ronald McDonald Disc
1970s (plastic)
$10-$20

**McDonald's Ronald
McDonald Face**
1970s (metal, enameled)
$15-$30

McDonald's Valentine
1970s (plastic)(red & white)
$10-$20

**Melvin Purvis
Secret Operator**
1936 (Post)(metal)
$75-$175

Painted green top

24K gold fin-
ished base

**McDonald's Ronald
McDonald Figural**
1970s (plastic)
$20-$30

Melvin Purvis Birthstone
1930s (metal)
$75-$150

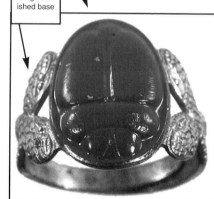

**McDonald's Ronald
Glow Disc**
1980s (plastic)
$5-$10

**Melvin Purvis Junior
G-Man Corps**
1937 (metal)(Post)
$25-$75

**Melvin Purvis
Secret Scarab**
1937 (Post-O)(same as Capt. Hawks
Secret Scarab) (rare)(24K gold finish)
Good $250
Fine $500
Near Mint $1200

**McDonald's Ronald
McDonald 3D face**
1970s (plastic)(yellow)
$20-$30

**Melvin Purvis Secret Scarab
Newspaper ad for ring**

Michael Jackson
1980s (metal, color)
$2-$4

Mickey Birthstone
1980s (in box)(metal cloisonne')
In Box $20
Ring Only $15

Mickey Mouse (see Disney)

Michael Jackson
1980s (metal, B&W photo)
$2-$4

Mickey Mouse Club
1950s (red/white/black
enamel)(metal)
$30-$60

Michael Jackson
1980s (metal on silver card)(photo)
On Card $10
Ring Only $4-$8

Mickey Mouse Club
1960s (plastic)
(Sugar Jets?)
$35-$70

Mickey Mouse Club
1980 (Nestles)(metal)
$40-$80

Mickey Mouse Club
1980 (Nestles)(metal)
$40-$80

Mickey Mouse Club
1980 (metal)
$40-$80

Mickey Mouse Club
1980s (round)(metal)
$10-$25

Mickey Mouse Club
1980s (round)(metal)
$10-$25

Mickey Mouse Club Flicker
1960s, "Mickey Mouse Club" to Mickey's face with "member" underneath (chocolate chip cookie premium)
$20-$40

Mickey Mouse Face
1947 (sterling silver)(store item)
$30-$60

Mickey Mouse Face
1970s (plastic)
$2-$5

Mickey Mouse Face
1980s (silver)
$20-$40

Mickey Mouse Face
1950s (plastic)(oval, paper)
$10-$20

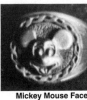

Mickey Mouse Face
1970s (pewter)
In Box $30

Mickey Mouse Face
1980s (gold plated)(in box)
$30-$60

Mickey Mouse Club Puzzle Dome
1950s (plastic)
$25-$50

Mickey Mouse Face
1970s (gold)(cloisonne')
$5-$10

Mickey Mouse Face with Name
1970s (metal, color)
$15

Mickey Mouse Face
1990s (metal, silver)
$5-$10

Mickey Mouse Face
1980s (in box)
In Box $15
Ring Only $4-$8

Mickey Mouse Face
1980s (color)(metal, cloisonne')
$5-$10

Mickey Mouse Face Ornament
1990s (gold)
$5-$10

Mickey Mouse Face
1995 (sterling)
$13

Mickey Mouse Face
1990s (metal/onyx)(10K
gold)(2 views)
$20-$40

Mickey Mouse Face
1990s (metal)(sun-
glasses)(cloisonne')
$4-$8

Mickey Mouse Face
1990s (metal)(dangle, gold)
$4-$8

Mickey Mouse Face
1995 (sterling)
$13

Mickey Mouse Face "M"
1990s (metal)(cloisonne')
$4-$8

Mickey Mouse Face
1990s (metal/onyx)
(10K gold)
$20-$40

**Mickey Mouse
Face Ornament**
1990s (metal)
$5-$10

Mickey Mouse Face
1995 (10k gold)
$70

Mickey Mouse Face
1990s (metal)(cowboy
hat)(cloisonne')
$4-$8

**Mickey Mouse Face-
Jeweled**
1990s (metal)
$20-$40

Mickey Mouse Face
1990s (metal)(cloisonne')
$4-$8

Mickey Mouse Face
1995 (10k gold)
$50

Mickey Mouse Face
1990s (metal)(cloisonne')
$4-$8

Mickey Mouse 3D Face
1990s (metal)(cut-out, silver
& gold versions)
$5-$10

**Mickey Mouse Face
Wrap-Around**
1990s (metal)(cloisonne')
$4-$8

Mickey Mouse Face
1990s (metal)
(cut-out)(silver)
$4-$8

**Mickey Mouse
15th Anniversary**
1980s (Disney
World)(metal)
In Box $150

205

Mickey Mouse Figure
1931-1934 (etched metal)
(1st Mickey ring)(Cohn & Rosenberger, Inc.)
GD $250
FN 375
NM $500

Mickey Mouse Figure
1980s
$10-$20

Mickey Figure
1994
$2-$4

Mickey Mouse Figure
1980s (gold color metal)
$5-$10

**Mickey Mouse
Figure, Baby**
1984 (metal cloisonne)
$10-$20

Mickey Mouse Figure
1935 (Brier Mfg.)(metal cloisonne' in
color)(2nd Mickey ring)(brass)(some came
w/Ingersol watch)
$200-$400

Mickey Mouse Figure
1980s (metal cloisonne')
$5-$10

**Mickey Mouse Figure,
Cowboy**
1970s (metal cloisonne')
$30-$60

Mickey Mouse Figure
1937 (Brier Mfg.)(metal cloisonne' in
color)(3rd Mickey ring)
$150-$300

Mickey Mouse Figure
1990 (w/stone)(small)
$5-$10

**Mickey Mouse
Figure, Santa**
1970s (metal, painted)
$20-$40

Mickey Figure
1960s (metal)(cloisonne')
$15-$30

**Mickey Mouse
Figure (small)**
1970s (metal, cloisonne')
$10-$20

Mickey Mouse Figure
1990s (w/stone)
(2 variations)(metal)
$5-$10 ea.

Mickey Mouse Figure, Small Black
1980s (metal)
(silver & gold versions)
$7-$15

Mickey Mouse Figure 3D
1970s (large)
(metal in color)
$20-$40

Mickey Mouse Happy Birthday
1980s (in box)(metal cloisonne')
In Box $20
Ring Only $5-$10

Mickey Mouse Figure 3D Mounted,
1950s (plastic)
$25-$50

Mickey Mouse Glass Dome
(brass)(gold color)
(red, black, yellow)
(Cleinman & Sons)
GD $250
FN $375
NM $500

Mickey Mouse Figure 3D
1960s (pewter)(metal)
$25-$50

Mickey Mouse Figure 3D
1960s (pewter)(metal)
$25-$50

Mickey Mouse Head Jewelry
1994 (in box)
In Box $40

Mickey Mouse Figure 3D
1960s (small)(metal in color)
$25-$50

Mickey Mouse Glow
1950s (square top)
(glow-in-dark)(silver)
$50-$100

Mickey Mouse Locket
1970s (metal, in color)(3)
$15-$30 ea.

Mickey/Minnie Heart
1970s (metal, painted)
$15-$30

Mickey/Minnie Heart
1992 (metal cloisonne')
$5-$10

Mickey/Minnie Heart
1970s (metal, painted)
$15-$30

Mickey Mouse Novelties
1970s (includes 8 rings)
Complete Set $75

**Mickey Mouse
Multiple Head**
1994
$4

Mickey Mouse Pearl Insert
1990s (metal)
$40-$75

Mickey Mouse Ring/Bracelet
1980s (in box)
Complete $50

Mickey/Minnie Love
1995 (10k gold)
$50

Mickey/Minnie Two Pieces
1970s (metal)(gold dangle)
$4-$8

Mickey Mouse Stuff
1994 (Mickey & Minnie on card)
Complete $10
Ring Only $2-$4 ea.

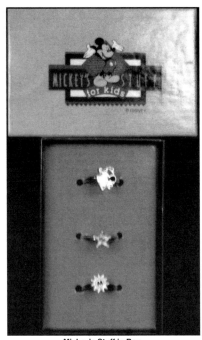

Mickey's Stuff in Box
1994 (metal)(3 diff. cloisonne')
Complete $15
Ring Only $2-$4 ea.

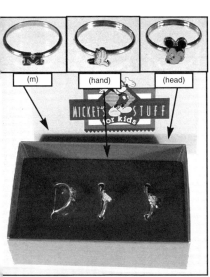

(m)   (hand)   (head)

Mickey Mouse Stuff
1994 (Box w/3 rings)
Complete $15
Ring Only $2-$4 ea.

**Mickey Mouse
Watch Ring**
1990s
In Box $100

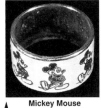

**Mickey Mouse
Wedding Band**
1970s (metal cloisonne)
(2 versions)
$10-$20 ea.

**Mickey Mouse
Wrap Figure**
1970s (metal)
$40-$80

Mighty Hercules Magic Ring
1960s (on card)(T.V.)(scarce)
Complete $300
Ring Only $100-$175

Mighty Morphin Power Rangers
1993 (5 rings on card)(plastic)
Complete $3

Mighty Morphin Power Rangers Disc
1990s (plastic)(color)
$1-$2

Mighty Mouse Disc
1977 (metal)(in color)
$2-$4

Mighty Mouse Disc
1977 (metal)(in color)
$2-$4

Mighty Mouse Disc
1977 (metal)(in color)
$2-$4

Milton Berle Photo
(see Real Photos)

Minnie Mouse
(see Disney)

Minnie Mouse Face
1980s (silver)(metal)
$5-$10

Minnie Mouse Face
1980s (gold)(metal)
$5-$10

Minnie Mouse Face
1970s (plastic)
$2-$5

Minnie Mouse Face
1980s (gold & silver
versions)(metal)
$5-$10

Minnie Mouse Face
1990s (metal)
(dangle, gold)
$4-$8

Minnie Face Ribbon
1990s (metal)
(cloisonne')
$4-$8

Minnie Mouse Figure
1980s (oval)(metal)
$10-$20

Minnie Mouse Red Face
1980s (metal cloisonne')
$10-$20

Minnie Mouse Face
1990s (metal)(cut-out,
small)(gold & silver ver-
sions)
$4-$8 each

Minnie Mouse Figure
1960s (metal)(store
item)(yellow & pink skirt
versions)
$25-$50

Minnie Mouse Figure
1990s (metal)
$5-$10

Minnie Mouse Face
1980s (metal)
$10-$20

Minnie Face Dome
1990s (metal/plastic)
(oval, color)
$5-$10

Minnie Mouse Figure
1960s (pewter)
$25-$50

**Minnie Mouse
Figure Cameo**
1980s (metal, in color)
$20-$40

**Minnie Mouse Face
with Stone**
1990s (metal)(gold)
$5-$10

Minnie Face "M"
1990s (metal)(cloisonne')
$4-$8

Minnie Mouse Figure
1970s (metal cloisonne')
$10-$20

**Minnie Mouse
Figure, Tennis**
1960s (metal)(cloisonne')
$15-$30

Minnie Figure Framed
1994 (metal, color)(in box)
In Box $15
Ring Only $5-$10

Minnie Watch Ring
1990 (with interchangeable bands)
Set $100

Minnie Mouse Locket
1970s (metal)(color)
$20-$40

Mirror
1980s (plastic)
.50-$1

Minnie Mouse Locket
1970s (metal in color)
(3 diff.)
$20-$40

Miss Dairylea
1960s (plastic)
$20-$40

Minnie Mouse Stamp
1992 (came in box as
shown)(5 diff.)
In Box $10 ea.

Minnie Mouse Locket
1970s (metal)(color)
$20-$40

Mr. Magoo
1975 (metal,
cloisonne')(U.P.A.)
$8-$15

Mr. Peanut
1950s (silver & gold,
color, metal)
$15-$30

Mister Softee Flicker
1960s "I Like Mister Softee"
to picture of Mr. Softee
(silver base)
$50-$100

Mr. Magoo set
1960s (3 rings, Mr. Magoo, Charlie & Waldo)
(5 diff. colors)
Set in Bag $25
Ring Only $4-$8 ea.

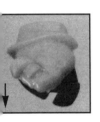

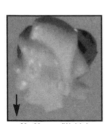

Mr. Magoo (Charlie)

Mr. Magoo (himself)
(2 diff.)

Mister Softee
1950s (plastic)
$10-$20

Mister Steak
1960s (plastic)(red on
yellow base)
$15-$30

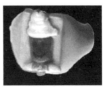

Mr. Magoo (Waldo)

Mr. Magoo
1960s (plastic)
$4-$8 ea.

Mister Softee
1970s (plastic)
(pink base)
$20-$40

Model Airplane club
1940s
$50-$100

Mr. T. Jewelry set
1983 (in package)
Complete $50

Monkey Flicker
1950s (Thick top)
$10-$20

Monkees Flicker (3a)
(side 1) "Mike" face to full
figure playing guitar

Monkees Flicker (1a)
(side 1) "Davy" face

Monkees Flicker (3b)
(side 2) "Mike" Face
to full figure playing guitar

Monkees Action Flicker Rings
1966 (on card)
On Card $150

Monkees Flicker (1b)
(side 2) "Davy" Face to full
Figure playing guitar

Monkees Flicker (4)
"Peter" Face
to full figure playing base

Monkees Flicker (2)
"Micky" Face
to full figure playing drums

Monkees Flicker (5a)
Four heads with heart
in the middle

Monkees Flicker (5b)
"I Love Monkees" Logo
o four heads w/heart in
middle

Monkees Flicker (8)
"I love Peter Micky" two
faces smilling to The
Monkees Davy Mike two
faces

Monkees Flicker (11)
Old fashioned camera
w/two guys holding flash to
two figures one standing,
one sitting

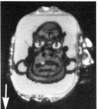

Monster Cartoon Flicker
Fat green one-tooth goon
with earrings to skinny
white guy with forehead
scar.

Monkees Flicker (6)
"I Love Monkees" Logo
/hearts to four figures in
water on surfboard

Monkees Flicker (9)
Davy & Micky playing guitar
& drums on unicycles to
Peter playing base on pogo
stick & Mike playing guitar
on skate board

Monkees Flicker (12)
"Official member Monkees
ring club" to four faces in a
red heart

Monkees Flicker
1966 (12 different)
All rings distributed in cereal
boxes sealed in paper
$30-$60 ea.

Monster Cartoon Flicker
White face phantom to red
face Frankenstein looking
character.

Monster (cartoon) Flicker
1960s (set of 3)(plastic)
Silver base $20-$40 ea.
Blue base $15-$30 ea.

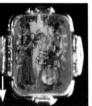

Monkees Flicker (7)
'eter" & "Micky" full figures
playing bass & drums to
Davy" & "Mike" full figures
playing guitars

Monkees Flicker (10)
"Monkees" logo to 4 figures
in Monkee Mobile

Monster Cartoon Flicker
Green face Frankenstein to
red face devil with pointed
teeth and big ears.

Top opens up to reveal
secret compartment

**Monster Cereal Secret
Compartment-Boo Berry**

Monster Cereal Secret Compartment-Count Chocula

Monster Card
1990s (plastic)(Dracula, Frankenstein, Mummy, Wolfman rings)
On Card $2

Monster Cereal Flick Count Chocula/ Frankenberry

Monster Cereal Secret Compartment-Frankenberry

Monster Cereal Flicker-Count Chocula

Monster Cereal Flicker-Count Chocula/ Frankenberry

Monster Cereal Flick Frankenberry

Monster Cereal Flick
1971-75 (plastic)(6 in s
(each ring came in blu
orange & yellow)
$50-$100 ea.

Monster Cereal Secret Compartment-Fruit Brute

Monster Cereal Secret Compartment
1976 (plastic)(4 in set)
(each ring came in blue, orange, pink & brown)
(Hasbro Toys)
(cereal premium)
$125-$250 ea.

Monster Cereal Flicker-Count Chocula

Monster Cereal Flicker-Frankenberry

Monster Flicker
1960s (silver base)(5
set)(ad run in Famou
Monsters mag.)
$15-$30 ea.

Monster Gumball (5)
1960s (plastic)(5 diff.)
$10-$20 each

Mork & Mindy Flicker (2)
1979 "Mork NA-NO, NA-NO
to "Hello Mindy"
$20-$40

Monster Fink Rings on Card
1960s (plastic)(frankenstein & Wolfman
Complete $25
Ring Only $2-$5 ea.

Mork & Mindy Flicker (1b)
1979 "Shazbot" to "Mork
Calling Orson"
$20-$40

Mork & Mindy Flicker (3)
1979 "Mork from Ork" to
"Mindy's Friend"
$20-$40

Monster Gumball (3)

Monster Gumball (1)

Monster Gumball (4)

Monster Gumball (2)

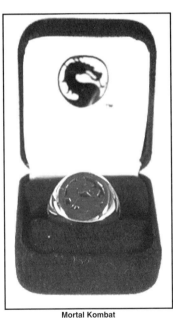

Mortal Kombat
1995 (bronze and gold versions)(in case)
Gold in Case $400
Bronze in Case $30

Mortal Kombat
1995 (sterling)(in case)
In Case $50

**Movie Star Photo
Allyson, June**
1940s
$15-$25

**Movie Star Photo
Fleming, Rhonda**
1940s
$15-$25

**Movie Star Photo
Bankhead, T.**
1940s
$15-$25

**Movie Star Photo
Flynn, Errol**
1940s
$15-$25

**Monte Cruz
Las Palmas Cigars**
1980s (Sterling silver w/red
film plastic enamel on
face)(Dunhill Co.)
$2-$5

Mouse Face
1970s (plastic)(Canada,
gumball)
$5-$10

**Movie Star Photo
Blythe, Ann**
1940s
$15-$25

**Movie Star Photo
Gable, Clark**
1940s
$20-$30

Montrose Lucky Skull
(see Skull)

**Movie Star Photo
Allyson, June**
1940s
$15-$25

**Movie Star Photo
Cooper, Gary**
1940s
$15-$25

**Movie Star Photo
Garson, Greer**
1940s
$15-$25

**Movie Star Photo
Granger, Farley**
1940s
$15-$25

**Movie Star Photo
Kelly, Gene**
1940s
$15-$25

**Movie Star Photo
Mature, Victor**
1940s
$15-$25

**Movie Star Photo
Peck, Gregory**
1940s
$15-$25

**Movie Star Photo
Grant, Cary**
1940s
$15-$25

Movie Star Photo
1940s (box closed w/ rings)

**Movie Star Photo
Hayward, Suzan**
1940s
$15-$25

**Movie Star Photo
Kelly, Gene**
1940s
$15-$25

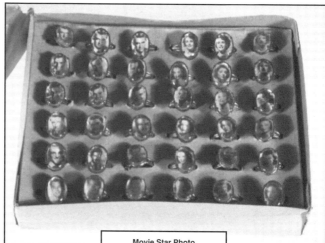

Movie Star Photo
1940s (box opened w/ 36 rings)

Movie Star Photo
Taylor, Elizabeth
1940s
25-$50

Movie Star Photo
Wayne, John
1940s
$25-$50

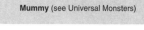

Movie Star Photo
(Starlett)
1940s
$15-$25

Movie Star Photo-other
Gibb, Andy
1980s
$5-$10

Top removes to expose ring seated inside the pyramid

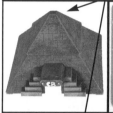

Movie Star Photo
(Starlett)
1940s
$15-$25

Ms Pac Man
1980s (metal)(color)
$15-$30

Mummy's
1995 (Gold ring encased in pyramid that opens at
top)(based on a design by Carl Barks)
(prototype, not sold)

Movie Star Photo
Curtis, Tony?
1940s
$15-$25

Mueslix
1970s (plastic)
(foreign, yellow)
$20-$40

Munster Flicker (Herman)
Picture of Herman to
"Herman Munsters"

Munster Flicker (Lily)
Picture of Lily to "Lily
Munsters"

Munster Flicker (Eddie)
Picture of Eddie & Wolfie
to "Eddie Munsters"

**Munster Flicker
(Grandpa Munster)**

Muppet-Gonzo
1970s (metal, enameled)
$12-$25

Muppet-Rowlf
1970s (metal, enameled)
$12-$25

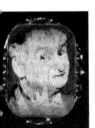

**Munster Flicker (Grandpa
Munster)**
Picture of Grandpa to
"Grandpa Munsters"

Munsters Flickers
1960s (silver base, set of 4)
(scarce)
$35-$75 ea.

**Munster Flicker
(Herman Munster)**

Muppet-Kermit
1970s (metal, enameled)
$15-$30

Mutant Ninja Turtles
(see Teenage--)

Mutley (see Wacky
Races)

**Munster Flicker
(Lily Munster)**

Munsters flickers
1960s (blue base, set of 4)
$25-$50 ea.

Muppet-Miss Piggy Large
1970s (metal, enameled)
$15-$30

Mysterymen of America
1992 (prototype)(metal)
(Bob Burden)
$15-$35

**Munster Flicker
(Eddie Munster)**

Muppet-Animal
1970s (metal, enameled)
$12-$25

Muppet-Miss Piggy Small
1970s (metal, enameled)
$15-$30

Mystic Horror Ring paper
(see Horror Rings)

Nabisco Compass
(see compass--)

National Baseball (see Baseball, Nationals)	New York Mets (see baseball)	

Navajo
1990s (metal/turquoise)
(Roy Rogers museum)
$50

Ninjack
1995 (silver & bronze
versions)
Silver - $35-$70
Bronze - $16-$32

New York State Police
1990s (metal, color)
$2-$4

Nixon (see President
Nixon)

Noogies (1)

Navajo Good Luck
1930s (metal, silver
color)(also see Kill the
Jinx, Swastika, and
Whitman, Paul)
$40-$80

New York World's Fair
(see World's Fair)

New York Yankees
(see baseball)

NFL (see Football)

New Kids On The Block
1980s (metal, photo,
4 diff., color)
$5-$10 ea.

NHL (see Hockey)

New York City YMCA
1930s (sterling)(HiY)
$30-$75

Nightmare
1982 (plastic)
(black over white)
$15-$30

Noid, The
1989 (on card)(plastic)
Complete on Card $10

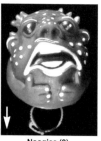

Noogies (2)

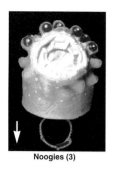

Noogies (3)

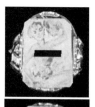

Old Man of the Mountains
1950s (metal)(square)
$5-$10

Nude Flicker
1960s (plastic)
$5-$10 ea.

Old McDonalds Farm
1960s (metal)(gold
metal base)(red/white
top, Butler, PA.)
$5-$10

Noogies On Card
1980s (4 diff., rubber)
On Card $12
Ring Only $5-$10 ea.

Official Gun and Hunting Ring
1960s (on card)
Complete $60
Ring Only $20-$40

Olive Oyl (see Post Tin)

Olympic Eagle (see Sam--)

Olympic Ring
1950s (aluminum)
$30-$60

Ovaltine Birthday
1930s (metal)(same as
Radio Orphan
Annie Birthday)
$100-$225

↓

↑
Pac Man
1980 (metal)(yellow)
$5-$10

Operator 5
1934 (rare)(metal)(6 known examples)(pulp)

Good - $3500
Very Good - $5500
Fine - $8500
Very Fine - $15,250
Near Mint - $22,000

Ovaltine Signet
1937 (metal)
$30-$75

Pac Man
1980s (metal)
(yellow w/eyes)
$5-$10

Pac Man
1980s (cereal)(metal)
$15-$25

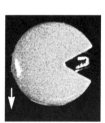
Owl Face
1970s (die stamped metal,
gold color, green eyes)
$5-$10

Pac Man (see Miss Pac
Man)

Operator 5
1995 (250 authorized,
stamped repro. &
numbered)(adjustable
w/certificate)
Complete $50

Orphan Annie
(see Post Tin & Radio--)

Paladin
(see Have Gun Will Travel

Orange Bird
(see Florida --)

Oscar Meyer Weiner
1960s (plastic)
(red & yellow)
$10-$20

Pan American Clipper
(see Kellogg's Picture)

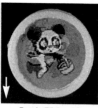
Panda Flicker (1)

Panda Flicker
1980s (set of 4)(plastic)
$5-$10 ea.

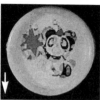
Panda Flicker (2)

Paratroopers (see
General Insignia)

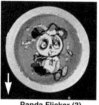
Panda Flicker (3)

Paris Eiffel Tower
1943 (metal)(square)
$25-$50

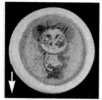

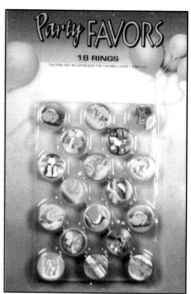
Party Favors Generic Pack
1990s (plastic, color)
On Card $5
Ring Only .25

Party Rings Carrousel Pack
1970s (plastic, color)
On Card $5
Ring Only .50

Party Rings Lisa Frank Pack
1990s (plastic)(generic, on card, color)
On Card $5
Ring Only .25

Peace Symbol
1960s (plastic)
(hand, gumball)
$2-$4

Pet Parade and Magic Pup Paper
1950s (large size)
$75-$85

Peace
1960s (oval, gold color)
$2-$5

Pepsi Cola
1980s (metal, in color)
with WHEAT CHEX or
RICE CHEX box top
$5-$10

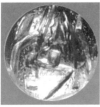

Peace Ball
1960s (metal)(gold color)
$2-$5

Magic magnetic ring collar makes magic pup do tricks

Peter Paul Face
1950s (plastic)
$15-$30

Peace Symbol
1960s (metal)
(hand, gold color)
$2-$4

Pet Parade Pup & Magic Ring
1950s (Wheat Chex)(w/magnet ring collar)
$60-$120

**Peter Paul
Glow-in-Dark
Secret Compartment**
1940s (metal)(also see
Sky King Radar)
$175-$375

Peter Paul Weather
1950s (also see Howie
Wing, Lone Ranger
Weather)(metal)
$25-$75

PF Flyer Decoder
1949 (plastic)
(green metal insert)
$20-$40

Phantom
1994 (silver)
$200

Phantom
1994 (Planet Studios)(silver metal)
In Case $60 ea.

Phantom Ring on Card
1991 (3 diff.)(metal),
Complete on Card $25 ea.

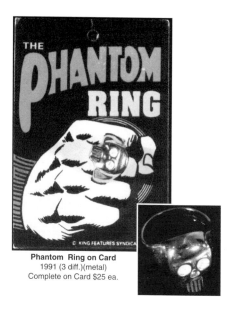

Phantom Ring on Card
1991 (3 diff.)(metal)
Complete on Card $25 ea.

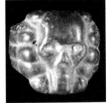

Pharoah Skull
1950s (w/eyes that
glow)(also see Egyptian
Sphinx)
$30-$60

Philadelphia Liberty Bell
1926 (metal)
$20-$40

Phantom Ring on Card
1991 (rings from card)(3 diff.)
(close-up view)
(see previous page)
Complete on Card $25 ea.

Phantom
1990s (gold color)(metal)
(distr. in England)
$50

Phantom (see King
Features, Post Tin &
Universal Monsters)

Pharoah
1950s (dark amber
see-through top)
$30-$60

Photo Ring Ad
1961 (16k gold plated, brass)
(Wilson Chemical premium)(Photo Ring
ad from Brave & The Bold Comics #34,
2-3/61, shown)
Ring $20-$40

Philadelphia Zoo
1950s (metal cloisonne')
$10-$20

Pinocchio
1950s (metal, gold color)
$50-$150

Pinocchio Figure
1970s (metal, cloisonne')
$40-$75

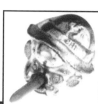

Pink Panther Face
1980s (plastic)(pink)
$8-$20

Pinocchio Figure
1960s (3D figure)
(metal in color)
$25-$75

Pinocchio (see Disney)

Pinocchio Tell The Truth
1940s (metal w/plastic nose)
GD $250, FN $375, NM $500

Pilot's Secret Compartment Ad from 1945
1945 (same as Captain Midnight Secret Compartment)(Army Air Corps star w/pilot's insignia)(top slides back to reveal secret compartment)(Brass base alloy)(golden color)
Ring $75-$175

Pirate Glow Skull
1940s (plastic)
$50-$75

Planet of the Apes
1970s (metal, green)
$100-$250

Pluto
1970s (plastic,
Canada, gumball)
$5-$10

Pluto
1980s (plastic)(paper disc)
$1-$2

Pirates of the Carribean
(see Skull)

Planet of the Apes
1970s (metal, green)
$100-$250

Pirates Of The Caribbean
1980s (metal)
$5-$10

Pluto (see Disney)

Pirates Of The Caribbean
1990s (metal, gold
w/red top)
$5-$10

Pluto
1950s (International, silver)
(colored & plain)
$50-$100

Rings join together

Pocahontas Best Friends
1995 (July)(Disney movie)
(2 joining rings on card)
On Card $4

Pittsburg Pirates (see
Bowman Gum)

Pluto
1950s (Glow-in-dark)
(intl. sterling)
$50-$100

Pocahontas Flit Flutter
1995 (Disney movie)(in box w/doll)
In Box $20

Police Sergeant Insignia
1960s (metal, silver color)
(on card)
On Card $15
Ring Only $5-$10

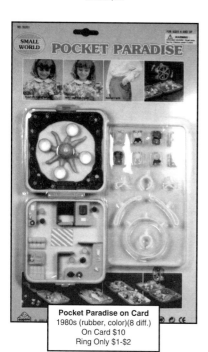

Pocket Paradise on Card
1980s (rubber, color)(8 diff.)
On Card $10
Ring Only $1-$2

Pointer Dog
1970s (die stamped
metal)(gold color)
$2-$4

Poll Parrot Face
1950s (gold & silver
versions)(metal)
$20-$40

Poll Parrot (see Howdy
Doody)

Poll Parrot Flicker
1950s (shows parrot flying)
$20-$50

231

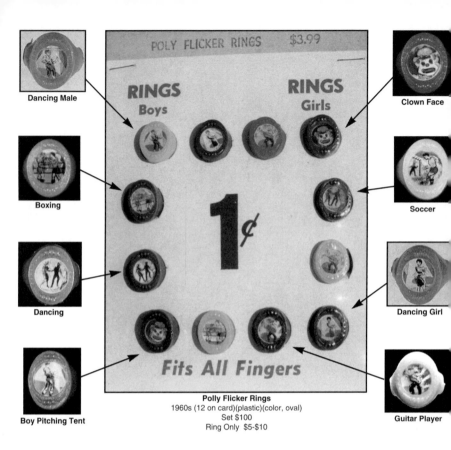

Dancing Male

Clown Face

Boxing

Soccer

Dancing

Dancing Girl

Boy Pitching Tent

Guitar Player

Polly Flicker Rings
1960s (12 on card)(plastic)(color, oval)
Set $100
Ring Only $5-$10

Polly Pocket
(see McDonald's --)

Polly Pocket (bagged set)
1990s
$15

Polly Pocket Ring Box
1990s (not offered in U.S.)
(plastic)(not shown)
$5

Polly Pocket (set 1)(2)
1990 (#5034)(plastic)(sports car)
$10

Polly Pocket (set 1)(4)
1990 (#5057)(plastic)(speed boat)
$10

**Polly Pocket
(set 1)(1)**
1990 (Throne)
(came in box)
(plastic)
$5-$10

Polly Pocket (set 1)(3)
1990 (#5051)(plastic)(stunt plane)
$10

Polly Pocket (set 1)(5)
1990 (#5058)(plastic)(dinner time)
$10

Polly Pocket (set 1)(6)
1990 (#5063)(plastic)(bath time)
$10

Polly Pocket (set 1)(8)
1990 (#5077)(plastic)(school time)
$10

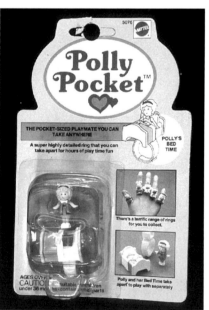

Polly Pocket (set 1)(7)
1990 (#5076)(plastic)(bed time)
$10

Polly Pocket (set 1)(9)
1990 (#5078)(plastic)(homework)
$10

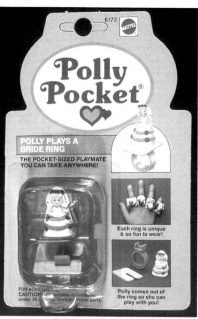

Polly Pocket (set 2)(1)
1991 (#6173)(plastic)(bride)
$8

Polly Pocket (set 2)(3)
1991 (#6175)(plastic)(pony)(change in package design)
$8

Polly Pocket (set 2)(2)
1991 (#6174)(plastic)(stroller)
$8

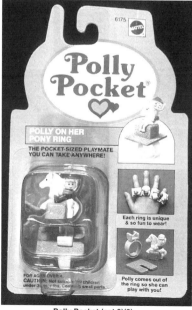

Polly Pocket (set 2)(3)
1991 (#6175)(plastic)(pony)(change in package design)
$8

Polly Pocket (set 2)(4)
1991 (#6178)(plastic)(princess)
$8

Polly Pocket (set 3)(2)
1993 (#6110)(plastic)(sammie/skateboard)
$6

Polly Pocket (set 3)(1)
1993 (#6094)(plastic)(suzy/safari)
$6

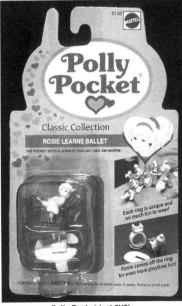

Polly Pocket (set 3)(3)
1993 (#6132)(plastic)(rosie/ballet)
$6

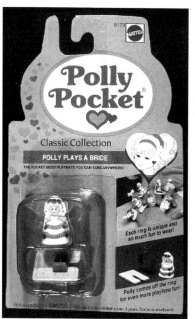

Polly Pocket (set 3)(4)
1993 (#6173)(plastic)(polly/bride)
(same as 1991 ring)(diff. package)
$6

Polly Pocket (set 3)(6)
1993 (#0797)(plastic)(midge/bumper car)
$6

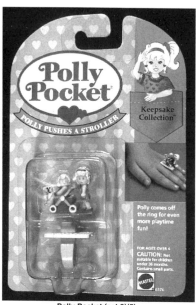

Polly Pocket (set 3)(5)
1993 (#6174)(plastic)(polly/stroller)
(diff. package)
$6

Polly Pocket (set 3)(7)
1993 (#9388)(plastic)(rose princess)
(diff. package)(scarce)
$10

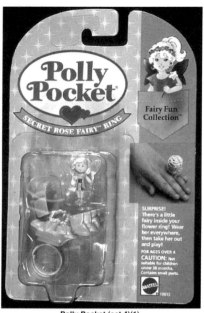

Polly Pocket (set 4)(1)
1993 (#10613)(plastic)(secret rose fairy)
$6

Polly Pocket (set 4)(3)
1993 (#10615)(plastic)(bed time)
$6

Polly Pocket (set 4)(2)
1993 (#10614)(plastic)(homework)
$6

Polly Pocket (set 4)(4)
1993 (#10616)(plastic)(bed time)
$6

Polly Pocket (set 4)(5)
1993 (#10617)(plastic)(sports car)
$6

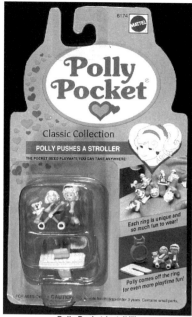

Polly Pocket (set 4)(7)
1993 (#6174)(plastic)(polly/stroller)
(repeat of 1991 ring)
$6

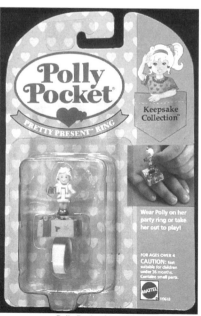

Polly Pocket (set 4)(6)
1993 (#10618)(plastic)(homework)
$6

Polly Pocket (ring w/ case) (set 5)(1)
1994 (#8156)(plastic)(bath time fun)
$10

239

Polly Pocket (ring w/case) (set 5)(2)
1994 (#8488)(plastic)(perfect piano)
$10

Polly Pocket (ring w/case) (set 5)(4)
1994 (#8743)(plastic)(50's diner)
$10

Polly Pocket (ring w/case) (set 5)(3)
1994 (#8571)(plastic)
(dazzling dressmaker)
$10

Polly Pocket (ring w/case) (set 5)(5)
1994 (#9081)(plastic)(Swan)
$10

Polly Pocket (ring w/case) (set 5)(6)
1994 (#9109)(plastic)(bathing beauty
pageant)
$10

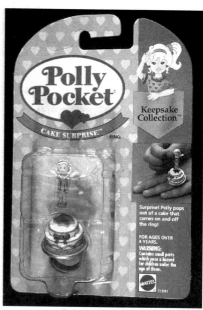

Polly Pocket (set 6)(2)
1994 (#11941)(plastic)(cake surprise)
$5

Polly Pocket (set 6)(1)
1994 (#10615)(plastic)(rose dream)
(repeat of 1991 ring w/diff. girl)
("caution" changed to "warning" on package)
$10

Polly Pocket (set 6)(3)
1994 (#11942)(plastic)(tanning time)
$5

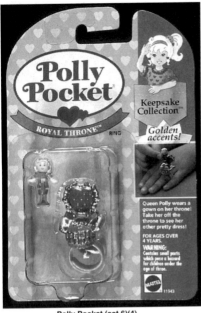

Polly Pocket (set 6)(4)
1994 (#11943)(plastic)(royal throne)
$5

Polly Pocket Gift Set
1990s
$10

Polly Pocket (set 6)(5)
1994 (#11944)(plastic)(racy roadster)
$5

**Ponderosa Steak
House**
1970s (plastic,
gold on white)
$4-$8

Popeye
1993 (staber)(Silver)
(36 produced)
$225

Popeye (see Post Tin &
Wimpy)

Popeye
1980s (Metal cloisonne')
$15-$25

Popeye Flicker
1960s (plastic)
$10-$20

Popeye Flicker
1960s (plastic, color)
$10-$20

Popeye Flicker (2)
1960s (Popeye to Olive
Oyl)(silver base)
$15-$25

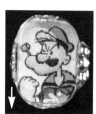

Popeye Flicker (3)
1960s (Popeye to
Sweet Pea)
(silver base)
$15-$25

Popeye Flicker (1a)
1960s (Popeye to Wimpy)
(blue base)
(side 1) $10-$20 ea.

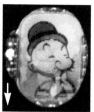

Popeye Flicker (1)
1960s (Popeye to Wimpy)
(silver base)
$15-$25

Popeye Flicker (1b)
1960s (Popeye to Wimpy)
(blue Base)(side 2)
$10-$20 ea.

Popeye Flicker
1960s (4 diff.)(blue base)
$10-$20 ea.

Popeye Flicker (4)
1960s (Popeye to
bucktooth nephew)
(silver base)
$15-$25

Note: Modern V-base,
$5-$10 ea

Popeye Vending Machine Ring Paper
1960s (in color)
$15-$30

Top swivels open to reveal
secret compartment and
paper code

Popsicle Boot
1951 (with paper
code)(plastic)
Complete $100
Without Paper $37-$75

Popsicle Skull (see Skull)

Porky Pig
1970 (hand painted)(metal)
$7-$14

Porky Pig Flicker
(see Arby's, Daffy Duck &
Looney Tunes)

243

Post Tin Rings

1948 (unbent examples with no rust are rare)
1949, 1952 (cereal premiums)(Post Raisin Bran
& Corn Flakes)(in color)(priced below)

Post Tin - Lillums, $5-$25

(All from Post's Raisin Bran)

Post Tin - Orphan Annie, $10-$50

Post Tin - Andy Gump, $5-$25

Post Tin - Dick Tracy, $20-$100

Post Tin - Perry Winkle, $5-$25

Post Tin - Harold Teen, $5-$25

Post Tin - Skeezix, $5-$25

Post Tin - Herby, $5-$25

Post Tin - Smilin' Jack, $10-$50

Post Tin - Smitty, $5-$25

Post Tin - Smokey Stover, $5-$25

Post Tin - Casper, $5-$25

Post Tin - Winnie Winkle, $5-$25

Post Tin - Dagwood, $10-$50

1949

(All from Post's Toasties Corn Flakes)

Post Tin - Felix the Cat, $20-$100

Post Tin - Alexander, $5-$25

Post Tin - Flash Gordon, $20-$100

Post Tin - Captain, $5-$25

Post Tin - Fritz, $5-$25

Post Tin - Casper, $5-$25

Post Tin - Hans, $5-$25

Post Tin - Henry, $5-$25

Post Tin - Mama, $5-$25

Post Tin - Inspector, $5-$25

Post Tin - Olive Oyl, $10-$50

Post Tin - Jiggs, $5-$25

Post Tin - Phantom, $20-$100

Post Tin - Little King, $10-$50

Post Tin - Popeye, $20-$100

Post Tin - Mac, $5-$25

Post Tin - Snuffy Smith, $10-$50

Post Tin - Maggie, $5-$25

Post Tin - Swee'pea, $10-$50

Post Tin - Tillie The Toiler, $5-$25

Post Tin - Dale's Brand (Roy Rogers), $8-$40

Post Tin - Toots, $10-$50

Post Tin - Deputy Sheriff (Roy Rogers)
$8-$40

Post Tin - Wimpy, $10-$50

Post Tin - Roy Rogers, $10-$60

1952

(All from Post's Raisin Bran)

Post Tin - Roy's Boots, $8-$40

Post Tin - Bullet (Roy Rogers), $8-$50

Post Tin - Roy's Brand, $8-$40

Post Tin - Dale Evans, $10-$60

Post Tin - Roy's Holster, $8-$40

Post Tin - Roy's Saddle,
front and back view, $8-$40

President Nixon Flicker
1970s (Faces of Nixon &
Mao Tse Tung to Faces of
Nixon & Cho En Lai with
Great Wall of China in
background.)
$15-$30

Prince Albert
1960s (metal)
$4-$8

Puzzle (see Quaker Puz)

Post Tin - Sheriff (Roy Rogers), $8-$40

Post Tin - Trigger (Roy Rogers), $8-$40

Quake Friendship Figural, Captain,
1960s (plastic, diff. colors)(also
see Quisp Figural)(cereal)
In Package $650
Ring Only -
GD $250, FN $425, NM $600

Post Propeller
1960s (plastic)
$25-$35

Power Rangers (see
Mighty Morphin)

President Nixon Flicker
1972 (President Nixon's
visit to Peking 21st Feb.
1972 to faces of Nixon)
$15-$30

Quake Leaping Lava
1960s (green plastic w/clear top)(contains real
meteorite)(also see Quisp Meteorite)(cereal)
In Package $600
Ring Only -
GD $250, FN $400, NM $550

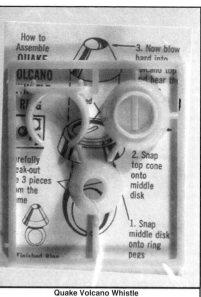

Quake Cereal Box Ad
1960s (back of cereal box)

Quake Volcano Whistle
1960s (complete in package)(plastic)(cereal)
In Package $600
Ring Only - GD $250, FN $400, NM $550

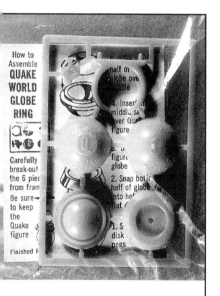

Quaker
1940s (metal)(Quaker Oats)
$75-$200

Quaker Jingle Bell
1950s
$15-$30

Quaker Friendship
1950s
$50-$100

Quaker Meteor
1950s (w/meteorite enclosed)
$15-$30

Quake World Globe
1960s (complete in package)(plastic)(rare)(cereal)
In Package $1500
Ring w/ figure GD $750, FN $1075, NM $1400

Quaker Pencil Sharpener
1950s
$15-$30

Quaker Crazy Ring Pap
1950s
$20-$40

Quaker Puzzle
1950s
$10-$20 ea.

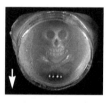

Quaker Puzzle
1950s (tic tac toe)
$15-$30 ea.

Quaker Siren
1950s
$15-$30

Quaker Crazy Ring
(above)
1950s (10 diff.)
(priced individually)

Quaker Whistle
1950s
$15-$30

Quaker Ship-in-Bottle
1950s (Also see Capt. Crunch)
$15-$30

Quaker Water Pistol
1950s
$15-$30

Quaker Initial Ring
1939 (metal)
$100-$250

Quick Draw McGraw (also see Hanna-Barbera)

(also see Baba Looey and Zorro for other glove and ring sets)

Quick Draw McGraw
1960s (w/Huckleberry Hound)
Ring $37-$75

Quisp Friendship Figural
1960s (plastic)(assembled)
Ring Only -
GD $1000, FN $1500, NM $2000

Quisp Friendship Figural (also see Quake Figural)

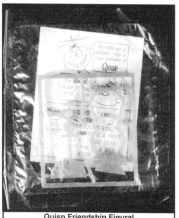

Quisp Friendship Figural
1960s (cereal)(packaged on tree w/papers)
In Package $2200

Contains real authentic meteorites inside package

HEY KIDS get 3 different rings in other packages of **QUISP**

Buy **quake** and get MY rings - THEY'RE BETTER!

Quisp Meteorite
1960s (plastic)
In Package $600
Ring Only -
GD $250, FN $375, NM $500

Quisp Space Disk Whistle
1965-72 (plastic)
In Package $600
Ring Only -
GD $250
FN $375
NM $500

Quisp Space Gun
1965-72 (plastic)
(with 4 bullets)(diff. colors)
In Package $600
Ring w/Bullet -
GD $250
FN $375
NM $500

Quisp
1995 (metal, fantasy piece)
$1

Quisp Cereal Ad
1960s (back of cereal box)

Rabbit Flicker
1950s (thick top)(plastic)
$15-$30

Rabbit Flicker
1970s ("v" base, silver)
$2-$5

Rabbit/Tennis Flicker
1970s (plastic, color)
(see Golf)
$2-$5

252

Radio Orphan Annie Face
1930s (metal, gold color)
$50-$100

Radio Orphan Annie Face
1980s (metal cloisonne')
$10-$20

Top contains two openings and a diagonal mirror inside enabling the viewer to look around corners

HERE'S YOUR Orphan Annie BIRTHDAY RING

LOOK INSIDE! See the Birthday Sentiment, Sign and Flower for the Month in Which You Were Born!

from
RADIO'S LITTLE ORPHAN ANNIE
180 North Michigan Avenue
Chicago, Illinois

HERE ARE THE BIRTHSTONES AND BIRTHDAY SIGNS, FLOWERS AND SENTIMENTS FOR EACH MONTH OF THE YEAR!

You can have lots of fun reading this list—and seeing what flower, sign and sentiment goes with **your** birthday—and the birthdays of your father and mother and all your friends!

MONTH	*BIRTHSTONE	FLOWER	SENTIMENT	SIGN
January	Garnet	Snowdrop	Constancy	Good Health, Victory
February	Amethyst	Carnation	Sincerity	Against Intoxication
March	Aquamarine	Violet	Wisdom	Social Success
April	White Sapphire	Easter Lily	Upright	Happy Marriage
May	Green Spinel	Hawthorn	Esteem	Fame, Immortality
June	Alexandrite	Rose	Wealth	Purity, Innocence
July	Ruby	Daisy	Freedom	Good Fortune
August	Peridot	Water Lily	Friendship	Prudence
September	Sapphire	Poppy	Truth	For Beautiful Thoughts
October	Rose Zircon	Cosmos	Hope	Power of Learning
November	Golden Sapphire	Chrysanthemum	Loyalty	Removes Fear
December	Zircon	Holly	Success	Soul Cheerer

* Modern list of birthstones approved by the Association of Stone Dealers.

HOW TO GET MORE RINGS

If your brother or sister or friend want to get one of these Orphan Annie Birthday rings when they see you wearing yours—tell them here's all they have to do. Just their name and address and BIRTHDAY plainly on a piece of paper— showing the **month** in which they were born. Then send it underneath the lid of a can of Ovaltine—and also a 10c piece! Mail it to—Little Orphan Annie, 180 N. Michigan Avenue, Chicago, Illinois! But tell them they'll have to act fast—because only a limited supply of these simulated birthstones are imported from Europe—so this other holds the supply of rings last!

Radio Orphan Annie Birthday Paper
1930s
Complete $50-$60

adio Orphan Annie (see Post Tin)

Fitted prongs

Note rare unbent (unfitted) prongs

Radio Orphan Annie Birthday
1936 (metal)(gold color)
(same as Ovaltine Birthday)
$50-$100

Radio Orphan Annie Face
1936 (rare unbent prongs)
(metal, gold color)
$120

Radio Orphan Annie Mystic Eye
1930s (same as Lone Ranger Ntl. Defender)(metal)
$105-$210

Radio Orphan Annie & Sandy
1980s (metal cloisonne')
$10-$20

The altitude of enemy planes can be determined by matching size of peep-through holes with plane

Small metal plates pivot out to reveal small peep holes for viewing planes

Radio Orphan Annie
Secret Guard
Altascope
1940s (very rare)
(Less than 10 known, one in near mint)(World War II premium)
Good - $3000
Very Good - $5500
Fine - $8000
Very Fine - $14,500
Near Mint - $21,000

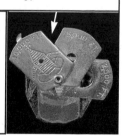

Radio Orphan Annie Face
1980s (metal cloisonne')(movie)
In Box $30
Ring Only $10-$20

Radio Orphan Annie
Secret Guard Initial
1940s (rare)(gold color metal)(red letter)(also see Walnettos Initial)
Good - $1250
Fine - $2500
Near Mint - $5500

Magnifying glass on top swings out

Radio Orphan Annie Secret Guard Magnifying
1940s (rare)(metal)
(also see Valric The Viking)
Good - $1125
Fine - $2250
Near Mint - $4500

Ad for Radio Orphan Annie Secret Guard Magnifying & Secret Guard Initial Rings
1940s (ad from back cover of early 1940s ROA premium booklet)

Radio Orphan Annie Silver Star
1930s (metal)(also see Empire State Building)
$200-$450

Radio Orphan Annie Secret Message
1930s (metal)
$150-$300

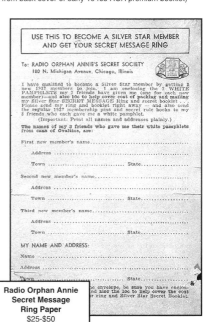

Radio Orphan Annie Secret Message Ring Paper
$25-$50

255

Complete with top intact

Ring showing top and inside together

Ring without top

**Radio Orphan Annie
Triple Mystery**
1930s (secret compartment)
Complete -
Good - $300 Fine - $600 Near Mint - $1200
Ring with top missing - $50-$100

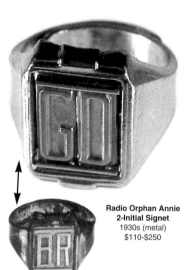

**Radio Orphan Annie
2-Initial Signet**
1930s (metal)
$110-$250

How Your 2-Initial Signet Ring Makes Personal Seals Like This

Your Orphan Annie Two-Initial Ring is a true Signet Ring. It will make your own *personal seal* in wax — in a way that no one can counterfeit.

Of course, when you use your ring as a seal, it prints your initials *backwards*—so it makes a fine secret seal that your friends will always recognize.

Here's how to use your ring to make your personal seal:

1. Just let some candlewax or sealing wax drip on the flap of your envelope.

2. Wet the front of your ring with your tongue. This keeps the ring from sticking to the wax.

3. Then press the front of your ring firmly down into the wax—while it's still soft.

4. Lift the ring—and you see the impression of your own initials in the wax, sharp and clear—and printed BACKWARDS!

Once you make this seal on a letter, nobody can tamper with

Radio Orphan Annie 2-Initial paper (1)

How To Care For Your 2-Initial Signet Ring

Your Orphan Annie Signet Ring was specially made up to your order—with your two initials set in the top.

The ring is made of a special gold-colored metal-finished with genuine 24-karat gold plate. Then, it coated with lacquer to help protect the gold. The initials and top section are solid nickel silver.

If you wear your ring every day, it will stay bright. However, if you don't happen to wear it for awhile and it becomes dull—you can make it shiny again by rubbing it a few times over any soft, rough surface, such as a carpet.

NOTE:—Your initials are "set" in this ring something like the way jewels are set in rings. You should always take off a "set" ring of this type when you wash your hands, because soap can get under an around the initials and keeps them from shining

**Radio Orphan Annie
2-Initial paper (2)**

Made to Fit You Automatically

If your ring is a little too small in size when you get it, you can simply pry it open a little at a time until it is the correct size. In case it is too large—it can be squeezed together until it fits your finger exactly

(See Next Page)

FOTOFRAME COUPON—SEND IN NOW!

Radio's Little Orphan Annie, Dept. S. R.
180 N. Michigan Avenue
Chicago, Illinois

I am enclosing all of the thin round aluminum seal from under the lid of a can of Ovaltine, together with ten cents (10c). (Wrap dime in seal.)

Please send me a genuine Silver-Plated Fotoframe.

(This offer expires May 1, 1937. Good in U. S. A. only.)

My name is
Street address
State City

Here's the Orphan Annie
2-INITIAL
SIGNET RING
WE MADE UP TO YOUR ORDER

INSIDE—See How To Make Your Seal With This Ring. ALSO—How To Get Gift To Surprise Your Mother on Mother's Day!

Radio Orphan Annie 2-Initial paper (3)
1930s
Complete $60-$80

Raggedy Ann Face
1980s (metal, cloisonne')
$10-$20

Raggedy Ann Figure
1980s (metal, painted)
$5-$10

Range Rider (T.V.)
1950s (aluminum w/brown leather tag)(rare)
Complete -
GD $275, FN $415, NM $550

Randolph Scott Photo
(see Real Photos)

Raggedy Ann
1980s (metal)(in color)
$5-$10

Range Rider (T.V.)
1950s (metal)
$100-$200

Rat Fink
1950s (complete in bag w/card)
(plastic, various colors)
In Bag $20
Ring Only $5-$10

Rat Fink
1960s (complete in bag)(plastic,
various colors)
In Bag $20
Ring Only $5-$10

**Real Photos
Berle, Milton Photo**
1950s (plastic)(B&W)
$10-$20

**Real Photos
Cassidy, Hopalong Photo
(William Boyd)**
1950s (plastic)(B&W)
$12-$25

**Real Photos
Hopalaong Cassidy**
1970s (metal)(B&W)
$6-$12

Ranger Rick (T.V.)
1950s (metal)
(2 views shown)
$50-$100

**Real Photos
Autry, Gene Photo**
1970s (metal)(B&W)
$6-$12

**Real Photos
Autry, Gene Photo**
1950s (plastic)(B&W)
$10-$20

**Real Photos
Benny, Jack Photo**
1950s (plastic)(B&W)
$10-$20

Real Photos Card with rings
1940s, 1950, 1960s (store)(round)(cowboy & T.V. stars)
Set $250
Ring $10-$20 ea.

**Real Photos
Cooper, Gary Photo**
1950s (plastic)(B&W)
$10-$20

**Real Photos
Godfrey, Arthur Photo**
1950s (plastic)(B&W)
$10-$20

**Real Photos
Hope, Bob Photo**
1950s (plastic)(B&W)
$10-$20

**Real Photos
MacArthur,
Douglas Photo**
1950s (plastic)(B&W)
$10-$20

**Real Photos
Crosby, Bing Photo**
1950s (plastic)(B&W)
$10-$20

**Real Photos
Grable, Betty Photo**
1950s (plastic)(B&W)
$12-$25

**Real Photos
Kennedy, Jackie Photo**
1950s (plastic)(B&W)
$10-$20

**Real Photos
McCarthy, Charlie Photo**
1950s (plastic)(B&W)
$10-$25

**Real Photos
Durante, Jimmy Photo**
1950s (plastic)(B&W)
$10-$20

**Real Photos
Hayes, Gabby Photo**
1950s (plastic)(B&W)
$10$20

**Real Photos
Kennedy, John Photo**
1950s (plastic)(B&W)
$5-$10

**Real Photos
McCrae, Joel Photo**
1950s (plastic)(B&W)
$10-$20

**Real Photos
Gleason, Jackie Photo**
1950s (plastic)(B&W)
$12-$30

**Real Photos
Hayworth, Rita Photo**
1950s (plastic)(B&W)
$10-$20

**Real Photos
Louis, Joe Photo**
1940s (plastic)(B&W)
$20-$40

**Real Photos
McCrae, Joel**
1950s (thick top, plastic)
$25-$75

**Real Photos
Rogers, Roy Photo**
1950s (plastic)(B&W)
$15-$35

**Real Photos
Sinatra, Frank Photo**
1950s (plastic)(B&W)
$10-$20

**Real Photos
Wayne, John Photo**
1950 (rectangle)(metal)
$50-$100

**Real Photos
Winchell, Paul &
Jerry Mahoney Photo**
1950s (plastic)(B&W)
$10-$25

**Real Photos
Rogers, Roy Photo**
1950s (plastic)(B&W)
$15-$35

**Real Photos
Starrett, Charles Photo**
1950s (plastic)(B&W)
(round)(store)
$10-$20

Red Ball Super Space Decoder
1950s (plastic)
In Bag, on Tree $40
Ring Only $15-$30

**Real Photos
Scott, Randolph Photo**
1950s (profile)
(plastic)(B&W)
$10-$20

**Real Photos
Sullivan, Ed Photo**
1950s (plastic)(B&W)
$10-$20

**Real Photos
Scott, Randolph Photo**
1950s (plastic)(B&W)
$12-$25

**Real Photos
Wayne, John Photo**
1950s (plastic)(B&W)
$20-$45

Top swings out to reveal
secret compartment

**Red Goose Secret
Compartment**
1940s (plastic & metal)
$115-$225

Red Ryder
1940s (metal)
$20-$40

Ren & Stimpy (Ren)
1990s (metal
cloisonne')(dangle)
$4-$8

Rin Tin Tin (3)
Geronimo

Rin Tin Tin (6)
Major

Rin Tin Tin (9)
Rinty & Rusty

Ren & Stimpy (Stimpy)
1990s (metal
cloisonne')(dangle)
$4-$8

Rin Tin Tin (4)
Horse

Rin Tin Tin (7)

Rin Tin Tin (10)
Rusty

Republic F-84E
Thunderjet
(see Kellogg's Picture)

Rin Tin Tin (5)
Lt. Rip Masters

Rin Tin Tin (8)

Rin Tin Tin (11)
Sgt. Biff

Republic XF-91
Thundercepter
(see Kellogg's Picture)

Rin Tin Tin
1960s (plastic)
(12 diff.)(Nabisco Rice Honeys cereal premium)
(also see Kellogg's Picture Rings)
$10-$20 ea.

Rin Tin Tin (1)
Cpl. Boone

Rin Tin Tin (2)
Fort Apache

EAT
NABISCO
SHREDDED
WHEAT
JUNIORS®

Enjoy the tastiest, toastiest flavor
ever ... in the neat-to-eat spoon-size!
It's the cereal the Spoonmen love.

WATCH RIN TIN TIN
AND THE SPOONMEN
EVERY WEEK ON TV

HERE IT IS!
YOUR
RIN TIN TIN

MAGIC RING!

Rin Tin Tin Magic paper (front)
1950s

YOUR NEW MAGIC RING —

☆ Fits any finger

☆ Contains hidden ink pad

☆ Includes extra strips of message paper

☆ Has magic pencil that writes invisible messages on white paper

Use this coupon to get more MAGIC RINGS. They're great gifts to give your friends.

RING
P. O. Box 95, New York 46, N. Y.

Please send .... MAGIC RING(S). (25¢ and box top for each).
Each ring complete with magic pencil and message paper.

NAME_____

ADDRESS_____

CITY_____ZONE_____STATE_____
PLEASE PRINT PLAINLY

WRITE INVISIBLE MESSAGES LIKE A SECRET AGENT

Rin Tin Tin Magic paper (back)
1950s
Complete $110-$135

Rin Tin Tin Magic Ring
1950s (with pencil)
Complete with scarce paper & pencil $750
Ring Only $150-$350

Ring Pops
1990s (in bag)
$2-$5

Ring Raiders
1980s (68 diff.)(on cards)
On Card $10 ea.
Ring Only $2-$4

Ring Watch
1992 (plastic)(2 diff., cat & dog)(digital quartz)
$2 ea.

RinGun paper
1940s
$35-$45

RinGun (shoots caps)
1940s (metal)
On Card $50-$65
Ring Only $15-$20

Robin Collapsible
1960s (rubber)
(See Batman Collapsible)
$10-$60

Robin Hood Shoes
1950s (scarce)(silver)
$175-$350

Rita Hayworth Photo
(see Real Photo)

Robin Dome
1970s (metal)(small, color)
(see also Aquaman)
$10-$20

Robin Logo
1980s (Nestles)(square)
$25-$50

Robot
1990s (metal,
fantasy piece)
$5-$10

Road Runner (see Looney
Tunes)

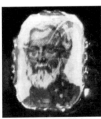

Robert E. Lee Flicker
1960s (Robert E. Lee face
to soldier carrying a confed-
erate flag. May be part of a
larger Civil War set)
$20-$40

Robin Head (3D)
1980s (metal)(gold color)
$45-$90

Robin Logo
1980s (nestles)(rect.)
$25-$50

Robot
1986 (rubber, blue)
(Roy Rogers/Marriott)
$10-$20

Robin & Nest Flicker
1960s (plastic, color)
$5-$10

Robin Logo
1980s (nestles)(round)
$25-$50

Robin Hood
1970s (plastic)(silver)
$20-$35

Robot (1)

Robot (2)
1970s (plastic, Canada, gumball, 2 diff.)
$5-$10 ea.

Robot Flicker (A)

Robot Flicker (B)
1980s (plastic, color, "V" base)
$2-$5

Rocket (see Tom Corbett Rocket Rings)

Rocket (1)

HOW TO OPERATE
ROCKET-TO-THE-MOON RING

Here is your ROCKET-TO-THE-MOON RING, complete with 3 luminous plastic "rockets." You'll find it easy to operate and lots of fun, if you follow these directions. Rockets are luminous—they will glow brighter in the dark if you first expose them to a bright light.

1. Squeeze ring so that it fits snugly (note that it is adjustable in this respect).

2. To cock the firing bar, push bar down as far as it will go, using thumb on one end and first finger on the other, pressing down equally on both ends. Then twist bar clockwise until it catches in the notches of launching barrel.

3. To insert "rocket," place "rocket" in launching barrel, with pointed end up and bottom resting snugly against firing bar.

4. To fire "rocket," trip firing bar by moving one end forward (as shown in picture above).

5. Ring is built to carry one "rocket" in launcher when not in use (as shown in picture above). To do this, simply cock firing bar and lock it in place (as in step 2 above). Then push "rocket" into carrying slot, release the firing bar, and "rocket" will be held securely in place.

Do a Friend a Good Turn or Get an Extra Ring for Yourself!

Give order blank below to your pal or to some other boy or girl so that they, too, can get a ROCKET-TO-THE-MOON RING.

"GOOD TURN" ORDER BLANK
Fill out and send at once.

KIX, Box 1085, Minneapolis, Minnesota

Please send me _____ ROCKET-TO-THE-MOON RING (S). For each one I enclose 20c in coin and a KIX box-top.

NAME _____
PLEASE PRINT
STREET _____
CITY _____ ZONE ____ STATE _____

(Offer Good in U. S. A. Only—Offer Expires June 1, 1951)

Rocket To The Moon Paper
1951 (paper is thin & unstable)(rare)
$135-$185

Rocket (2)
1970s (plastic, 2 diff., Canada, gumball)
$5-$10 ea.

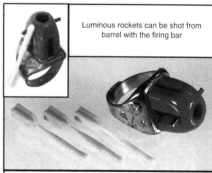

Luminous rockets can be shot from barrel with the firing bar

Rocket-To-The-Moon
1951 (w/3 glow-in-dark rockets)(gold & silver)(red top)(believe to be a Lone Ranger premium)
Complete $600-$1500
Ring Only $200-$600
Rocket Only - $135-$300

Rockettes Flicker
1960s (round, plastic)
$5-$10

Rockettes Flicker
1960s (rectangle)
$10-$20

Rockettes Flicker
1960s (oval, plastic)
(Also see Polly Flicker
Rings)
$5-$10

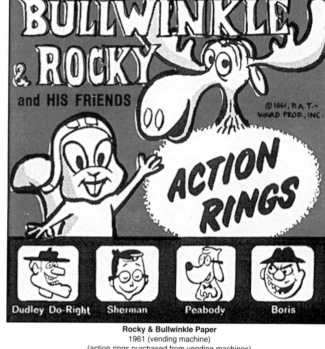
Rocky & Bullwinkle Paper
1961 (vending machine)
(action rings purchased from vending machines)
(in color)
$30-$45

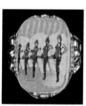
Rockettes Flicker
1990s (Rockettes dancing in
a line)(modern "v" base)
$2-$5 ea.

Rocky Figure
1969 (metal, painted)
$20-$40

Rocky Figure
1993 (metal cloisonne')
$10-$20

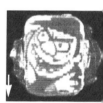
**Rocky & Bullwinkle
Flicker (1b)**
1961 (Boris)(side 2)(gold
base)(color)
$25-$60

Rocky (see Bullwinkle)

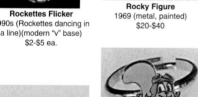
Rocky Figure
1993 (metal cloisonne')(right
& left profile exists)
$5-$10

**Rocky & Bulllwinkle
Flicker (1a)**
1961 (Boris)(side1)(color)

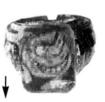

**Rocky & Bullwinkle
Flicker (2b)**
1961 (Bullwinkle)(gold
base)(color)
$25-$50

**Rocky & Bullwinkle
Flicker (3a)**
1961 (Dudley)(Side
1)(color)

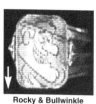

**Rocky & Bullwinkle
Flicker (3b)**
1961 (Dudley)(side 2)(gold
base)(color)
$25-$60

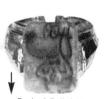

**Rocky & Bullwinkle
Flicker (4a)**
1961 (Mr. Peabody)
(side 1)(gold base)(color)

**Rocky & Bullwinkle
Flicker (4b)**
1961 (Mr. Peabody)
(side 2)(gold base)(color)
$25-$50

**Rocky & Bullwinkle
Flicker (5a)**
1961 (Rocky)(color)
(side 1)(gold base)

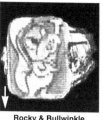

**Rocky & Bullwinkle
Flicker (5b)**
1961 (Rocky)
(side 2)(gold base)(color)
$25-$50

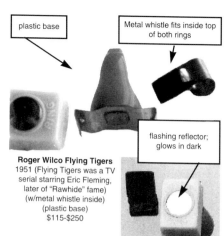

plastic base

Metal whistle fits inside top
of both rings

flashing reflector;
glows in dark

Roger Wilco Flying Tigers
1951 (Flying Tigers was a TV
serial starring Eric Fleming,
later of "Rawhide" fame)
(w/metal whistle inside)
(plastic base)
$115-$250

**Rocky & Bullwinkle Flicker Ring comic ad
from Charlton comics**

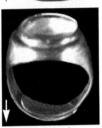

top variation A

Roger Wilco Rescue Paper
1949
$50-$75

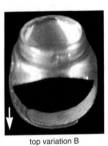

top variation B

Roger Wilco Magniray
1940s (metal)(two top variations)
$30-$75

Roman Coin
1980s (metal)(replica)
$5-$10

Romper Room T.V.
1960s (gold color)
(aluminum)
$20-$60

Rootie Kazootie Lucky Spot
1940s (rare)(metal)
GD $250
FN $500
NM $750

Name "Roger" on metal base

Romper Room T.V.
1960s (silver color)
(aluminum)
240-$60

Rootie Kazootie T.V. Flicker
1950s (metal)
$75-$175

flashing reflector; glows in dark

Roger Wilco Rescue
1949 (metal base)
(w/metal whistle inside)
$75-$200

Ronald McDonald (see McDonald's--)

Rosalie Gimple
1940s (gold color metal)(scarce)
$125-$300

ROY ROGERS "King of the Cowboys"
says—
Here's a chance for you and your pals to
GET EXTRA
"BRANDING IRON" RINGS
with any one of your initials made
into a Western Brand!

STAR OF
REPUBLIC PICTURES

"Pardner, take your pick of these Western Brands so you can 'brand' your schoolbooks, cap, balls, gloves, and other belongin's with the initial of your first, middle or last name.

"Look at the name under each brand and you can tell how a cowpoke out on the range would read your brand if he spotted it on a steer!"

Your Pardner,
Roy Rogers

WHILE
SUPPLY LASTS
ONLY 15¢
AND ONE BLUE STAR FROM
QUAKER OR MOTHER'S OATS PACKAGE

QUAKER AND MOTHER'S OATS
ARE THE SAME

**Roy Rogers Branding Iron
Ring Paper**
1950s
$50-$65

Roy Rogers Saddle
1950s (metal)
GD $250
FN $385
NM $525

Roy Rogers Store
1950s (silver metal)
$50-$100

**Roy Rogers
Branding Iron**
1950s (metal)(white cap)
$150-$300

Roy Rogers Hat
1950s (scarce)(metal)
GD $400
FN $625
NM $850

Roy Rogers on horse
1950s (silver)
$125-$300

Rudolph
1940s (metal)(scarce)
$100-$200

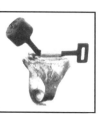

**Roy Rogers
Branding Iron**
1950s (black cap)(metal)
$100-$225

Roy Rogers Microscope
1950s (also see Sky King
Magni-glo)(metal)
$50-$110

Roy Rogers on horse
1950s (oval)(silver)
$125-$300

Saddle
1980s (metal)(silver color)
$2-$4

Saddle ring, Smith Brothers ad
1951 (in All Star Comics #57, 2/51)

Saddle, Generic
1950s (plastic)(generic, gumball)
$4-$8

Saddle, Goudy Gum
1950s (metal)
(saddle spins)
$40-$80

Saddle
1980s (bronze)
(Frontierland)
$5-$10

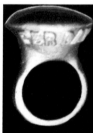

Salesman Door Knocker
1950 (large & heavy)(meta
$50-$100

Saddle, Generic
1950s (metal)
$10-$20

Saddle, Smith Brothers
1951 (Cough Drops premium)(airplane aluminum)(a real scale model of a western saddle)
$25-$50

Sam the Olympic Eagle
1984 (on card, color)
On Card $40
Ring Only $15-$30

Sam The Sheep Dog (see Looney Tunes)

San Francisco Expo
1939 (silver metal)
$30-$60

Wheat Honeys cereal box
1961 (with Savage Tribal ring offer)
Cereal box Complete $100

Schoenbrunn Village, Ohio
1950s (metal cloisonne')
$5-$10

Congo

Nigeria

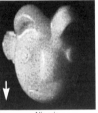

West Africa
Savage Tribal
1961 (plastic)(set of 6)
(Nabisco Wheat or Rice Honeys)
$10-$20 ea.

French West Africa

Scarab (see Capt. Hawks & Melvin Purvis)

Scarab
1930s (metal)
$10-$20

Schlitz
1970s (metal)
$5-$10

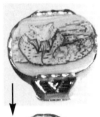

Scorpion/Snake Flicker
1980s (plastic, color)
$5-$10

Scotty Flicker
1960s (metal, gold base)
(Hong Kong Star)
$5-$10

Sears Christmas Flicker
1960s ("Sears has every-thing" picture of four small trees to face of Santa) (silver base)(2 versions)
$10-$20

Sears Christmas Flicker
1960s (blue base)
$5-$10

Secret Compartment
(see Pilot's --)

Secret Compartment
1950s (generic)
(Cleinman & Sons)
$20-$40

Secret Compartment
1960s (generic)
$10-$20

Shadow
1994 (gold w/diamond inset)(25 produced) (Diamond Comic Distr.)(numbered)
$800

Shadow
1994 (silver)(Diamond Comic Distr.) (numbered)
$200

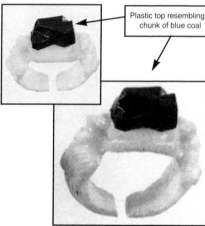

Plastic top resembling chunk of blue coal

Shadow Blue Coal Ring
1941 (glows-in-dark)(plastic) (blue top resembling a chunk of coal)
GD $200, FN $400, NM $600

Secret Agent Lookaround
1930s (Brass w/same base as R.O.A. Mystic Eye & Lone Ranger National Defenders) (Very rare) (a proto-type)
GD $250
FN $375
NM $500

Secret Service
1950s (gumball) (plastic)(also see Treasury Agent)
$20-$40

Shadow Blue Coal Advertising sticker
1941 (color)(gummed back)
$50-$150

HERE IS YOUR *Shadow* RING
PRESENTED WITH THE COMPLIMENTS OF 'blue coal'

INSTRUCTIONS FOR "CHARGING" YOUR RING
SO THAT IT WILL GLOW IN THE DARK

To charge your "Shadow" Ring so that it will glow in the darkness, hold it close to a lighted electric bulb for a half minute or more. The longer you hold the ring to the light, the longer and brighter it will glow. And

you may recharge it as often as you wish. The ring can also be charged by holding it in the sunlight. BUT DO NOT EXPOSE THE RING TO THE DIRECT RAYS OF THE SUN FOR TOO LONG!

TO MAKE YOUR RING LARGER

(1) Put the ring in hot water (not boiling hot) for about five minutes. (2) Take it out of the water and gently

bend it until it fits your finger. (3) After bending it to the correct size, put it in cold water for one minute.

YOU ARE NOW A MEMBER OF THE SHADOW "STOP CRIME" CLUB
(See other side for special order blank)

YOU ARE NOW A MEMBER OF *The Shadow* "STOP-CRIME" CLUB

USE THIS BLANK TO ORDER ADDITIONAL
"Shadow" RINGS

If you want to order additional "Shadow" Rings for your own use or for gifts, send the order blank below to: "The Shadow", P.O. Box No. 5, Madison Square Station, New York City. Simply enclose 10c for each ring you order.

Please send me _____ rings. Enclosed is _____ cents

NAME _____

Print Name and Address

ADDRESS _____

CITY _____ STATE _____

THIS OFFER EXPIRES DECEMBER 31st, 1941

Shadow Blue Coal Ring Paper
1941 (very rare)
Paper - $500-$650

CONTENTS—MERCHANDISE
Third Class Mail

Postmaster: This parcel may be opened for postal inspection if necessary.

from: D. L. & W. COAL CO.
120 Broadway, New York, N.Y.

Return Postage Guaranteed

'blue coal'

The Shadow

Sec. 562, P. L. & R.
U. S. POSTAGE
1c PAID
New York, N. Y.
Permit No. 11922

Katharine Hoffman
111 E. Market St.
Williamstown, Pa.

Shadow Blue Coal Envelope
(see above for price)
Envelope Only $300-$400

TUNE IN ON—

The Shadow

For the best in thrilling radio entertainment tune in every Sunday afternoon. Presented by

'blue coal'

See your newspaper for time and station

Shadow Blue Coal
Advertising sticker
1941 (color)(gummed back)
$60-$120

273

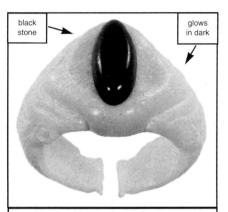

black stone

glows in dark

Shadow Carey Salt
1947 (black stone)(glows-in-dark)(also see Buck Rogers
Ring of Saturn, Jack Armstrong Dragon Eye & Shadow
Blue Coal)
GD $500, FN $850, NM $1200

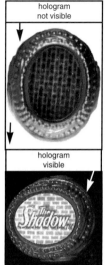

hologram
not visible

hologram
visible

Shadow Hologram
1994 (Shadow toy coupon
offer)(Kenner)
Ring Only - $25

gold base   silver base

red
stone

Shadow Movie
1994 (High quality ring
w/tin box and slip jacket in
color)(released at time of
movie)(gold & silver
versions)
Box $25
Gold Ring Only $400
Silver Ring Only $100

silver base

Red stone
ring on finger

gold base

Shadow Crossed Guns
1984 (High quality ring
with Shadow wearing ring)
Silver Ring Only $100
Box $25

WHO KNOWS WHAT EVIL LURKS IN THE HEARTS OF MEN?
The Shadow

Shadow Crossed Guns
1984 (High quality ring
with Shadow wearing ring)
Gold Ring Only $400
Box $25

FREE!
SHADOW™AGENT
HOLOGRAM RING
WHEN YOU BUY
ANY TWO SHADOW™TOYS
To receive your free hologram ring:
1) Buy any two Shadow toys.
2) Cut out proof of purchase seals.
3) Write your complete name, address and
zip code on a 3x5 card.
4) Send the card and two proof of purchase seals to:
Shadow Ring Offer
P.O. Box 2235
Young America, MN 55553-2235
Offer Expires 1/31/96. Allow 12-16 weeks for delivery.
Void where prohibited, taxed or otherwise regulated.

514294-00

FREE!
SHADOW™AGENT
HOLOGRAM RING
WHEN YOU BUY
ANY TWO SHADOW™TOYS
Offer Expires 1/31/96. Peel Here For Details ➤

Shadow Hologram
1995 (Shadow toy coupon offer)(color)
Coupon Only - $2

Shmoo Lucky Rings
1950s (metal)(on card)
Card w/rings - $600
Ring Only $30-$60 ea.

Shazam
1995 (metal, color)
(fantasy piece)
$1

Shield
1930s (metal)(generic)
$25-$45

Shield
1970s (plastic, Canada,
gumball, color)
$5-$10

Shark
1990s (metal, gold color)
$5-$10

Shelly Winters (see Movie
Star Photo)

Shield
1940s (metal)(blank top)
$10-$20

Ship in bottle
(see Quaker)

Shirley Temple Face
1930s (metal)(scarce)
GD $300
FN $425
NM $550

Shirley Temple Face
1990s (metal, silver
color)(fantasy)
$1

Shoe Shine
1950s (gumball)(plastic)
$20-$45

Sir Ector
(see Sword in the Stone)

Siren (see Quaker)

Siren Whistle
1995 (plastics)
(orange & green)
$1

Siren Whistle
1970s (metal)(Taiwan)(no
in package)(heart base)
In Package $25
Ring Only $6-$12

Signet (generic)(ad in Showcase Comics #26, 5-6/60)
Ring $20-$40

Siren Whistle in package
1960s (elephant base)
(gold & silver versions)
(metal)
In Bag $25
Ring Only $6-$12

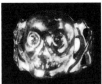

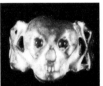

Skeleton Flicker
dancing skeleton in a
graveyard moving back &
forth
$10-$20

Skull
1939 (gold w/red
eyes)(metal)
$50-$125

Skull (foreign)
1940s (2 diff.)(top-green
back, bottom-yellow
back)(metal)
$30-$75 ea.

Skull
1940s (gold
w/black eyes)
$50-$125

Skull
1940s (silver w/green
eyes)(metal)
$50-$125

Skeleton Rings
1990s (Boxed set)
Complete in Box $15

Skull
1940s (metal)
$50-$125

Skull-Montrose Lucky
1940s (metal)
$50-$110

Skull
1960s (metal)
$20-$50

Skull-Popsicle
1949 (silver w/sparkling
jewel-like red eyes)
(see above for ad)
$50-$110

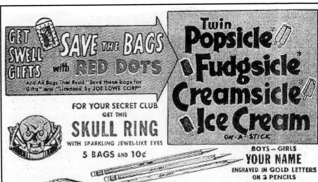

Skull Ring, Popsicle ad in Sensation Comics #90, 6/49

Skull
1960s (metal)
$20-$50

Skull
1970s (metal)(fantasy)
$1

Skull
1970s (metal)
$8-$15

**Skull, Pirates Of
Carribean**
1980s (gold)(metal)
(Jeweled eyes)(Disney)
$10-$20

**Skull, Pirates of the
Caribbean**
1980s (Silver)(metal, blank
eyes)(Disney)
$10-$20

Skull
1970s (metal)
$8-$15

Skull
1970s (metal)
$8-$15

**Skull, Pirates Of
Carribean**
1980s (gold)(metal)
(eyes blank)(Disney)
$10-$20

**Skull, Pirates of the
Carribean**
1980s (silver)(metal)(jeweled eyes)(Disney)
$10-$20

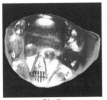

Skull
1970s (metal)
$8-$15

Skull Flicker
(see Monster Flicker)

Skull, Pirates Of Carribean
1980s
$5-$10

Sky Bar Pilot
1940s (metal)
$150-$325

Sky Birds
1940s (Army Air Corps.)
(silver finished metal w/gold
finished Air Corps.
insignia)(Sky Birds Bubble
gum box top offer)(Goudy
Gum Co.)
$50-$100

Green colored
plastic jewel

Sky King Aztec Emerald Calendar Ring
1940s (metal/plastic)(24 Karat gold plated)
GD $300, FN $625, NM $950

**Sky King Aztec Emerald
Calendar Ring Paper**
1940s (scarce)(complete)
$125-$150

Front lens magnifies 2x

**Sky King Electronic
Television Picture**
1940s (metal)(with 4 photos of Clipper, Penny, Jim & Martha
that can be placed over portrait of Sky King in base of
ring)(Sky King picture glows-in-dark)
Ring Only $50-$125
Indiv. Photos - $25 ea.

SEE Sky King's picture glowing through the TELEVISION VIEWER SCREEN! Magnifies picture 2 times...looks like a real Television Screen!

Get it Kids! Nothing like it before! **SKY KING'S**

ELECTRONIC TELEVISION *PICTURE* RING

ELECTRONIC-GLO PICTURE of Sky King's set in ring glows in the dark, like a real television image! Actually works electronically—"charge" the picture by holding it to a light, facing the electrons out of their normal position, in the dark, the electrons return to their normal position, giving off light! It will amaze you and your friends!

Has SECRET COMPARTMENT inside for hiding messages!

EXTRA PICTURES WORK LIKE MAGIC—pictures of Clipper, Penny, Martha and Jim Bell that you can wear in the ring! They're amazing—they come blank, but when you rub them with the wet 'presto' pad, pictures appear like magic! They fit right into the ring, so you can have a different picture in it every day!

DETECTO-SCOPE is built right into ring—magnifies 3 times for detecting fingerprints or secret writing!

It's the most amazing ring ever! Think of it—the magnified Electronic-Glo Picture of Sky King actually glows in the dark, like a real television image! This ring *looks* like a real television set, too, with its magnifying Television Viewer Screen. And you get four different Magic Picture Settings to wear in the ring, too—you can wear a different one every day. There's just never been anything like Sky King's Electronic Television Picture Ring before!

A real beauty—made of strong gold-like metal, with big Television Viewer Screen. Fits any size finger.

Easy to get—just follow the simple instructions. Send for yours *today*, while this amazing offer lasts!

☆ Listen to my air adventures! Hear how the Electronic Television Picture Ring helps me solve exciting adventure mysteries! For plenty of thrills, tune in "The Adventures of Sky King," every other week-day evening, 5:30 to 6:00 on your local ABC station.

Sky King

There are two kinds of Peter Pan Peanut Butter—smooth Peter Pan with the red jar top, and Peter Pan Crunchy Peanut Butter with the green jar top. You can send in the disc or liner from either kind of Peter Pan for your Television Picture Ring.

Send for your Ring TODAY! Only 15¢ with one disc or liner from PETER PAN Peanut Butter jar. (THIS OFFER GOOD ONLY IN U.S.A.)

SEND this coupon TODAY!

Dear Sky—With this coupon I am sending 15¢ and one round aluminum disc or the paper jar top liner from inside a Peter Pan Peanut Butter jar, for my Sky King's Electronic Television Picture Ring. (Note: If you want more than one ring, send one disc or liner and 15¢ for each Electronic Television Picture Ring you want.)

PRINT NAME AND ADDRESS PLAINLY IN PENCIL

NAME ....

STREET ADDRESS ....

CITY .... ZONE .... STATE ....

Mail to SKY KING, BOX 3636, CHICAGO 77, ILLINOIS

Sky King Electronic Television Picture Ad
1940s

Here's your Sky King *ELECTRONIC TELEVISION Picture* RING
. . . . and here's how to use it:

To make Sky King's picture glow in the dark like a real television image, hold ring to a light, then take it into a dark place. Picture will actually glow electronically through the Television Viewer Screen which magnifies image.

Secret Compartment for hiding messages! Just lift up Television Viewer Screen and slip message in.

To make pictures of Clipper, Penny, Jim and Martha appear like magic, cut dotted lines on the blank strips. Then rub the squares with the "presto" pad dipped in water. Then trim the pictures to fit in the ring.

Detecto-scope built into ring magnifies 2 times! Use it for detecting fingerprints or decoding tiny secret messages!

REMIND MOM TO HAVE PLENTY OF PETER PAN PEANUT BUTTER AROUND—IT'S SKY KING'S FAVORITE!

Now there are *two* delicious kinds of Peter Pan—smooth Peter Pan in the red top jar, and Peter Pan Crunchy Peanut Butter in the green top jar. And if you want another ring, send a round aluminum disc or the paper liner from under a Peter Pan Peanut Butter jar top and 15c for each Television Picture Ring you want together with your name and address to Sky King, Box 3636, Chicago 77, Illinois.

Sky King Electronic Television Picture Ring Paper
1940s
$50-$75

Sky King Kaleidoscope Ring
Aluminum tube with viewing lens. Multiple images of Sky King can be seen inside while rotating the tube. The base is gold finished brass attached to a black metal saddle holding the tube. A very rare prototype ring. Less than 5 known.

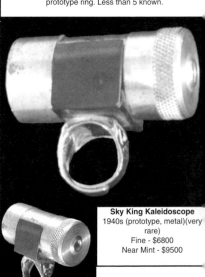

Sky King Kaleidoscope
1940s (prototype, metal)(very rare)
Fine - $6800
Near Mint - $9500

Here's Your Sky King Magni-Glow Writing Ring from Peter Pan

. . . and here's how to use it:

Secret Stratospheric Pen in ring writes at any altitude, or under water, in red ink!

Built-in Detecto-Scope magnifying glass for detecting fingerprints or decoding messages!

Mysterious Glo-Signaler gives a strange green light! You can send blinker signals with it!

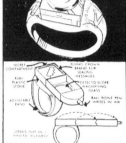

Remember to have mom get some more Peter Pan Peanut Butter—it's Sky King's Favorite.

Now there two delicious kinds of Peter Pan to choose from. Smooth Peter Pan in the red top jar and in the green top jar Peter Pan Crunchy Peanut Butter.

Sky King Magni-Glo Writing
$35-$50

Sky King Magni-Glo Writing Ring
Opens in three hinged sections. Contains a secret compartment & magnifying glass hidden in a ruby red base. At night coded eerie green blinker light pulses can be sent.

Sky King Magni-glo Writing
1940s (also see Roy Rogers Microscope)(metal)
$50-$100

Sky King Magni-Glo Writing Ad
1940s

281

Sky King Mystery Picture Ring Ad
1940s

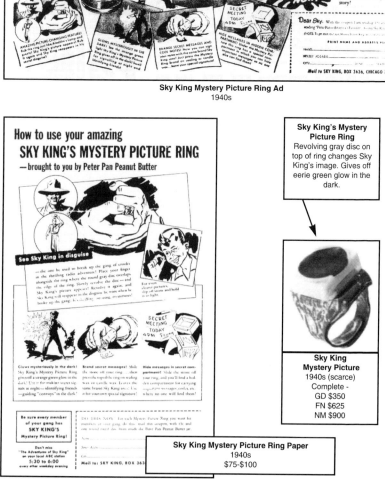

Sky King's Mystery Picture Ring
Revolving gray disc on top of ring changes Sky King's image. Gives off eerie green glow in the dark.

Sky King Mystery Picture
1940s (scarce)
Complete -
GD $350
FN $625
NM $900

Sky King Mystery Picture Ring Paper
1940s
$75-$100

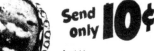
Kids! Get Sky King's mysterious
NAVAJO TREASURE RING

plus a handy present for Mom —

Send only **10¢**

Sky King's mysterious Navajo Treasure Ring— looks like the one Sky found bearing the mysterious clues that helped him find the long-lost Navajo turquoise mine! A strange and beautiful Ring in genuine Navajo Indian design, with a sky-blue stone that looks like real turquoise set in gleaming silver-like metal. The mysterious, centuries-old Navajo symbols on the sides are the clues Sky King deciphered to reveal the whereabouts of the fabulous lost Navajo mine! A Ring you'll be proud to wear, that your friends will envy! Order yours today! Fits any size finger.

For You!

For Mom!

Handy Plastic Re-Seal Jar Cap—
A stay-on-tight, but easy-to-remove, cover for Peter Pan Peanut Butter Jars. Turns empty Peter Pan or other drinking glasses into valuable food savers. You get this Re-Seal Jar Cap for Mom at no extra cost with every Navajo Treasure Ring you order for yourself— you get both. Send only 10 cents! Order today!

Special for Peter Pan Peanut Butter users!
Just send your name, address, and 10¢ — that's all! You will receive a beautiful Navajo Treasure Ring for yourself, plus a present for Mom—a handy plastic Re-Seal Cap for Peter Pan Peanut Butter!

Buy a jar of Peter Pan
Send this coupon today!

Dear Sky King:

Don't miss my radio adventures— fun, thrills, and adventures galore on "The Adventures of Sky King" every other

Sky King Navajo Treasure Ring Ad
1950s

Sky King Navajo Treasure Ring
1950s (turquoise colored stone, silver colored base)(Advertised on back cover of Danger Trail comic book #1, 1950)
$75-$150

| Gold colored base | Top glows in dark and slides off to reveal secret compartment |

Sky King Radar
1940s (metal)(also see Peter Paul Sec. Compt.)
$75-$150

"Hey kids! Here's your Sky King Radar Signal Ring !!!"

Makes mysterious symbols!
Place any cut-out symbol on stone, and hold stone up to bright light. Remove the cut-out, and the symbol will appear on the stone in the dark!

Stone glows in the dark!
Makes a mysterious bluish light! And to make it glow even brighter, hold stone close to bright electric light before taking it into a dark place!

Sky King's own insignia
—the Winged Propeller—appears on each side of the ring!

Band is simulated gold!
Handsome, gold-like finish. Looks and sparkles like real gold! Bright, long-lasting.

Stone is removable!
To remove it, just slip it off sideways.

Secret compartment!
In underside of stone. For secret messages, codes, etc. Nobody would suspect it was there!

Flying Crown Brand insignia
Appears when stone is removed. By pressing it on sealing wax or candle wax, you leave the mark of the Flying Crown Brand. Use it for sealing private letters, secret club papers, etc.

Ring fits any size finger!
Band can be adjusted to fit you perfectly!

Sky King Radar Paper
1940s
$50-$75

283

Sky King Tele-Blinker Ad
1950s

Here's your Sky King
2-WAY TELE-BLINKER RING
and here's how to use it

to send signals . . .

1. Place the ring on your trigger finger with windows facing out.

2. Push metal box down. The blinker will appear bright enough to be seen for at least 70 feet—and for night signaling, it glows in the dark. When you release the pressure, the blinker snaps up again to the "off" position. Notice also that when you signal there is a clicking sound like a telegraph key so that you can send sound signals when you can't be seen—or even over the phone.

3. Make dots or dashes by pushing the box down quickly for dots and slowly for dashes. There is a short "action" code on top the tele-blinker Or you can use the Morse Code below

A •—	F ••—•	K —•—	P •——•	U ••—
B —•••	G ——•	L •—••	Q ——•—	V •••—
C —•—•	H ••••	M ——	R •—•	W •——
D —••	I ••	N —•	S •••	X —••—
E •	J •———	O ———	T —	Y —•——
				Z ——••

to receive signals

Just pull out the jointed 3-power telescope and watch your partner's tele-blinker flash messages to you in dots and dashes. You can use your tele-blinker to view distant objects also.

flashes recognition signal

On the opposite side from the two windowed tele-blinker, Sky King's Flying Crown brand appears when you press the top of the ring. Release it and it disappears.

Remind Mom to Have Plenty of Peter Pan Peanut Butter on Hand —It Is Sky King's Favorite!

There are two delicious kinds of Peter Pan—smooth Peter Pan in the red top jar and Peter Pan crunchy in the green top jar

To get another 2-WAY TELE-BLINKER RING, send the round aluminum disk*or the paper liner from under a Peter Pan peanut butter jar top and 25c together with your name and address to SKY KING, Box 3636, Dept. D, Chicago 77, Ill. (Good only in U.S.A. Expires March 13, 1950.)

**Sky King
Tele-Blinker Paper**
1950s
$60-$75

Luminous blinker and a clicking sound is activated by pushing top up and down

Telescope extends for viewing distant objects. 3-power magnification

Sky King Teleblinker
1950s (metal)
$75-$160

Sky Strike Ring Fighters (Ja-Ru)
1989 (plastic (3 diff.)
On Card $15
Ring Only $2-$4

Sliding Whistle
(see Tom Mix--)

Sliding Whistle
1940s (generic)(rare)(metal)
$150-$250

**Sleeping Beauty
Prince Phillip**
1960s (hard plastic)
(Disney)(also see weapon)
$20-$40

Smile
1950s (Orange flavored
drink)(aluminum)
$30-$60

Smile (see Happy Face)

Smile Flicker
1950s (Orange flavored
drink)(plastic)
$30-$50

Sleeping Beauty Ring Ad
1960s

285

Smilin' Jack (see Post Tin)

Smith Brothers
(see U.S.--)

**Smith Brothers Good
Luck Initial**
(see Good Luck--)

Smurfs
1980s (4 diff.)(meta
cloisonne')(color)
$10-$20 ea.

Smilin' Jack
1964 (Canada Dry)(plastic)
$50-$100

Smith Brothers Saddle
(see Saddle)

Smitty (see Post Tin)

Snake Flicker
(see Scorpion/Snake

**Smith Brothers
U.S. Army Air Corps.**
1940s (Cough
Drops)(metal)
$40-$80

Smokey Bear
1990s (2 diff.)
$1

Smokey Stover
(see Post Tin)

**Smith Brothers
U.S. Marine**
1940s (Cough
Drops)(metal)
$40-$80

Smokey Stover
1964 (still on tree)(Canada
Dry)(plastic)
(also see Smilin' Jack)
$50-$100

**Smith Brothers
U.S. Navy**
1940s (Cough
Drops)(metal)
$40-$80

Smurf Card
1980s
On Card $35

286

Snap
(white hat)(rubber)
GD $200
FN $375
NM $550

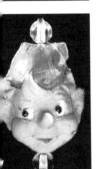

Crackle
(red hat)(rubber)
$100-$300

Pop
(yellow hat)(rubber)
GD $250
FN $450
NM $650

Snap, Crackle, & Pop
1950s(3 ring set)
(Kellogg's)(rare)
(priced above)

Sneezy Mouse (see Looney Tunes)

Snoopy (see Lucy)

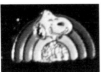

Snoopy
1980s (metal)
$10-$20

Snoopy
1980s (metal cloisonne')
$10-$20

Snoopy
1980s (metal cloisonne')
$10-$20

Snoopy & Woodstock
1980s (metal cloisonne')
$10-$20

Snoopy on Bike
1980s (metal cloisonne')
$10-$20

Snoopy w/Basketball
1970s (metal cloisonne')
$10-$20

Snoopy w/Flower Pot
1970s (metal cloisonne')
$10-$20

Snoopy w/Helmet
1970s (metal cloisonne')
$10-$20

Snow White (see Disney)

Snow White & 7 Dwarfs
1938 (brass metal, painted)(Doc)
$50-$150

Snow White & 7 Dwarfs Happy
1970s (metal, painted)
$10-$20

Snow White & 7 Dwarfs Sleepy
1990s (in color, metal)
$2

Snow White Dome Happy
1990s (metal)(round)
On Card $5
Ring Only $3

Snow White Dome Dopey
1990s (metal)(round)
On Card $5
Ring Only $3

Snow White Snow White
1990s (metal)(round)
On Card $5
Ring Only $3

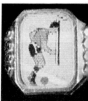

Soccer Flicker
1960s (gold base, metal)
(Hong Kong Star)
$10-$20

Soccer Flicker
(see Polly Flicker Rings)

Sock It To Me
(see Laugh-In)

Snuffy Smith
(see Post Tin)

Soccer Flicker
1960s (gold base, metal)
(Hong Kong Star)
$10-$20

Snow White & 7 Dwarfs
1994 (metal on card in color)
On Card $5
Ring Only $3

Soupy Sales Rings on card
1960s (4 rings)
Complete $125

Soupy Sales Flicker
1960s "Soupy Sales" to
:ture of Soupy with fingers
touching his head.(silver
base)(side 1 & 2)
$15-$25

Space (see Apollo)

Space Rings
1960s (vending machine paper)
(in color)(scarce)
$20-$30

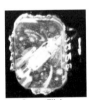

Space Flicker
1960s Outerspace scene
with rocket ship to farther
view of ship with Saturn in
background
$15-$35

Space
1960s (10 diff.)(vending
machine)(plastic)
$5-$15 ea.

Space Flicker
1960s Rocket ship ready
to take off to rocket ship
taking off
$15-$35

white plastic cap glows in dark & removes revealing the radioactive chamber

Space Patrol Cosmic Glow
1950s (plastic)
(red & blue)
GD $400
FN $625
NM $850

Space Patrol Hydrogen Ray Gun
1950s (plastic/metal)(Rice Wheat Chex cereal premium along with the Space Patrol periscope)(not offered on TV show)
$150-$325

Space Ring
1950s (sparkles like meteor dust)
(rings in various colors)(plastic)(on card)
Set $100

Space Patrol Hydrogen Ray Gun paper
(scarce)(both sides illustrated)
$125-$150

Space Flicker
1960s (plastic)
$10-$20

Who is it?

Buzz Corry?

One of the Gang?

...Could be YOU!

Wear this official

SPACE PATROL **OUTER SPACE HELMET**

You can see out . . . but nobody can see in . . . because of Mystic Strato-Viewer that SPACE PATROLLERS use! . . . Fresh-air oxygen tubes printed right on helmet . . . Solar golden color!

Keeps your identity a secret!

To get yours, send only 25¢ (no stamps, please) and 1 box top from any one of these Ralston cereals: Wheat Chex, Rice Chex, Regular or Instant Ralston, with your name and address to Outer Space Helmet, Box 987, St. Louis, Mo.

Offers good only in U.S.A. and may be withdrawn at any time. Void wherever prohibited or restricted.

Talk about fast action, Space Patrollers!...

this **COSMIC ROCKET LAUNCHER**

has got it!

Slick red and yellow plastic rocket with an unbreakable snap-on scout car! Stainless steel launching gun sends rocket whooshing over 33 feet of special breakproof nylon cord! Scout car drops down at end of trip! Use it for window-to-window communications with a pal next door . . . special place inside scout car for secret messages!

To get yours, send only 25¢ (no stamps, please) and 1 box top from any one of these Ralston cereals: Wheat Chex, Rice Chex, Regular or Instant Ralston, with your name and address to Cosmic Rocket Launcher, Box 987, St. Louis, Mo.

Spaceman
1970s (metal)(rectangle)
$10-$20

Look like a space stranger! Wear a **MAN-FROM-MARS TOTEM HEAD**

with Magic Forehead Vision!

Makes you look just like the space men Commander Corry found on Mars! . . . You can see out, nobody can see in! . . . One face on front, another on back . . . Order for your whole gang. Stack several up and make a TOTEM POLE!

To get yours, send only 25¢ (no stamps, please) and 1 box top from any one of these Ralston cereals: Wheat Chex, Rice Chex, Regular or Instant Ralston, with your name and address to Totem Head, Box 987, St. Louis, Mo.

How to use your Hydrogen Ray Gun Ring that lets you **WATCH ATOMS BEING SPLIT!**

FIRING CAP

ATOMIC CHAMBER

OBSERVATION LENS

Tell your gang how to get a Hydrogen Ray Gun Ring!

For each Ring, send only 25¢ in coin (no stamps, please) and 1 box top from any one of these Ralston Cereals: Wheat Chex, Rice Chex, Regular or Instant Ralston, with your name and address to Hydrogen Ray Gun Ring, Box 987, St. Louis, Mo.

1. Take your ring into a real dark room.

2. Wait until your eyes get used to the dark—about 1 to 2 minutes.

3. Slide the Firing Cap off the back of the ring.

4. Hold the ring close to one eye, and look through the Observation Lens.

5. See the bouncing dots and flashes of light in the Atom Chamber! That's atomic power in action—the energy released by atoms as they're split!

PRINTED IN U.S.A.

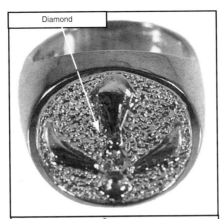

Diamond

Spawn
1993 (Image Comics)(gold)(w/diamond)(25 made)
$1050

Speak No Evil
1950s (3 monkeys)
(metal)
$20-$40

Speedy Gonzales
1970s (metal, enameled)
$10-$20

Space Patrol Printing
1950s (plastic)
W/Stamp Pad -
$300-$500
Ring Only - $150-$225

Spawn
1993 (Image Comics)
(sterling silver)(495 made)
$275

Spawn
1994 (metal, color)
(Image Comics/Gemstone
Publ. premium)
$5

Speedy Gonzales
1970s (hand painted)
(metal)(also see Looney
Tunes)
$6-$12

Space Patrol Siren Whistle
1950s (metal)
(gold & silver versions)
$75-$175

Space Shuttle
1982 (includes ring &
patch)(in box)
Set-$150
Ring Only - $80
Patch Only - $35
Box Only - $35

THE SPIDER RING

In October of 1933 a new action hero debuted on newsstands across America. His name was The Spider and he waged a relentless war against the overlords of crime. The Spider wore a black hat and cape and a trademark ring featuring a crimson spider.

THE SPIDER-MASTER OF MEN - became a pulp magazine sensation.

Clubs were the trend of the day and THE SPIDER Magazine wasted little time forming "The Spider League for Crime Prevention." Members were called SPIDERS and a column called "The Web" was featured in each issue of THE SPIDER Magazine. SPIDERS were to help Uncle Sam's G-Men ferret out criminals and alert constituted authorities.

SPIDERS could order a Spider ring for twenty-five cents in coin or stamps. The ring was just like the one The Spider wore when he left the mark of The Spider on the jaw of a despicable gangster.

Less than 20 of the original rings have been documented and a high grade example can bring a very high price. The Spider and Spiders are trademarks of Argosy Communications, Inc.

Red spider over black top

Spider
1930s (pulp character)(pulp & theater premium) (scarce)(silver base)(less than 20 known)

Good - $2000
Very Good - $3500
Fine - $4750
Very Fine - $6500
Near Mint - $9000

Spider
1995 (limited to 250) (Authorized stamped rep & numbered)(adjustible gold ring)
$50

ER MAGAZINE WILL COOPERATE!

Get the powerful national circulation of the Spider Magazine and other Popular Publications magazines working for you! The publishers have expressed a desire to get behind this ace serial and help you plug it locally. Use every angle offered. Don't miss a thing! "The Spider Returns" is being pre-sold in a series of large space ads in Spider Magazine calling attention to the picture. These display ads will catch the eye of the very people who will want to see the Spider in action on your screen! This is what the Spider Magazine is doing . . . It's up to you to tell these readers about your playdate by inserting a herald into each copy on the newsstands.

NG BILLBOARDS!

magazine wholesaler to snipe your theatre copy on feature the Spider Magazine. Posters are approximate in size. Use a snipe with this copy: "SEE THE REEN . . . RIALTO THEATRE SATURDAY!"

CK NUMBERS

azine wholesaler for back numbers of the Spider in at least two weeks in advance of opening-chapter direct attention to "The Spider Returns." Be sure copies. For name of the wholesaler who handles in your community, write Rogers Terrill, c/o Spider · 42nd Street, New York City.

EWSSTANDS

ed lobby hangers as flashy newsstand display cards. on fer complete description and prices.) Spot cards town . . . take advantage of this perfect movie-

ORGANIZE LOCA

open to you in organizing your own Spider club. luct kids into your club by having them attend

SPIDER RINGS

The Spider's official ring proved so popular during the run of "The Spider's Web", that it is again offered exhibitors for their campaign on "The Spider Returns".
Price: In lots of 15, $3.75, or at a rate of 25 cents each. (Single rings cost 50 cents each. Rings will be shipped postpaid. Be sure to get your order in immediately as the supply is LIMITED!

SPIDER PENCILS

Another top-notch novelty for your campaign, a beautiful mechanical Spider pencil, available in mixed colors, containing a small rubber stamp of the Spider's mark in the top section! Here is a novelty that is bound to win favor with both youngsters and adults . . . and it'll call direct attention to your playdate.
Price: $2.40 per dozen. Send cash with order, or order C. O. D. for either rings or pencils.

Order rings and pencils direct from:
Rogers Terrill, Spider Magazine, c/o Popular Publications
205 East 42nd St., New York City

Spider Ring ad
from a 1939 Spider pulp magazine. Note: The Spider was a masked pulp character very popular during the 1930s & 1940s

Spiderman (vitamins)

Spiderman (vitamins)
1975 (metal)(Marvel Ent.
Group)
$30-$60

Spiderman (silver)
1993, (limited to
50)(Marvel Ent. Group)
Near Mint - $450

Spiderman Face
1980s (green)
(Marvel Ent. Group)
(see Marvel)(green top,
white base)
$30-$60

Spiderman (bronze)
1993 (limited to 50)(Marvel
Ent. Group)
Near Mint - $250

Spy Set
1960s (plastic)(mirror
ring on card)
On Card $20

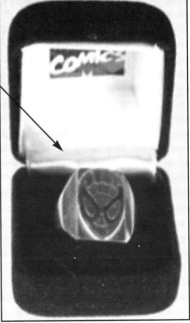

Spiderman (gold)
1993 (limited to 12)(Marvel Ent. Group)
Near Mint - $3,000

Spiderman
1994 (Marvel Ent. Group)(1200 minted)
Near Mint - $100

Squirt Party Favors
1995 (on card)
On Card $2

Star Trek
1979 (emblem)(on tree)
(McDonalds)
(plastic, set of 4)
$75

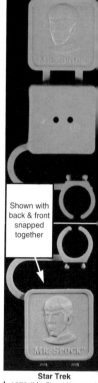

Shown with
back & front
snapped
together

Star Trek
1979 (Mr. Spock)(on tree)
(McDonalds)(plastic,
set of 4)
$75

Stanley Club
1940s (green stone,
gold metal)(radio)
$150-$350

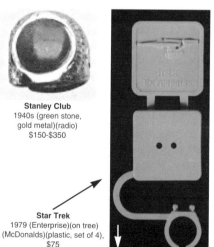

Star Trek
1979 (Enterprise)(on tree)
(McDonalds)(plastic, set of 4),
$75

Star Trek
1979 (Kirk)
(on tree)(McDonalds)
(plastic, 4 diff.)
$75

Star Trek Enterprise
1970s (plastic, Canada,
gumball)
$5-$10

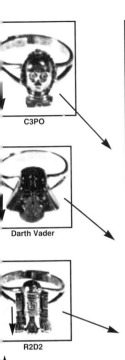

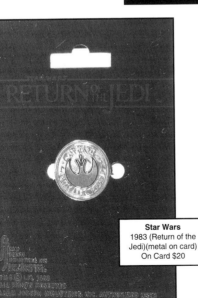

C3PO

Darth Vader

R2D2

Star Wars
977 (set of 3)(came in box
on previous page)
$2-$4 ea.

Star Wars (set in box)
1977 (warehouse find)(set of 3)
In Box $15
Ring Only $4 ea.

Star Wars
1983 (Return of the
Jedi)(metal on card)
On Card $20

Star Wars (8 diff.),
1980s (C3PO, Fighter,
Force (lg.),
Force (sm.), R2D2,
Vader, X-Wing, Yoda),
$7-$15 ea.

State of California
1941 (metal)(metal)(same
base as Spider
& Operator 5)
$30-$60

Starriors
1984 (on card)(2 rings)
(Includes comic book)
Complete $65
Ring Only $30 ea.

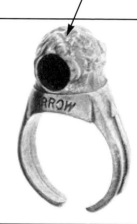

Lens magnifies photo of Straight Arrow, his palomino Fury and yourself in the secret golden cave

**Straight Arrow
Golden Nugget Ring**
1951 (Nabisco Shredded Wheat premium)
(w/photo inside)(see Golden Nugget Cave)
(Versions exist without photo of sender)
Complete $125-$250
Base without insides $15-$20

Stimpy
(See Ren & Stimpy)

Story Book
1960s (metal)
$50-$125

Stay-Puft Marshmallow
1980s (metal)(2 views of
same ring)(enameled)
$5-$10

Steer Head
1940s (generic)(metal)
$30-$60

**Straight Arrow
Gold Arrow Ring**
(Bandana slide)
1940s
$25-$50

Here's your **STRAIGHT ARROW**

GOLDEN NUGGET *Secret Picture* **RING!**

SEE THE INSIDE OF MY SECRET CAVE
*There you will find
your picture with my
Palomino, Fury, and me!
Straight Arrow*

This sensational Golden Nugget Secret Picture Ring is an official emblem of the Straight Arrow Tribe. Be sure to wear it at all times, to identify yourself to other tribe members.

Tell all your friends and fellow tribesmen about this wonderful new ring. Make sure they get theirs right away. Coupon on the reverse side tells how!

Handy coupon on back for a friend!

Straight Arrow Golden Nugget Paper
1940s (rare)(see next page for price)

Straight Arrow Golden Nugget Paper
1940s (rare)
$200-$250

Straight Arrow Gold Arrow Instructions
1940s (rare, less than 10 known)
(in color)
$300-$350

Straight Arrow Golden Nugget Ring Ad
ad from All Star Comics #57, 2/51

AMAZING VALUE!

BE THE FIRST IN THE STAMPEDE FOR THIS

STRAIGHT ARROW
GOOD LUCK
RING

NOT A TOY –
A REAL RING
SOLID
INDIAN BRONZE

ONLY 10¢ AND A NABISCO SHREDDED WHEAT BOX TOP

The breakfast full of POWER from Niagara Falls

NABISCO SHREDDED WHEAT

Baked by NABISCO NATIONAL BISCUIT COMPANY

- Raised curved profile of Straight Arrow himself!
- Shines—without polishing!
- Adjustable—fits any finger!
- Straight Arrow's mystic pass words secretly engraved!
- Indian good luck charm!
- Original—Exclusive!
- No other like it!

LOOK! Full-faced curved head of Straight Arrow embossed in solid metal!

HONEST INJUN!
THIS RING IS REAL JEWELRY!

A real ring with no gadgets to break! You'll wear it proudly, show it off to all your friends. Straight Arrow himself wears his always! Hear his adventures, with the ring, on the exciting Straight Arrow radio show. Look in your local paper for time and station.

HURRY! LIMITED TIME ONLY!

NABISCO SHREDDED WHEAT
Box 200, New York 46, N. Y.
Please rush me my STRAIGHT ARROW RING. I enclose 10¢ and a NABISCO SHREDDED WHEAT box top. (Please print)

Name
Address
City _____ Zone ___ State

Straight Arrow Good Luck Ring
ad from All Star Comics #52, 4-5/50

Straight Arrow Good Luck Ring
1950 (solid Indian bronze)(Nabisco Shredded Wheat & radio premium)
$25-$50

Sunbeam Bread Flicker
1950s (Sunbeam Bread Girl holding piece of bread to her eating the piece of bread.)
$20-$40

Sunday School Attendance
1940s (metal)(4-leaf clover w/heart & cross design)
(in color)
$20-$40

Sundial Shoes
1940s (see Fireball Twigg)(metal)
$30-$60

Strawberry Shortcake
1980s (enameled metal, color)
$5-$10

Street Sharks Card
1995 (plastic, color)
(5 diff.)
On Card $5
Ring Only $1

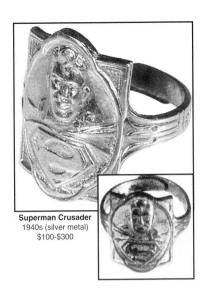

Superman Crusader
1940s (silver metal)
$100-$300

Superman Emblem
1979 (blue logo)(Nestle)
$25-$50

Superman Emblem
1970s (movie)(metal)
(red logo)
$25-$50

Superman Emblem
1993 (sold at Warner
Bros. stores)
Complete in Box $50

Superman Ring
1970s (In box w/clear top & full color paper display)
(3 diff.)(metal)
In Box $40
Ring Only $15-$30

Superman Emblem Dome
1970s (metal, color)
$10-$20 ea.

Superman Emblem
1990s (enameled metal)
$5-$10

Superman Dome Ring
1970s (In box w/clear top & full color paper display)
(3 diff.)(metal)
In Box $40
Ring Only $15-$30

Superman Emblem
1979 (plastic)(red,yellow,
blue)(came w/Superman
Action figure)
$20-$40

Superman Emblem
1990s (metal)
$10-$20

Superman Emblem paper wrapper
1979 (Nestle)
$50-$60

Super F-87 Jet Plane
(Kellogg's ad for ring)

Super F-87 Jet Plane Paper
(1948)(page 1)(see below)

HOW TO BE A CHAMP PILOT WITH YOUR "F-87" SUPER JET PLANE:

YOUR FIRST TAKE-OFF. Your Super Jet Plane comes to you all set to fly. Just slip the ring on your finger — with nose of plane pointing away from you. Aim it. Then press down quickly with finger nail on the Secret Launching Trigger — located to the right of the plane. Zoom! Away your plane streaks — (Be sure to hold trigger down until plane is launched to avoid tail surfaces striking trigger or finger.)

GET READY TO RE-LAUNCH! To replace plane on your ring, simply slide the hollow tail of your plane over the launching pin on the ring. Push plane back gently until it "clicks" in place. Zoom 'er again!

ENGINE TROUBLE? If you have a little difficulty launching your plane, examine your launching pin. It may be bent down too far. If so, bend it slightly upwards.

WIN DISTANCE RACES! You and your friends will want to race your jet planes.

Find the Proper Launching Angle

So here's how to get the *most distance* from your plane. Make repeated test flights at different launching angles until you discover which angle lets your plane fly the *farthest*. Then always launch your plane from this angle.

WIN LANDING CONTESTS!

It's fun to pretend you're landing your plane on a carrier. But it's tricky to do it right. Cut a piece of paper in the shape of a carrier 12 inches long, 3 inches wide. Place this cut-out carrier on the floor or a table. Then practice coming in *low* and *slow* — *not high or fast*. With practice, you can become an expert "flat top" flyer.

ZOOM THE LOOP!

Here's a trick that will amaze your friends — but it takes practice! Make a loop of wire about 12 inches across. Hang this loop from a lightcord or low tree branch about 5 feet above the ground. Then practice zooming your plane through the loop — close to it at first, then farther away.

WIN "DOGFIGHTS"!

It's fun to "dogfight" your jet planes — and here's how to do it: First, your friend will zoom his plane into the air. Then, you "shoot him down" from the side with your plane. If you miss, he gets a chance to shoot at your plane. Here's a tip: aim ahead of the plane — *not at it*.

BOOM THE BALLOON!

Blow up a toy balloon and tie it to a lightcord or low tree branch. Let it swing back and forth — then zoom your plane at it. BOOM! If you miss, your friend gets a chance to zoom it.
Tip: When the balloon is swinging, always shoot ahead of it — not at it. Aim at the center of the balloon — not at the top or bottom.

Do not point jet plane at yourself or anyone else!

GET YOUR FRIENDS TO FORM A SUPER JET PLANE RING SQUADRON!

Super F-87 Jet Plane Paper
1948 (page 2)(Scarce)
$125-$150

Kellogg's Corn Flakes box top premium. Plane and ring base should be displayed in un-cocked position to preserve the launching spring.

Secret launching trigger when pressed zooms plane away. Plane can be reloaded by sliding over the launching pin until it clicks in place.

Super F-87 Jet Plane
1948 (offered on Superman radio & other shows)(shoots plastic plane; spring loaded)(previously believed to be a Superman premium)
$125-$250

Superman Figure
1990s (enameled metal)
$10-$20

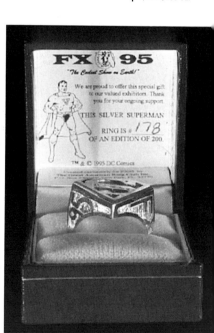

Superman Flicker
1960s (8 diff.) (scarce)
$100-$250 ea.

© NATIONAL PERIODICAL PUBLICATIONS. Inc.

Get your official SUPERMAN ACTION RING here

Superman Flicker Paper
1960s (from vending machine) (rare)
$75-$125

FX 95
"The Coolest Show on Earth"

We are proud to offer this special gift to our valued exhibitors. Thank you for your ongoing support.

THIS SILVER SUPERMAN RING IS # 178 OF AN EDITION OF 200.

TM & © 1995 DC Comics

Superman FX
1995 (sterling)(200 produced)
In Box $125

Superman Magnetic Kryptonite Ring
1990 (plastic, Green top)(came in box with Superman figure.
Magnetic ring will push Superman down)
Complete in Package $50
Ring Only $30

(front of package)

(back of package)

Superman Metropolis
1980s (metal)
$10-$20

Superman Pep Airplane
(also see Super F-87 Jet plane)
Silver metal plane hooks onto a spring launch. When the lever
is pushed, the plane is propelled away

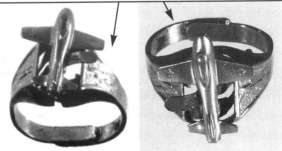

Superman Pep Airplane
1940s (cereal)(spring loaded)
$125-$250

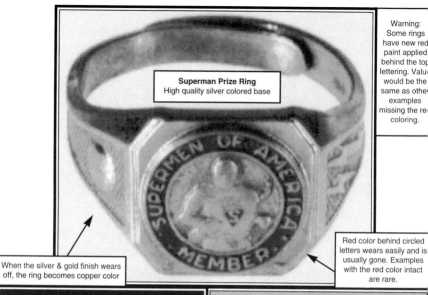

Superman Prize Ring
High quality silver colored base

Warning: Some rings have new red paint applied behind the top lettering. Value would be the same as other examples missing the red coloring.

When the silver & gold finish wears off, the ring becomes copper color

Red color behind circled letters wears easily and is usually gone. Examples with the red color intact are rare.

Superman Prize Ring
1940s (membership)(rare)(gold plated center
w/red color behind circled letters) (promoted in Suprman & Action Comics)(1600 issued in 1940)
(examples have sold in Good for $22,500, Fine for $50,000, VF for $80,000 & $100,000)
(Only 12 known, one in near mint)(most are in good to fine condition)

Good - $10,000
Very Good - $20,000
Fine - $35,000
Very Fine - $70,000
Near Mint - $100,000

Note: This ring is very rare with only 12 examples known, one in near mint.
It is currently the most valuable ring listed.

Superman Candy
ring with top in place

Superman Seceret Compartment
1940 (candy premium)(Note: Superman
image printed on paper in red and blue
and is affixed to inside of top) (rare)
(16 known with 5 in VF to NM)

Good - $5,000
Very Good - $10,000
Fine - $15,000
Very Fine - $25,000
Near Mint - $40,000

Radiating eye
below lightning bolt

Initial of person
that ordered ring

Top shown
flipped over

Top snaps off here

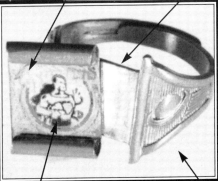

Gold colored brass finish

Superman image
on paper (blue & red ink) on back side of top piece

Superman Candy
ring with top removed.

Front side

Back side

Superman Candy Ring Coupon
1940 (front and back of actual coupon that was sent in for the Superman Candy
ring)(75 coupons were needed or 10 coupons and 10 cents to receive ring)
$25-$50

Gold colored brass finish

This ring was made from the candy ring. Superman's image was stamped over the eye on the candy ring top.

Top snaps off to reveal secret compartment (see Superman candy ring)

Superman breaking chains below lightning bolt on top; blank on reverse side. See gum ring paper on next page

Superman Secret Compartment Gum Ring
1940s (gum premium)(rare - only 10 known, none in near mint)

Good - $7,500
Very Good - $15,000
Fine - $20,000
Very Fine - $35,000
Near Mint $50,000

silver color metal

Superman Tim "Good Luck" Ring
1949 (Given away at department stores)(scarce)(silver color metal)
(only one known in NM, most examples exist in low grades)
Good - $1,500
Very Good - $3,500
Fine - $6,000
Very Fine - $10,000
Near Mint - $14,000

SUPER-GUM for SUPER-MEN

Super-gum is a good, big, husky chew with a delicious flavor. Chewing it helps to keep teeth strong and healthy. Dentists recommend this type of gum for young folks.

THE **SUPER BUBBLE GUM**

Helps keep teeth strong and healthy!

Start a Collection of thrilling . . . Colorful
ADVENTURE-STORY CARDS
Copyright 1940, SUPERMAN, INC.

Made by GUM, INC., PHILADELPHIA, PA.

JOIN THE SUPERMAN SUPERMEN OF AMERICA CLUB AND COMPETE FOR THESE VALUABLE PRIZES

Superman Secret Compartment Ring Gum Wrapper
1940 (rare)(in color)(5 coupons and 10 cents was required
to receive the gum ring)
GD $500, FN $625, NM $750

SNELLENBURGS INVITES YOU TO ANOTHER BIG PARTY!
Celebrating the 6th Birthday of the Superman-Tim Club

FUN! GIFTS!

TIME: SATURDAY, FEBRUARY 19th
PLACE: BROADWOOD HOTEL
BROAD AND WOOD STREETS

— TWO PERFORMANCES —
Morning: 10 sharp until 12 noon.
Afternoon: 2 sharp until 4 o'clock.
State your preference when you get your ticket at club headquarters.
SNELLENBURG'S :: THIRD FLOOR

EXCITING STAGE SHOW . . . IT'S TERRIFIC!
"UNCLE JIM", YOUR RADIO FRIEND!
SURPRISE GIFTS . . . LOADS OF 'EM!

And listen to this:

A SUPERMAN-TIM "GOOD LUCK" RING
FOR EVERY BOY AT THE PARTY!!
(We drew it extra large so you'd see the secret code letters on the side!)

REMEMBER! EVERY FELLOW MUST HAVE A TICKET!

Superman Tim Ring Ad
1949

Supermen of America Can
1995 (Silver)(shown)(Note: All rings came in a colorful can
with certificate, pinback and papers. The two gold rings
came with a Superman syroco each.)
Complete in Can $100

Supermen of America Syroco
1995 (came with both gold ring versions -
see at right)

Supermen of America
1995 (Gold w/diamond)
(member)(50 made)
(w/Superman syroco)
$750

Supermen of America
1995 (gold)(200 made)
(Action Comics)
(w/Superman syroco)
$400

Supermen of America
1995 (silver w/diamond)
(member)
$300

Supermen of America
1995 (silver)
(Action Comics)
$100

Swan Princess
1970s (plastic, 4 diff.)
On Card $30
Ring Only $6

Sir Ector

Squirrel

↑ **Sword In The Stone**
1960s (8 diff.)(plastic)
$10-$20 ea.

Sylvester
1990s (metal, cloisonne)
$5-$10

Tales of the Texas Rangers
1950s (TV)(aluminum)
(came w/membership kit)
$10-$20

Swastika Good Luck
1920s (metal)(Symbols of good luck: Swastika, horse-shoe, 4-leaf clover)(Also see Kill the Jinx--, Navajo Good Luck & Whitman, Paul)
$30-$60

Sweeney (see King Features)

Sword in the Stone (1)

↑ **Sword in the Stone (2)**
1960s (see Sleeping Beauty)(soft plastic)(3 diff.)
$10-$20 ea.

Fish

Tale Spin Flicker
1980s (Winky)(plastic, Disney)
On Card $10
Ring Only $2 ea.

Target Comics Ring
1940s (sterling silver)
$30-$60

Note: Also known as a Chinese **Good Luck Ring**, sold through Johnson Smith & Co. Catalogues in 1929. Symbols on ring stand for health, happiness, prosperity & prolonged life.

Tarzan
1930s (metal)(rare)
GD $200
FN $350
NM $500

Tarzan Flicker
Tarzan face to full figure shooting bow & arrow (re letters)
$5-$10

Free Prizes for You

Target Comics

. . . wants you for a regular reader—so we are going to do something for you that no other comic magazine has done before—we are going to give you Free Prizes just for reading TARGET COMICS.

On this page are six prizes you can get absolutely free. For a complete list of Prizes just send a letter or a penny postal card to TARGET COMICS, 525 West 52nd Street, New York City, and say, "Please send me your Target Comics Prize List." Do this today!

Here's How You Get Your Prizes →

In each issue of TARGET COMICS there will appear a coupon similar to the one on this page. Clip these coupons and save them. The Prize List will tell you how many of these coupons you will need for each prize.

Double Value Target Comics Coupon

The coupon on this page has DOUBLE VALUE — in other words, it is worth twice as much as the ones which will appear in the future issues of TARGET COMICS. Save this coupon — DO NOT MAIL THE COUPON WHEN YOU SEND FOR YOUR PRIZE LIST.

This offer is void in any state or municipality where the redemption of coupons is prohibited, taxed, or restricted.

Win prizes by reading every issue of TARGET COMICS.

DOUBLE VALUE TARGET PRIZE COUPON

This coupon, clipped from the first issue of TARGET COMICS, will be redeemed at double the value of coupons appearing in future issues. Write for your Prize List to TARGET COMICS 525 West 52nd Street,

Target Ring
(ad from Target Comics #1, Feb, 1940)

Tarzan Flicker (1)
Tarzan swinging on vine 1 Tarzan punching out a native
$10-$20

Tarzan Flicker (2)
Tarzan looking over his shoulder at spear throwing natives to Tarzan captured by two black natives
$10-$20

Tarzan Flicker (3)
Tarzan lifting a boulder in front of a waterfall to Tarza punching another guy.
$10-$20

Tarzan Flicker (6)
Tarzan landing from a vine
to Tarzan approching a
black natve whose
back is to us.
$10-$20 ea.

Tarzan Flicker
1960s (silver & gold
versions)(plastic)
(all individually priced)

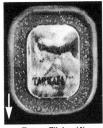

Tarzan Flicker (4)

Tarzan Flicker Paper
1960s (vending machine)
(in color)
$35-$50

Tarzan Flicker (5)

Tarzan Flicker (1)

Tarzan Flicker (4a)

Tarzan Flicker (6)

Tarzan Flicker
1960s (blue plastic base)
$10-$20 ea.

Tarzan Flicker (2)

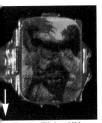

Tarzan Flicker (4b)
Tarzan squaring off with a
gorilla to Tarzan having
gorilla in a headlock.
$10-$20 ea.

Tarzan Flicker (5)
Tarzan yelling to Tarzan
caught in vines.
$10-$20 ea.

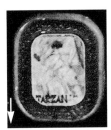

Tarzan Flicker (3)

Tazmanian Devil
1990s (pewter)
$20

Tazmanian Devil
1990s (metal)
(10 Karat gold)
$50

Bat swings to
hit baseball

Ted Williams
1940s (Baseball)
(metal & plastic)
GD $300
FN $612
NM $925

Tee Pee
1990s(metal)(copper)
(Custer's Battlefield)
$5

Here's my new NABISCO Shredded Wheat "Baseball Action Ring" which I hope you will enjoy.

By following these simple suggestions you can keep it in good condition for a long time: Adjust it to the exact size of your finger. Always keep it out of water and take it off when playing games.

I am sure some of your friends will want a ring like yours and I am therefore attaching a coupon which they can use.

Good luck to you!

Ted Williams

Send your name and address with 1 NABISCO Shredded Wheat Box top and 15¢ in coin (not stamps) to
NABISCO, DEPARTMENT "D"
BOX 372, NEW YORK 8, N.Y.
PLEASE PRINT CLEARLY!

NAME.....................
ADDRESS.................
CITY........STATE.......
Offer good in U. S. A. only.

BOYS and GIRLS NOTICE!

I want you to have the most possible fun with my NABISCO SHREDDED WHEAT "Baseball Action Ring." Here are a few simple suggestions:

1. **Remember it is a precision instrument. Treat it carefully and it will perform for you indefinitely.**

2. **I am a "southpaw" which means that I hit the ball left-handed. The small arrow on the white plastic base shows you the direction to which to flip the lever.**

3. **The wire supporting the baseball is part of the mainspring. If it should slip out of the tiny notch at the front of the ring, you can replace it in a jiffy.**

Yours for a better batting average with NABISCO SHREDDED WHEAT.

Ted Williams

Ted Williams Coupon & Paper
1940s (scarce)
Complete $150-$200

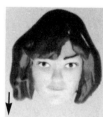

Teenage Mutant Ninja Turtles (April O'Nell)

Teenage Mutant Ninja Turtles (Leonardo)

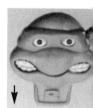

Teenage Mutant Ninja Turtles (Raphael)

Teenage Mutant Ninja Turtles (Donatello)

Teenage Mutant Ninja Turtles (Michael)

Teenage Mutant Ninja Turtles (Rock Steady)
(set continues on second page following)

Teenage Mutant Ninja Turtles Cereal Box
1990s (front & back illustrated)(Distr. in Canada only)
Complete $200

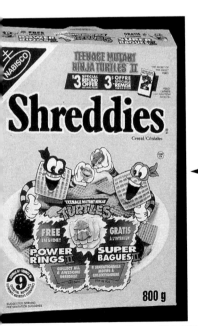

Teenage Mutant Ninja Turtles Cereal Box
1990s (front & back illustrated)(Distr. in Canada only)
Complete $250

Teenage Mutant Ninja Turtles (Splinter)

Tennessee Jed Look-Around
1940s (metal)(rare in VF-NM)
GD $150
FN $325
NM $500

Terry & the Pirates
1950s (plastic)(Sugar cereal)
$40-$80

Teenage Mutant Ninja Turtles (Shredder)

Teenage Mutant Ninja Turtles
1990s (8 diff.)(rubber in color)(cereal premiums; cereal only distr. in Canada)
Turtles - $25-$55 ea.
Others - $30-$60 ea.
In Pkg. add $5

Terry & the Pirates Gold Detector Ring Ad
1940s

Teenager Flicker
1960s (plastic, round)
$5-$10

Tekno Comix Logo
1994 (metal)(secret compartment)
$10

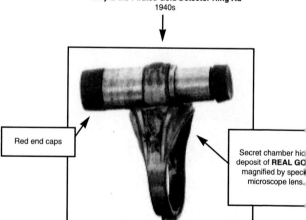

Red end caps

Secret chamber hides deposit of **REAL GOLD** magnified by special microscope lens.

Terry & the Pirates Gold Detector
1940s (metal)
$50-$150

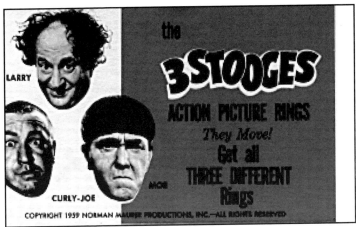

The 3 Stooges Flicker Paper
1960s (vending machine paper)(in color)
$20-$40

Texas Rangers
(see Tales of the--)

Three carrots
(see carrots)

**Three Stooges Flicker
(Larry)**

**Three Stooges Flicker
(Moe)**

Three Stooges Flicker
1959 (3 diff.)
$10-$20 ea.

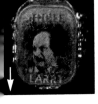

**Three Stooges Flicker
(Curly)**

Thunderbird
1930s (rare) (see Lone
Wolf)
$200-$400

Thundercats Flicker
1986 (in package)(plastic secret compartment ring)(Burger
King premium)(top slides off to reveal secret compartment)
In Package $30

Thundercats Flicker
1987 (villain)(red plastic with a sliding cover that is transparent red plastic that slides over image)(Telepix)
$15-$30

Timothy (Disney)
1950s (oval)
(International sterling)
$50-$100

Tom & Jerry (Jerry)
1972 (metal,
enameled)(M.G.M.)
$12-$25

Thundercats Flicker
1986 (plastic secret compartment flicker ring)(Burger King
premium)(top slides off to
reveal secret compartment)
$15-$30

Timothy (Disney)
1950s (square)
(International sterling)
$50-$100

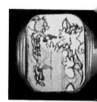

Tom & Jerry Flicker
1970s (blue plastic base
$10-$20

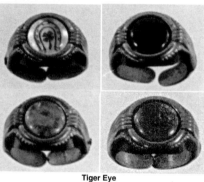

Tinkerbelle
1970s (plastic)
$5-$10

Tiger Eye
(4 diff.) (blue, green, and red tops)
1960s (plastic)
$25-$50 ea.

Tillie The Toller
(see King Features & Post
Tin)

Tim (see Superman Tim)

Tim Ring
1930s (rare)(metal)
(sold at Tim Stores)
GD $150
FN $400
NM $650

Tom & Jerry (Tom)
1972 (metal,
enameled)(M.G.M.)
$12-$25

Tom Corbett Face
1950s (silver color meta
$50-$100

Tom Corbett Rocket Rings
(ad from Action Comics #163, 1951)

Tom Corbett Rocket (4)
Sound-Ray Gun

Tom Corbett Rocket (5)
Space Academy

Tom Corbett Rocket (6)
Space Cadet
Dress Uniform

Tom Corbett Rocket (7)
Space Cadet Insignia

Tom Corbett Rocket (8)
Space Cruiser

Tom Corbett Rocket (1)
Girl's Space Uniform

Tom Corbett Rocket (2)
Parallo-Ray Gun

Tom Corbett Rocket (3)
Rocket Scout

Tom Corbett Rocket (9)
Space Helmet

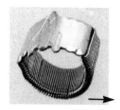

Tom Corbett Rocket
1950s (metal)
$175-$350

Tom Mix Circus
1930s (metal)(see Bill
West & Cowboy
Riding Horse)
$10-$20

Tom Corbett Rocket (10)
Space Suit

Tom Corbett Rocket (11)
Strato Telescope

Tom Corbett Rocket (12)
Tom Corbet Space Cadet

Tom Corbett Rocket
1951 (plastic)(12 diff.)
(Kelloggs Pep cereal)
$10-$20 ea.

FREE!!! FREE!!! FREE!!! FREE!!!
TOM MIX DEPUTY RING
SAVE 75 TOM MIX CERTIFICATES AND GET A 14 KT.
white gold finished TOM MIX DEPUTY RING. - You then become a
TOM MIX DEPUTY. - A full fledged fearless champion of law and order

THE TOM MIX DEPUTY RING IS A BEAUTIFUL REPRODUC-
TION OF THE DEPUTY SHERIFF SHIELD AS USED IN THE
WILD DAYS OF THE WEST. IT IS BEAUTIFULLY FINISHED
IN 14 KT. WHITE GOLD. TOM MIX CERTIFICATES ARE
ONLY ATTACHED TO TOM MIX CHEWING GUM WRAP-
PERS.

SEE INSTRUCTIONS BELOW.

SAVE your TOM MIX CERTIFICATES

HOW TO OBTAIN SIZE OF RING

Cut off on dotted line   Cut off on dotted line

TOM MIX CERTIFICATE
FREE
TOM MIX DEPUTY RING
DETERMINE THE SIZE OF THE RING DESIRED AS INSTRUCTED ABOVE AND WRITE
IT ON A NOTE TOGETHER WITH YOUR NAME AND ADDRESS AND PLACE IT
WITH 75 TOM MIX CERTIFICATES AND MAIL TO NATIONAL CHICLE CO. 504
MAIN ST. CAMBRIDGE, MASS., U. S. A. AND YOU WILL RECEIVE A 14 KT. WHITE
GOLD FINISHED TOM MIX DEPUTY RING. PLACE THE PROPER POSTAGE ON YOUR
ENVELOPE. YOUR POSTMAN WILL TELL YOU.
THIS CERTIFICATE IS VOID IN STATES WHERE PREMIUMS ARE PROHIBITED
THIS CERTIFICATE IS NOT REDEEMABLE AFTER JUNE 30, 1935.

TOM MIX CERTIFICATE

Tom Mix Deputy Ring
Certificate
1935 (color)
$75-$100

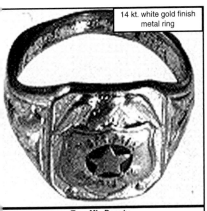

14 kt. white gold finish metal ring

Tom Mix Deputy
1935 (rare)(Tom Mix chewing
gum premium)(75 certificates needed to get
ring)(each attached to a Tom Mix chewing gum
wrapper)(scarce)
Good - $1375
Fine - $2750
Near Mint - $6000

SIGNET RING

A lucky Signet Ring just like Tom wears. 24-carat gold plated. *With your own initial* set in simulated gold over a special onyx black panel. Fits any finger. For one Ralston (hot cereal) box top and 10¢ or two box tops.

Tom Mix Lucky Initial Signet Paper
Complete $60-$80

Tom Mix Lucky Initial Signet
1930s (24 kt. gold plated)
(customer had his own initial placed on
top of ring)
$100-$250

Tom Mix Elephant Hair Good Luck
1940s Ring (ad from comic book shown above)(rare)
Ring $100-$200

Dear Straight Shooter:

Here is your Tom Mix "Look-Around" Ring from the Ralston Straight Shooters Radio Program.

We know you're going to have a lot of fun with it, and surprise your friends by being able to see around corners and over your shoulder ... without turning your head!

Here's the way to use your "Look-Around" Ring. Put it on your *left* hand with the "crossed pistol" design toward the ends of your finger. Now, the open peephole above the T-M Bar insignia will be toward your thumb. This is the part you look through—and you can see objects to the left and slightly in back of you.

Your "Look-Around" Ring is adjustable to fit any finger size. To make it smaller, squeeze the overlapping prongs together. To make it large, spread them apart.

Your Straight Shooter Pal,

Tom Mix

Tom Mix Look-Around Paper
1940s
$75-$100

Diagonal mirror enables viewer to look around corners

Tom Mix Look Around
1940s (metal)
$75-$150

TOM MIX MAGNET RING

Magnet in head of ring picks up pins, paper clips and other small metal objects!

← Fits any finger. Just squeeze ring together here to make it smaller.

For Better Breakfasts . . . It's

RALSTON

ONE—Instant Ralston, cooks in 10 seconds.

TWO—Regular Ralston, cooks in 5 minutes.

THREE—Shredded Ralston, the delicious *bite-size* ready-to-eat cereal.

Whole Grain Cereals in the Red-and-White Checkerboard Packages.

C2403A-9-46   Printed in U. S. A.

Tom Mix Magnet Ring Paper
1940s
$30-$40

Magnetized steel top

Blowing through top of ring creates whirring sound

spinner missing

Tom Mix Magnet Ring
1940s (metal)
$45-$100

Tom Mix Musical Ring
1940s (metal)(also see Jack Armstrong Egyptian Whistle ring)
Complete $100-$200

Tom Mix Nail
1930s (metal)(same form as Gene Autry Nail)(signed)
$20-$40

ANSWERS to TOM MIX mysteries

THE TELEVISION MURDER: Photograph of Mintmore (Frame 3) shows he needed thick glasses. Why didn't he have them on if he was watching Television when shot? Window glass shows bullet was fired from inside room. Hole is always smaller on side where bullet enters.

THE PHONE BOOTH MURDER: If man was talking on phone when shot, receiver would not be on hook. Bullet entered head on side that would have been toward back wall of booth.

THE SELF-DEFENSE MURDER: Bruises show murderer used own hands to fake marks on neck. If someone had choked him, the little-finger mark would have been at the bottom of the neck . . . not at top.

THE MATCH MURDER: Matches torn from left side of match book shows left-handed man. Watch on right wrist of one suspect shows he is left-handed.

THE MURDERED TRAPPER: If cabin was 50° below, man couldn't have written suicide note with pen. Ink would have frozen instantly.

Your friends can also get a
TOY TELEVISION SET
and MUSICAL RING

Hot RALSTON

Instant RALSTON

USE THIS COUPON

TOM MIX, Box 808,
Checkerboard Sq., St. Louis 1, Mo.   C14   Printed in U. S. A.

I enclose 20¢ and one Ralston box top. Please send Toy Television Set and Musical Ring to . . .

Name_____

Address_____

City_____ State_____

(Offer good . . . . any time.)

Tom Mix Musical Ring Paper
1940s
$75-$100

Tom Mix Signature Ad
1940s (color)

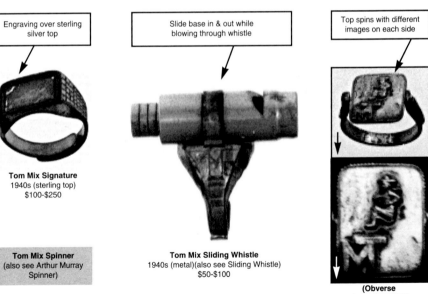

Engraving over sterling silver top

Tom Mix Signature
1940s (sterling top)
$100-$250

Slide base in & out while blowing through whistle

Tom Mix Sliding Whistle
1940s (metal)(also see Sliding Whistle)
$50-$100

Top spins with different images on each side

(Obverse shows Tom Mix)

Tom Mix Spinner
(also see Arthur Murray Spinner)

(Reverse shows Tony)

Tom Mix Spinner/Stamp
1930s (rare)(metal)(used for stamping emblems on paper)(multiple views shown)(less than 10 known)
Good - $600
Fine - $1200
Near Mint -$2500

Tom Mix Straight Shooters
1936 (gold Metal)
$60-$125

Tom Mix Straight Shooters Variant
1936 (gold Metal)(From Robbins archives)(Very rare)(only 6 known)
$175-$350

Tom Mix Target
1930s (metal)(Marlin Guns)
$100-$250

Tom Mix & Tony photo viewed through lens

Tom Mix Stanhope Image
1930s (metal)
$150-$400

Tom Mix Straight Shooter paper
1936,
Complete $60-$80

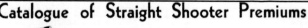

Catalogue of Straight Shooter Premiums

STRAIGHT SHOOTER RING
This ring is a beauty. Every Straight Shooter should own one. Has Tom Mix' TM Bar Brand in raised letters on top and a six shooter and steer's head on the sides. Glitters like gold! Fits any finger. FREE for only 1 Ralston Box Top.

Tom Mix Straight Shooter Ring paper
(from catalogue)
Complete Catalogue Value $75-$100

322

Tom Mix Tiger-Eye Ad

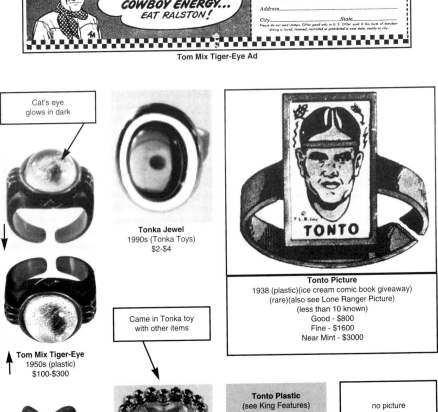

Cat's eye glows in dark

Tonka Jewel
1990s (Tonka Toys)
$2-$4

Tom Mix Tiger-Eye
1950s (plastic)
$100-$300

Came in Tonka toy with other items

Tonto Picture
1938 (plastic)(ice cream comic book giveaway)
(rare)(also see Lone Ranger Picture)
(less than 10 known)
Good - $800
Fine - $1600
Near Mint - $3000

Tonto Plastic
(see King Features)

no picture available

Tony the Tiger's Secret Word Changer
1970 (Kellogg's premium)(plastic)
(has a wheel that turns to reveal secret words).
$10-$20

Tonka Cat
1991 (plastic, purple)
$2-$4

Tonka Jewel Heart
1992 (plastic)
$2-$4

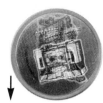
Transformers (2)

Transformers (6)

Transformers (8)
1980s (plastic, color)
(flickers)(8 diff.)
$2-$4 ea.

Toucan On Perch
1990s (plastic, 12 diff.)
$10 ea.

Transformers (3)

Transformers (7)

Treasury Agent
1950s (gumball,
plastic)(also see Secret
Service)
$20-$40

Toucan On Perch
1990s (plastic, 12 diff.)
$10 ea.

Transformers (4)

Treasure Rocks
1994 (in box)
(Hasbro Toy)
In Box $2

Transformers (1)

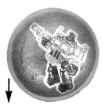
Transformers (5)

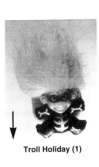

Troll Holiday (1)

Troll Holiday (2)

Troll Holiday (3)

Troll Doll
1960s
$15-$25

Troll Doll
1992 (5 diff.)(each doll
has var. hair colors)
$2 ea.

Troll Holiday (4)
1970s (rubber, 4 diff.)
$5 ea.

Troll Rings
1992 (on card)
With Card $6

Troll Rings
1992 (on card)(rings diff. than card at left)
With Card $6

Turtle-Keep on Trucking
1970s (plastic, Canada)
$2-$4

TWA
1960s (plastic)
(oval, blue on white)
$2-$4

Tweety Bird (see Looney Tunes)

Tweety Bird
1980s (metal cloisonne')
(Warner Bros.)
$5-$10

Tweety Bird
1980s (metal cloisonne')
$5-$10

Tweety Bird Dome
1980s (metal)(small)(color)
$10-$20

Tweety Bird
1980s (metal cloisonne')
(Warner Bros.)
$5-$10

Twinkie Shoe
1940s (metal)
$100-$250

Twinkie The Kid
1970s (snack cake)
$2-$5

Twist Flicker
(see A Go-Go Discotheque
Dancer Rings)

Uncle Creepy
1970s, (Warren) (metal)
(also see Cousin Eerie)
$100-$200

Ultraman Cartoon
1980s (metal cloisonne')
$15-$30

Underdog
1970s (metal cloisonne)
$75-$150

U.N.C.L.E. Flicker
(see Man From --)

Twist Flicker
1960s (plastic)
$2-$5

Uncle Sam Hat
1960s (plastic, USA, color)
$2-$5

Ultraman Figure
1980s (metal)
$15-$35

Underdog
1970s (plastic)
(silver over red)
$100-$275

LET'S TWIST
FLICKER RING

Twist Flicker paper
1960s (rare)(in color)
$20-$30

Ultraman Large Face
1980s (metal)
$40-$80

Underdog
1970s (plastic)
(black over yellow)
$100-$250

Ultraman Small Face
1980s (metal)
$50-$110

United Nations
1940s (metal)
$15-$30

327

Universal Monster Flicker Paper
1960s (vending machine paper)(rare)(in color)
$30-$40

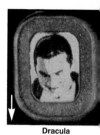

Dracula

Monster

Mummy

Phantom

Universal Monster Flicker
(The Creature)
(both images shown)

Universal Monster Flicker
(Dracula)
(both images shown)

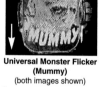

Universal Monster Flicker
(Mummy)
(both images shown)

Universal Monster
Flicker
1960s (original silver
base)(scarce)
(set of 6)(the 2 Casper
flickers may be part of set)
$50-$100 ea.

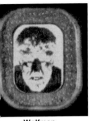

Wolfman

Universal Monster Flicker
(plastic)(blue base)
1960s (scarce)
$40-$80 ea.

Universal Monster Flicker
1960s (Mummy/Wolfman)
$20-$40

niversal Monster Flicker
960s (Creature/Wolfman)
$20-$40

Universal Monster Flicker
1960s (Phantom of the
Opera/Wolfman)
$20-$40

niversal Monster Flicker
960s (Hunchback of Notre
Dame)
$20-$35

**Universal Monsters
Flicker**
960s (monster/Werewolf)
$20-$35

USA Astronaut Flicker
1960s (in color)(plastic)
$20-$40

U.S. Air Force Academy
1960s (metal cloisonne')
$15-$30

USA/KKK Ring (100%)
1920s (flips to reveal KKK)(1st moveable
ring)(rare)(metal)(2 diff. bases known)

GD $200, FN $350, NM $500

Note: The Ku Klux Klan was a very popular group during the
1920s with members reaching the U.S. Supreme Court.
Large public parades were common and many KKK items
were produced. This ring was probably for children. They
could wear the ring displaying the "100% USA" during the
day and revealing their secret identity "KKK" at night while
at the secret meetings.

U.S. Air Force
1960s (metal)
$2-$4

U.S. Air Force Store Card
1950s (plastic)
$10-$20

U.S. Air Force Store Card
1950s (plastic, green)
$10-$20

U.S. Army Air Corps.
(see Smith Brothers)

U.S. Army Store Card
1950s (plastic)
$10-$20

U.S.Army Store Card
1950s (plastic)
(white on blue)
$10-$20 ea.

U.S. Army Gumball
1940s (gumball)(metal)
$5-$15

U.S. Keds
1960s (metal)
(see Kolonel Keds)
$55-$110

U.S. Marshal
1930s (rare)(metal)
GD $300
FN $475
NM $650

U.S. Marine Corps.
(see Smith Brothers)

U.S. Marshal
1990s (metal)(Dept.
Justice, color)
$5-$10

U.S.Army Store Card
1950s (3 variations)(plastic)
$10-$20 ea.

U.S.Army World War I
1918 (sterling)(childs adj.)
$50-$100 ea.

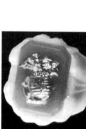

**U.S. Marine Corps.
Store Card**
1950s (plastic)
$10-$20

U.S. Navy
(see Smith Brothers)

U.S. Army
1950s (metal)
$15-$30

**U.S. Marine Corps.
Store Card**
1950s (plastic)
$10-$20

USN Gumball
1940s (gumball)(metal)
$5-$15

U.S. Army
1950s (metal)
$10-$20

**U.S. Capitol
Washington D.C.**
1950s (metal
cloisonne')(round)
$10-$20

U.S. Marine Corps.
1950s (plastic)
$10-$20

U.S. Military Ad
1940s (Smith Bros.)(metal)(same ring base as
the Kellogg's baseball game ring
Ring Only - $40-$80

U.S. Navy Store Card
1950s (3 variations)
$10-$20 ea.

Valentine Flicker
(see Cupid, Heart-Arrow &
Heart Throbs flicker)

Less than
10 known

Magnifying glass swings
out to the side

**Valric Of The Vikings
Magnifying**
1940s (All Rye Flakes
premium)(less than 10
known)(very rare)
(also see Radio Orphan
Annie Magnifying)
Good - $1750
Very Good - $2625
Fine - $3500
Very Fine - $5250
Near Mint - $7500

Vote '72 (2)
1972 (metal)(round,
domed)(2 diff.)
$2-$4

Victory Ring
1940s
$2-$4

Volcano (see Quake...)

Wacky Races-Mutley
1970s (metal)
$10-$20

Vincent Price 3D Face
1990s (pewter)(only 12
made)(licensed)
$375-$750

Walnettos Initial
1940s (metal)(same base
as R.O.A. Initial)
$100-$350

Vote '72 (1)

Walnettos Initial Saddle
1940s (metal)
$30-$60

Valric Of The Vikings Ad

Washington D.C.
50s (metal, onyx & silver)
$10-$20

Weapon, Gun
1960s (red over silver)
(plastic)
$5-$10

Weapon, Knife
1960s (blue over
silver)(plastic)
(also see Sleeping Beauty)
$5-$10

Weather Bird
1950s (metal)
(shoes)
$75-$200

Watch Flicker
1960s (Face of Elgin
watch with hands
flickering around)
$5-$10 ea.

Western Flicker
1960s (plastic, circular)
(green & blue plastic bases
known)(set of 5)
(all wrapped in clear plastic)
$10-$20 ea.

Watch Ring, Adjustable
1960s
$10-$20 ea.

333

Western Ring Series
1960s (plastic, 11 rings w/bases on card)
$125 complete

Wheat Chex Decoder
1982 (paper)(plastic base)
$5-$10

Wheaties
(see Compass)

Whistle
(see Kazoo & Quaker)

Whistle Police
1960s (plastic, large,
gumball)
$7-$15

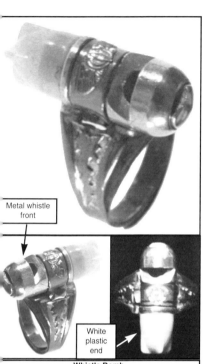

Metal whistle front

White plastic end

Whistle Bomb
1940s (glow-in-dark)(rare)(metal)
Good $300
Fine $800
Near Mint $1500

Whistle Bomb
1953 (metal)
$20-$40

Whitman, Paul Good Luck
1930s (bakelite)(band
leader)(Whitman figure on
sides of ring)(also see
Navajo Good Luck &
Swastika)(same as Kill The
Jinx ring)
$125-$250

Whistle Bomb (also see
Lone Ranger Atomic Bomb)

Wile E. Coyote (see
Looney Tunes)

**William Boyd
(Hopalong Cassidy)**
(see Real Photos)

Wimpy
1950s (silver color metal)
(in color)(also see King
Features & Popeye)
$75 - $150

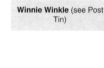

Winnie The Pooh
1970s (metal cloisonne')
$20-$40

Winnie Winkle (see Post
Tin)

Witchipoo (see H.R. Puff n'
Stuff)

**Wizard of Oz Flicker
(Dorothy)**
1967 (plastic)
(shows both images)
$15-$25

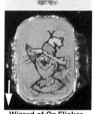

**Wizard of Oz Flicker
(Scarecrow)**
1967 (plastic)
(shows both images)
$15-$25

**Wizard of Oz Flicker
(Tin Man)**
1967 (plastic)
(shows both images)
$15-$25

**Wizard of Oz Flicker
(Witch)**
1967 (plastic)
$15-$25

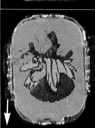

**Wizard of Oz Flicker
(Wizard)**
1967 "Off to See The
Wizard" with picture of OZ in
background to full cartoon
figure of cowardly lion
$15-$25

Wizard of Oz Flicker
1967 (plastic)(set of 12)
(priced above)(uncut sheets
exist from warehouse)

Wizard of Oz Flicker
1970s (green base, green
flicker)
$10-$20

Wizard of Oz Flicker
1970s (blue base, green
flicker)
$10-$20

Wolfman (see Universal
Monsters)

Woman Dancer Flicker
1950s (thick top)
$10-$20

Wonder Bread
1960s (plastic)
$5-$10

Wonderman
1939 (gold colored
metal)(Wonderman comic
premium?)(rare)
(value determined by
identification)

Wonder Woman Logo
1980s (metal)
$35-$70

Wonder Woman Logo
1980s (metal)
$35-$70

Wonder Woman Logo
1980s (metal)
$35-$70

Woodstock
1980s (metal, enameled)
$10-$20

Woodstock
1980s (metal cloisonne)
$10-$20

Woody Woodpecker
1977 (metal, enameled)
$10-$25

Woody Woodpecker
1970s (plastic)
$5-$10

**Woody Woodpecker
Club Stamp**
1960s (2 diff. colors)
(Kelloggs Rice Krispies
cereal premium)(plastic)
$75-$150

World's Fair
1933 Chicago (metal)
$15-$60

World's Fair
1933 Chicago (metal)
$15-$60

Woody Woodpecker
1970s (plastic)
$5-$10

World War I (see U.S.
Army)

World's Fair
1933 Chicago (metal)
$15-$60

World's Fair
1933 Chicago(silver/blue
top)(metal)
$20-$75

Woody Woodpecker
1980s (metal cloisonne')
$10-$25

World's Fair
1893 Columbia Expo (1492-1892) (sterling)(1st child's
adj. premium ring?)(same image used on coin)(Rare)
$150-$300

World's Fair
1933 Chicago (metal)(blue
over silver)
$40-$100

Woody Woodpecker
1992 (metal cloisonne')
(left & right profiles)
$5-$10

World's Fair
1933 Chicago (metal)
$15-$60

World's Fair
1933 Chicago
(Indian head) (bronze)
$15-$50

World's Fair
1934 Chicago
(Indian head)(pewter)
$15-$50

World's Fair
1934 Hall of Science
(Chicago)(metal)
$15-$50

World's Fair
1995 New York
(dome)(note: 1939 shown
on ring)(fantasy piece)
$1

World's Fair
1934 Chicago (metal)
$15-$50

World's Fair
1934 Chicago (metal)
$15-$50

World's Fair
1935 San Diego (metal)
$15-$50

World Fair
1939 (New York)(metal,
blue)
$15-$50

World's Fair
1934 Chicago (metal)
$15-$60

World's Fair
1934 Chicago (metal)
$15-$50

World's Fair
1939 New York (metal)
$15-$50

World's Fair
1939 (New York)
(plastic top)
$15-$40

World's Fair
1934 Chicago (metal)
$15-$60

World's Fair
1934 Chicago (metal)
$15-$50

World's Fair
1939 (New York)
(silver metal)
$15-$50

World's Fair
1939 (plastic)(New York)
(white, blue, green, orange
tops; silver, gold metal base
versions)
$60-$150 ea.

World's Fair
1968 San Antonio (metal)
$15-$30

Writer's Club
1940s (metal)(premium)
$50-$100

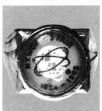

World's Fair
1964-65 New York
(dome)(plastic, color)
$10-$20

World's Fair Flicker
1964 (plastic)(New York)
$5-$10

World's Fair Flicker
"Souvenir of the New York
Worlds Fair 1964-1965" to
picture of the globe
sculpture
$10-$20

Wyatt Earp Marshal
1950s (metal)(Cheerios)
$40-$80

Wyatt Earp Paper
$35-$50

X-Men Gold
1993 (Diamond Comics Distr.)
(w/diamond chip, 25 made)
$750

X-Men Xavier Institute Class Ring
1994 (excellent detail)
Gold (10K, 250 made) - $400
Sterling (2,500 made) - $75
Bronze finished pewter (unlimited) - $20

X-Men Silver
1993 (Diamond Comics Distr.)
$100

X-Men Wolverine Mask
1980s (plastic)(black/yellow)
$5-$10

X-Men Class Ring
1994
$10-$20

X-O
1993 (Valiant Comics)
(metal)
In Case $80

Yellow Kid gold ring fits in slide-out secret compartment

Yale University
1940s (metal)
$15-$30

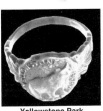

Yellowstone Park
1950s (sterling)
$15-$30

Yogi Bear (see Hanna Barbera)

Yogi Bear Figure
1960s (metal, in color)
$15-$30

Yellow Kid
1995 (100th Anniversary statue with gold ring)(limited to 100 made)
(ring only available with statue)(design by Randy Bowen)
Complete $2000
Ring Only $800

Yogi Bear
1960s (aluminum)
$15-$30

Yogi Bear Figure
1970s (metal)(enameled)
$20-$40

Yogi Bear
1970s (plastic, Canada,
gumball)
$5-$10

**Yogi Bear's
Jellystone Park**
1960s (metal, in color)
$15-$30

Good Luck

to you while you wear this ring!

Notice! The band of this handsome "Your Name"
Ring brings you two "good luck" symbols:

THE HORSESHOE: Ancient people believed that the horse brought good luck. Lord Nelson, when he fought the famous battle of Trafalgar had a horseshoe nailed to the mast of his ship VICTORY. When you see a horseshoe nailed to the door of a house these days, the owner put it there for luck!

THE FOUR-LEAF CLOVER: If you've ever tried to find a four-leaf clover growing in the field, you know how rare it is. No wonder the belief arose that good luck soon came to the person who found one. Today the four-leaf clover is worn as a charm by many people who believe in its wonderful magic. We want it to bring good luck to you—that's why we put it on "Your Name" Ring, together with the lucky horseshoe.

HERE IT IS!

Kellogg's luminous
"YOUR NAME"
RING

Everybody will want one

We know you'll be proud as punch to wear this ring and to show it to your friends. Naturally, when they see it, they will want one, too. You can be the one to show them how to order this ring. Here's how:

We're printing *two* coupons on this folder one for *you*, so you can order more of these wonderful rings, and one called the Kellogg's "Friendship Club" coupon which you can tear off and give to a *friend*. This coupon gives all the information your friend will need.

This ring glows in the dark

This ring is *luminous* which means that the name will GLOW in the dark. We know you will want to test your ring right away. So do this:

I   Hold the "Your Name" Ring under a strong light for a minute or two ...

II   Then turn off all the lights, or hold the ring in a dark corner ...

III The script letters of your name will glow in a bright bluish green!

Your Name Good Luck Paper
1950s (Kellogg's)
$30-$40

Yosemite Sam
1970s (metal, enameled)
$6-$12

Yosemite Sam
1980s (metal, in color)
$15-$30

Your Name Good Luck
1950s (metal)(Kellogg's)
(Luminous)
$20-$50

Zorro (Z)
1960s (plastic)(vending machine)
$30-$60

Zorro Ring Paper
1960s (vending machine paper)(scarce)
$20-$35

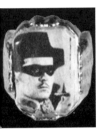

Zorro Photo
1960s (plastic)
$15-$30

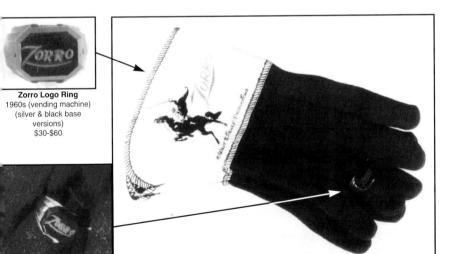

Zorro Logo Ring
1960s (vending machine) (silver & black base versions)
$30-$60

Zorro Logo Ring & Glove set
1960s (ring sold with Zorro glove)(silver base version)
$50-$100

another Star in the Gemstone Universe

Football, Steelers
1970s, $30

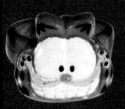

Garfield
1978, $15

General Insignia
1960s, $15

Gene Autry Horseshoe Nail
1950, $250

Ghost Busters, Slimer
1992, $8

Girl Scouts
1930s, $275

Gleason, James
1940s, $100

Howdy Doody Face
1950s, $150

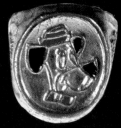

Huckleberry Hound
1960s, $100

McDonald's Grimace
1970s, $30

Howdy Doody Glow
1950s, $250

Icee
1970s, $50

Have Gun, Will Travel
1960s, $25

Huckleberry Hound Flicker
1950s, $40

Incredible Hulk
1980s, $150

Hot Wheels
1970s, $20

Huckleberry Hound
1960s, $100

Jack Armstrong Baseball
1939, $650

Hill Valley
(Back To The Future
1994, $20

Jesus Flicker
1960s, $20

Kellogg's Picture
1950s, $40

LET'S PRETEND

PRICE 39¢

JUNIOR
AIR STEWARDESS
DRESS-UP SET

FOR EVERY JR. AIR STEWARDESS FROM 3 TO 8 YEARS
No. 3108 FOLEINMAN & SONS, PROV., R. I., MADE IN U.S.A.

Junior Air Stewardess
1970s, $10

REAL FLYING ACTION

AGES 5 AND OVER

MICRO ACTION
JET RING SQUADRON™

- ADJUSTABLE HEIGHT AND POSITION
- REMOVABLE FREE WHEELING JETS

© FUNRISE, INC. 1989, ENCINO, CA. 91316
MADE IN CHINA
ITEM NO. T0500

Jet Ring Squadron
1989, $15

Keebler Elf
1970s, $60

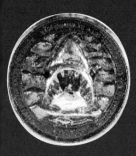

Jaws
1975, $2

Kellogg's Picture
1950s, $40

John Kennedy Flicker in vending capsule
1960s, $20

Kool-Aid Aztec Treasure
1930s, $200

**Lone Ranger Mari
Corps. Sec. Comp**
1940s, $850

**Laugh-In
package w.
ring**
1960s, $20

**Laurel &
Hardy (Hardy)**
1951, $600

Land of the Lost card
1991, $25

Looney Tunes (Tweety Bird)
1995, $5

Laugh-In Flicker
(square version)
1968, $75

Man From Uncle
1960s, $20

Macy's Santa
1960s, $25

Mask Movie on card
1994, $50

Melvin Purvis Jr. G-Man
1937, $75

Mickey Mouse
1935, $400

Michael Jackson
1980s, $10

Mister Softee Flicker
1960s, $100

McDonald's, Ronald
1970s, $30

Mickey & Minnie Heart
1970s, $30

McDonald's, McFries
1975, $30

Mickey Mouse Club
1980, $80

**Minnie Mouse
Figure Framed**
1994, $15

McDonald's Polly Pocket
1994, $4

**Mickey Mouse Wedding
Band**
1970s, $20

**Monster Cereal Flicker
Count Chocula**
1971-75, $100

Munsters Flicker-Lily
1960s, $75

**Monster Cereal Flicker
Count Chocula**
1971-75, $100

**Monster Cereal, Count
Chocula**
1976, $250

Mr. Magoo
1975, $15

Monster Cereal, Fruit Brute
1976, $250

Mueslix
1970s, $40

Mr. T Jewelry Set
1983, $50

Monster Fink
1960s, $25

Muppets-Kermit
1970s, $30

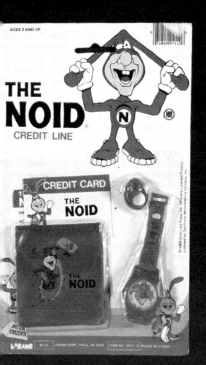

The Noid
1989, $10

Police Sergeant
1960s, $15

Poll Parrot
1950s, $50

Popeye Flicker
1960s, $20

Noogies
1980s, $12

Post Tin Group
1948, (varying prices)

Quisp Ray Gun
1965-72, $600

Post Tin Group
1949, (varying prices)

ROA Face
1980s, $30

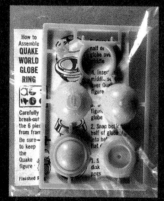

Raggedy Ann Face
1980s, $20

Quake Figural
1960s, $650

Quake World Globe
1960s, $1500

Range Rider
1950s, $550

Quake Leaping Lava
1960s, $600

Quisp Meteorite
1960s, $600

Ranger Rick
1950s, $100

Robot Flicker
1980s, $5

Romper Room
1960s, $60

Red Goose Shoes
1940s, $225

Sam, The Olympic Eagle
1984, $40

ROA Mystic Eye
1930s, $210

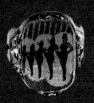

Rockettes Flicker
1990s, $5

Rootie Kazootie
1940s, $750

Scorpion Flicker
1980s, $10

Ren & Stimpy
1990s, $8 each

Shadow Blue Coal sticker
1941, $150

Robin
1980s, $90

**Rocky & Bullwinkle
(Dudley)**
1961, $60

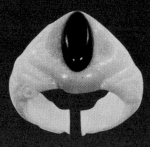

Shadow Carey Salt
1947, $1200

Shadow-Movie, gold
1994, $400

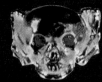

Skull
1960s, $50

**Space Patrol
Hydrogen Ray Guin**
1950s, $325

Spawn, gold
1993, $1050

Shadow, gold
1984, $400

Sky King Aztec
1940s, $950

Smilin' Jack
1964, $100

Speedy Gonzales
1970s, $20

Shmoo
1950s, $600

Sky King Navajo
1950s, $150

Snoopy
1970s, $20

Stanley Club
1940s, $350

Skull
1940s, $125

Sky Strike
(set of 3)
1989, $15

**Snap, Crackle, Pop
(Snap)**
1950s, $550

Superman F-87 Jet
1940s, $250

Smurfs
1980s, $20

Superman
1979, $40

Superman Gum Wrapper
1940s, $750

Teenage Mutant Ninja Turtles Cereal Box
1990s, $200

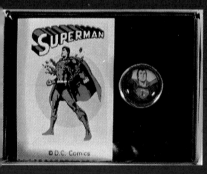

Target Comics
1940s, $60

Tennessee Jed
1940s, $500

Target Comics
1970s, $40

Superman Flicker
1960s, $250

Superman
1979, $50

Three Stooges Flicker ring & paper
1960s, $40 (paper), $20 (ring)

Tom & Jerry Flicker
1970s, $20

Tom Mix Target
1930s, $250

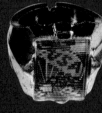

U.S.A. Astronaut Flicker
1960s, $40

FREE!!! FREE!!! FREE!!! FREE!!!

MIX DEPUTY RING

SAVE 75 TOM MIX CERTIFICATES AND GET A 14 KT. white gold finished TOM MIX DEPUTY RING. - You then become a TOM MIX DEPUTY. - A full fledged fearless champion of law and order.

Tom Mix Deputy Ring Certificate
1935, $100

Transformers
1980s, $4

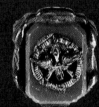

U.S. Airforce Store Card
1950s, $20

Tweety Bird
1980s, $10

U.S. Army, 1918
1918, $100

Tom Mix Lucky Initial
1930s, $250

Tom Mix Stanhope
1930s, $400

Ultraman
1980s, $30

Tom Mix Straight Shooters (showing two variants)
1936, $350

Universal Monsters Phantom
1960s, $80

U.S. Army Store Card
1950s, $20

USA/KKK
1920s, $500

Woody Woodpecker
1977, $25

X-Men, Gold
1994, $400

Watch Flicker
1960s, $20

Wonder Woman
(round)
1980s, $70

World's Fair Columbia Exposition
1893, $300

Yellow Kid, Gold
1995, $800

Whistle Bomb
1940s, $1500

Wonder Woman
(square)
1980s, $70

World's Fair 1933
1933, $100

Yosemite Sam
1970s, $12

Writers' Club
1940s, $100

Wizard of Oz-Tin Man
1967, $25

Wonderman
1939, (no price listed)

Wonder Woman
(rectangle)
1980s, $70

Zorro Paper
1960s, $35

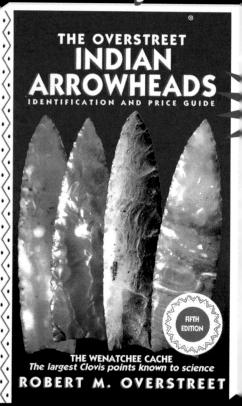

Discover the excitement inside

PREVIEWS

every month, from detailed advance information on the latest coming comics and collectibles to...

- ▼ **The Splash Page**—Full-color news on the hottest comics!
- ▼ **PREVIEWS Contests**—Your chance to win original art, limited-edition comics, and more!
- ▼ **PREVIEWS Comics**—Exclusive full-color comics serials available nowhere else!

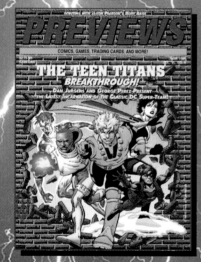

NOW SHOWING

from Dark Horse-
The Return of Tarzan
and
from Topps-
Mars Attacks:The Perils of Perilman

- ▼ **PREVIEWS Presents**—Exclusive comics sneak-previews!
- ▼ **PREVIEWS Interviews**, starring top creators and personalities in comics and beyond!
- ▼ Full-color **Gems of the Month**!

PREVIEWS

The excitement's inside a fine comics shop near you!

PREVIEWS is a publication of Diamond Comic Distributors, Inc., the industry's leading distributor of new comics and related merchandise.